A Political and Diplomatic History of the United States

An Interpretive View

Publication of this book was assisted by a grant from the Ministry of Education, Science and Culture, Japan

This book was originally published in 1975 by the University of Tokyo Press under the title *Amerika seiji gaikoshi*.

UTP 3031–36283–5149
ISBN 0–86008–249–0
Printed in Japan

For Professor Yasaka Takagi

Contents

Contents

Foreword

The publication of this book marks the beginning of a program
to make available to western scholars the work of Japanese scholars in various fields of American studies. This book, and others to
follow, is evidence of the great growth of American studies in
Japan since World War II. A beginning was made soon after
Japan's "opening" to the west more than a century ago. Japanese
who became political and intellectual leaders traveled to and
some were educated in the United States. Japanese began writing
books and translating more and more books about the United
States into Japanese.

The beginnings were small but the foundations were laid for the
rapid expansion of American studies since 1945. Today hundreds
of courses in American literature, history, economics, political
science, law and other subjects are given in colleges and universities throughout Japan. The courses are given by Japanese scholars, many of whom have received part of their training in the
United States and most of whom have visited the United States
more than once to carry on research in a wide variety of fields. The
results of that research are being published in an increasing number of monographs and books, but since they are written in Japanese, most scholars in the United States are unable to benefit from
them.

Nor are they able to benefit from the fact that people in any
society are influenced by their own history, traditions, and assump-
tions when they try to explain the history, traditions, and assump-
tions of other societies. Thus Japanese writing about the United
States are influenced by a civilization quite different, if neither
better nor worse, than the civilization of the western world. We

may not see ourselves as others see us, or agree with or like what they see, but their interpretations should serve us well in the never-ending task of trying to understand where we have been and where we are going.

Such is the case with this brief book. Outwardly it is conventional in form and the factual framework is traditional. But this is a book to be read for its insights and interpretations, sometimes in a sentence or two. For example, the author reminds us in passing of what we too often forget: that the United States was a "backward" and "relatively minor" nation for several years after independence. Later on he comments that the problem of the American army in Vietnam was like that of the British army when it struggled with an army of American farmers during the American Revolution.

As a citizen of a nation whose remarkable ethnic unity was established hundreds of years before Columbus discovered America, the author is intensely interested in the racial, ethnic, and national diversity of the people of the United States, and its consequences. Thus, he explains the so-called "Red Hunt" after World War I as follows: "For American society, which had neither racial nor cultural unity, an artificial unity of belief was essentially indispensable" and "the specter of xenophobia and threats from the outside were raised in the desperate efforts to maintain ideological unity." And in commenting on the "McCarthyism" of the 1950s he writes that "from a broader perspective, it was, after all, deeply connected with the American nation's inevitable need for artificial unity, composed as it is of various races and nationalities."

As a citizen of a nation whose origins date back nearly 2,000 years, and which had a powerful central government before the first English colonies were founded, the author looks upon the United States as a very young nation indeed, in fact one which did not reach "adulthood" until the two hundredth anniversary of the Declaration of Independence. After summarizing the crises through which the United States had passed he concludes the book:

> However, is not the crisis which America faces in the 1970s different from these? This crisis must be conquered not by expansion, but by self-restraint; not by self-confidence, but

by self-examination. Success in meeting the challenge will
be measured not by quantitative expansion, but by qualitative change. This in itself may indicate that "America has
come of age."

The above are but a few of the thoughtful and thought-provok-
ing interpretations throughout this all too brief book. We may or
may not agree with them, but they are well worth thinking about.

The University of Wisconsin: Madison   MERRILL JENSEN

Preface

"In recent years we have been hearing calls for the study of the United States from many quarters," wrote Inazo Nitobe in 1919. Nitobe, well known among Americans for his *Bushido: The Soul of Japan*, devoted his life to being "a bridge across the Pacific."[1] Indeed, a year before he wrote these words, Nitobe gave a series of lectures on American history following the opening ceremony of the Hepburn Chair in American Political and Diplomatic History at the University of Tokyo.

Alonzo Barton Hepburn, Chairman of the Board of the Chase National Bank, wrote a long letter to Eiichi Shibusawa, one of the leading Meiji-era businessmen, in June, 1917: "We must be a little more devoted to the cause of international good-fellowship, a little more in earnest in advocating peace on earth, good will toward men. As an influence in that direction I have in mind to present to the University of Tokyo, 100,000 yen . . . to endow an American professorship of International Law and Comity." The university authorities were delighted to accept the offer and suggested that, instead of another chair in international law (two of which had been established years earlier), "a chair such as that of American history in its broadest sense . . . would be not only desirable but also far more effective in promoting better mutual understanding between the American and Japanese peoples." Hepburn welcomed this suggestion, and accordingly the Hepburn Chair for the American Constitution, History and Diplomacy was established at the Faculty of Law, the University of Tokyo.

The opening ceremony was held in 1918, and it was followed by a series of lectures on American history, the American constitution, and American diplomacy by Inazo Nitobe, Tatsukichi

[1] "Beikoku kenkyu no kyumu" (The Urgent Need for the Study of the United States), *Jitsugyo no Nippon* (April 1, 1919), p. 23.

Minobe, and Sakuzo Yoshino, respectively.[2] These men were three of the leading liberals in prewar Japan. As the first holder of the chair, the young, promising scholar Yasaka Takagi was nominated and sent to the United States for a few years of study. Upon his return to Tokyo in 1924, Takagi began to lecture on American political and diplomatic history, and continued until 1950 when he retired from the university. His book *Beikoku seijishi josetsu* (An Introductory Treatise on American Political History), published in 1931, is a classic in American studies in Japan. However, outside the university walls, Japanese-American relations were becoming more and more strained. Takagi was desperately anxious to avoid the final catastrophe of war, and he conferred with such prominent political leaders as Premier Konoe and the Lord Keeper of the Privy Seal Kido on the one hand and U.S. Ambassador Grew on the other. Nonetheless, both Nitobe's appeal for American studies and Takagi's efforts to avoid the catastrophe were fruitless.[3]

A year before the outbreak of the Pacific War, my first encounter with American history came when I sat in a class given by Takagi. In the gloomy days preceding the war, my personal commitment to American studies was made. Yet, like most of the young men of that time, I joined the armed forces, and served in the Japanese Navy for four years. From an isolated front in the South Pacific, I returned to the academic world in 1946. Thanks to the Rockefeller Foundation, I had an opportunity to study in the United states, mostly at Harvard University, from 1951 to 1953. My memories of classes given by Samuel E. Morison, Arthur M. Schlesinger, Sr., and his son Arthur, Jr., Arthur Holcombe, V. O. Key, Jr., and Louis Hartz remain vivid. This was a time when McCarthyism was threatening American society from within and the Korean War was challenging it from without. I witnessed the

[2] Nitobe's lecture was published later as *Beikoku kenkokushi yo* (A Concise History of the Evolution of the American Nation) in 1919 by Yuhikaku Publishers.

[3] For more details on the endowment of the Hepburn Chair and the status of American Studies in prewar Japan, see Makoto Saito, "American Studies in Prewar Japan" in *Amerika kenkyu* (The American Review), vol. 4, 1970; the abridged version of it in Robert H. Walker, ed., *American Studies Abroad* (Greenwood Press, 1975); Marius B. Jansen, "American Studies in Japan," *American Historical Review*, January, 1965; and Joseph Bucklin Bishop, *A. Barton Hepburn: His Life and Service to His Time*, 1923. The chair is now officially titled the American Political and Diplomatic History Chair, but is still commonly called the Hepburn Chair for American History and Government.

way in which, while the tradition of freedom was most acutely treasured, this very freedom was also used as the symbol of unity for the society. Precisely because American society had its tremendous diversity of racial and ethnic groups, it seemed to me, the need for a common value system to unify Americans was urgent. The interrelationships between freedom and unity, diversity and integration, in American history thus almost inevitably became the central theme of my research. Upon my return to Japan, I began teaching the political and diplomatic history of the United States as Takagi's successor, and since then more than twenty years have passed.

This book was originally written as a text for Japanese students. While it was intended as a historical survey of American political development, the task of writing the history of some 370 years within a severely limited space necessitated rigorous selection of "facts," concise description, and free exercise of "interpretation." Undoubtedly, the premises of my work differ from those of American scholars. My writing is inevitably influenced by my educational background, daily surroundings, and socio-political environment. This book, therefore, is but one interpretation of American history.[4]

Today, when one examines the historiography of American history, one recognizes that there have been many different interpretations of the same "facts." Take, for example, the American Revolution. From the patriotic explanation of the Whig school represented by George Bancroft in the nineteenth century to the present "New Left" interpretation, new interpretations of the American Revolution have repeatedly been advanced. Indeed, in the field of American history, labels such as "new viewpoint," "new interpretation," "reconstruction," and "revisionism" are in frequent use. Needless to say, new "facts" based on new discoveries of historical materials play an important role in revising historical interpretations. The adoption of methodologies from the social

---

[4] In the original Japanese version, no documents were inserted for reference. I have edited and compiled a separate documentary source book (in English) for class use, *Amerika seiji gaikoshi kyozai* (University of Tokyo Press), and I have borrowed some of the documents from that volume to supplement my history. I am well aware that, due to space limitations, I have at places resorted to a rather sweeping presentation. Had space allowed, this text would be supplemented by notes or references to other writings of my own in which I have given them more detailed discussion.

sciences continues to shed new light on the established "facts," and new historical explanations are developed. It may simply be that history is bound to be rewritten. Nonetheless, one wonders if there is something uniquely American about the striking potential for diverse interpretations of American history.

In this connection, it should be noted that Americans, having left the *ancien regime* in Europe, experimented with a new social order on the new continent and since then have maintained a single socio-political system. One could argue that in American society, because of its basic continuity, history as "fact" has not yet completely become part of the past. This particular kind of contemporaneity manifests itself in writings not only about such recent events as the Cold War or the New Deal, but also about more remote ones such as the American Revolution and the Civil War. At the same time, precisely because of the continuity of American society, the frame of reference which regulates historical writing has maintained its fundamental homogeneity. At least since Independence, essentially one single value system has continued to prevail in American society, and American history has been characterized by the vigorous expansion of this basic value system in terms of space and time. Even what appear to be heated disputes over issues have centered mostly on the interpretation of this dominant value system, and have remained contests among branches of the same family.

Now, two centuries after independence, American society is encountering external limitations and deepening internal divisions. From the bitter experiences of the Vietnam War abroad and the Watergate Incident at home, the American people have learned a great deal and have demonstrated the ability to solve their problems with sophistication and wisdom. With these instances of discontinuity in their history, one could argue, the American people have at long last entered into a new era in which the past is no longer conceived as part of the present but as the past itself. In other words, America is coming of age.

In the course of preparing this English version, I have been assisted by a number of people. I am most grateful to Professor Shumpei Okamoto and Ms. Linda L. Sieg of Temple University for their painstaking and time-consuming work of translation. I would like to express my deep gratitude to Professor Merrill Jensen of Wisconsin University for his kindness in writing a foreword to this English version. His contribution to the promotion of American studies in Japan deserves special mention. A special kind of indebtedness is due to Ms. Susan Schmidt of the University of Tokyo Press for her expert editorial advice. With deep appreciation, I would like to thank the Institute for Advanced Study at Princeton, where the finishing touches were placed on this version. At the last stage of writing the preface and proofreading, Dr. Michio Umegaki of Princeton University kindly extended his help.

Finally, to Professor Yasaka Takagi, in recognition of his intellectual integrity and of my deep indebtedness to his scholarship and personality, I would like to dedicate this English version as well as the Japanese version. Without his guidance and encouragement for more than three decades, I would never have written this book.

Institute for Advanced Study, Princeton　　　　　　Makoto Saito
Thanksgiving Day, 1978

A Political and Diplomatic History of the United States

An Interpretive View

CHAPTER

1

The Colonial Period

The term "colonial period" usually refers to the years between 1607, when Jamestown, the first permanent English settlement on the American continent, was established, and 1763, when the Seven Years' War between England and France ended. Having insufficient space to describe in detail the history of that period, I want to confine myself here to presenting the limited background necessary for understanding the political and diplomatic development of the United States since the Revolution.

This is not to deny the importance of that historical period. The colonial era was not a mere prelude to the history of the United States; it shows a fundamental continuity with later American society and politics. A modern American history did not begin after the Revolution had fundamentally rejected and transformed the colonial society; it had already begun in the colonial period. In other words, American society of the colonial period can be seen as the prototype of modern American society, and the history of the colonial period should be understood not as the history of an expansion of European society, but as the history of the formation and development of a new society different from that of Europe.

It should be kept in mind that England was not the only power which established and managed colonies on the American continent in the colonial period. For example, after the "discovery" of America by Columbus, Spain had subjugated Mexico and in 1565 established the permanent settlement of St. Augustine in Florida. In the first half of the seventeenth century, France built up a vast North American colony which extended into midwestern Canada, with Quebec and Montreal as its control centers. During the same period, Holland established a colony in the vicinity of

3

present-day New York. In fact, among the great European powers of those days, England was a comparative latecomer in building its American colonies on the east coast.

Although one conventionally calls the pre-revolutionary United States the "English colonies," England controlled, not one unified American colony, but thirteen separate colonies, each with its distinctive characteristics and separate administrative apparatus. It is also worth noting that the West Indies were just as important to England as the North American colonies, at least during the seventeenth century.

From this point of view, the history of the American colonial period is also the history of world-wide rivalries among the powers for the establishment and management of colonies—the New World version of the relentless power struggles which were occurring in Europe—as well as one link in the British empire which was founded in the midst of these struggles. Thus, if one may prejudge here, American independence constituted a partial dismantling of the British Empire and signaled the beginning of the founding of the "American Empire."

We should also note the fate of the so-called American Indians, who were the original occupants of the continent. From this perspective, the history of the colonial period can be regarded as the history of the struggle between the indigenous "First Americans" and the major emigrants from Europe, the Anglo-Saxons. More realistically, it was the history of the subjugation of the Indians by the Anglo-Saxons. In this connection, it is extremely symbolic that the Seven Years' War in Europe, which ended in 1763, in American history is called the French and Indian War.[1] Keeping in mind this wider historical context, I shall confine my discussion here to a general survey of the establishment of the

---

[1] The Seven Years' War was a war in which the English colonists expelled the French influence from the North American continent and at the same time drove away the Indians. As Francis Parkman pointed out long ago: "The victory of Quebec was the signal of their [the French] swift decline. Thenceforth they were destined to melt and vanish before the advancing waves of Anglo-American power, which now rolled westward unchecked and unopposed" (Francis Parkman, *The History of the Conspiracy of Pontiac, 1851, The Works of Francis Parkman*, 1902, vol. XVI, p. ix). Parkman left behind extensive writings concerning the struggle between the French and the Indians against the English-Americans on the American continent, a struggle which was in a sense "completed" in 1890 at Wounded Knee. See Dee Brown, *Bury My Heart at Wounded Knee*, 1970 (Japanese translation, 1972).

English colonies as background to the history of the United States of America.

The Founding of the Colonies

Although jointly called the English colonies, the thirteen colonies were independent of one another and were established with different governing mechanisms and economic structures. Complex intertwining economic, social, and religious motives also lay behind the original establishment of these colonies. If we confine our attention exclusively to political motives and discuss them with extreme simplification, we can divide the colonies into two types—those which were established with the support of the home government and those established in opposition to it.

The former were created by the English ruling class in order to extend the power of England to the New World. Aristocrats and influential London merchants undertook these colonization enterprises with the support of the state power of the Tudor and Stuart monarchies in an attempt to establish the English mercantile system. Their mercantile enterprises in North America included the abortive colonization effort (1585) by Sir Walter Raleigh, favorite of Queen Elizabeth I; the founding of Jamestown in 1607; and other colonial settlements primarily in the South. Although private joint-stock companies carried out these colonization enterprises, they held charters which gave them considerable privilege and authority. The promoters of these enterprises were inspired by nationalistic pride in the growing power of England in competition with such advanced nations as Spain and France, and they collaborated closely with the monarchy. It was symbolic of this fact that the first successful settlement was named after King James I, who was then in power. In the matter of religion, as well, the colonies were naturally placed under the official Anglican Church. Though at first operated by the chartered companies, these colonies soon came under the direct control of the home government as royal colonies and became more clearly a part of the ruling system of the mother country.

In contrast, the colonies of the latter group were established in defiance, or at least in evasion, of the power of the state. These colonial settlements were first attempted by Puritans who were dissatisfied with the established Church of seventeenth-century England and rebelled against the religious conformity it imposed. These colonies were established mainly in the northeastern section, beginning with the Plymouth Plantation, founded in 1620 by a separatist group called the Pilgrim Fathers. Their aim was not to extend the old ruling system of England to the New World but rather, figuratively speaking, to establish a "New England" in opposition to the old England. That they aspired to create a new political society is evident in such passages of the Mayflower Compact, which the Pilgrims signed on board ship prior to landing on the American continent, as: "covenant and combine ourselves together into a civil Body Politick." The same determination was also expressed by the Puritans, who, when they established the Massachusetts Bay Plantation in 1630, already called it a "commonwealth," even before the establishment of the Commonwealth in the mother country. They were conscious that they were building "a city on a hill" that would become an example for the world.[2]

The attitude of the northern colonies toward the home government was also suggested by the class origin of their leaders. They were not nobles or rich merchants; rather, a good number of them came from the ranks of yeomanry. Many of the northern colonies were managed under the Corporate Colony system, which was subject to relatively less control by the mother country. In these colonies it was often customary for the governors to be popularly elected rather than appointed.

Under the influence of their differing natural environments, these two groups of colonies soon developed into regions with distinctive economic interests. The natural conditions of fertile soil, warm climate, and vast plains made the colonies in the south suitable for the cultivation of such staples as tobacco, rice, and cotton,

[2] When the Puritans, who in England were anti-establishment and nonconformist, separated themselves spatially from the established authority of the mother country and founded their own "commonwealth," they themselves became the established authority and conformists. The transformation by emigration also transformed heresy to legitimacy. Thus, in the new land, the new heresy, seeking freedom, again began to move spatially. The founding of Roger Williams's colony at Providence, Rhode Island, can be said to be typical of this process.

and led to the development of a plantation system based on slavery. The basic administrative unit generally adopted in the south was the county, which covered a comparatively large area. The growth of the plantation system gradually drove the middle-class independent farmers out of competition. Pushed into the mountain hinterlands, some of them eventually deteriorated into the so-called "poor white" class. In the plantation zone, a class division between the small number of planters, on the one hand, and the indentured servants and slaves who provided the labor force, on the other, was promoted and soon firmly fixed. The monocultural southern colonies, which needed capital for the purchase of land and slaves, often borrowed from merchants in the mother country, and their exclusive reliance on agricultural production made them dependent for their daily necessities and other materials on importation from England. This intensified the southern colonists' economic dependency on the English merchants who acted as both their creditors and monopolistic buyers. The southern colonies in this way came to constitute one important link in the English mercantile system.

Natural conditions in the north made it impossible to develop a plantation system such as that in the south. In the north's unfavorable climate and infertile soil, there existed mostly small farms which were sufficient only for self-subsistence. Consequently, large planters such as those in the south did not emerge, and independent farmers who cultivated more or less similar amounts of land formed the nucleus of the population. Administrative divisions also centered around the relatively small town system. The northern farmers had no agricultural products for export as did those in the south. Still, the growing northern colonies needed many commodities that had to be imported. In order to compensate for this imbalance, they embarked on intermediate or triangular trade. Thus, for the northern colonies, commerce and trade were vital enterprises and the means of capital accumulation. As a result, the dominant merchant class in coastal ports such as the city of Boston came to have an important voice in the northern colonies. With the growth of commerce and trade, such industries as shipping, fishing, and shipbuilding also developed in the north. These circumstances made the northern colonies economically less dependent upon the mother country than the southern colonies. Indeed, as their industries developed, the northern colonies became potential competitors of the mother country, and a force fundamentally in opposition to the English mercantile system.

Here we must note the existence of another group of English colonies which shared common characteristics with both the southern and northern groups. These colonies, New York, Pennsylvania, Delaware, and New Jersey, occupied a middle position geographically, politically, and economically. Neither self-governing nor royal colonies, they were private or proprietary colonies which the monarch granted to specific individuals. In agriculture, large manor farms co-existed with small farms. Because the main produce of these colonies was wheat and other grains, they were called the "bread colonies." Along with agriculture, commerce also developed rapidly; Philadelphia was North America's commercial center during the colonial period. In religion, the middle colonies manifested a tolerance which allowed different sects, including the Pennsylvania Quakers, to exist side by side, and provided the opportunity for such individuals as Benjamin Franklin to engage freely in wide-ranging political and intellectual activities.

The Colonial Policy of the Mother Country

As we noted earlier, England was competing on a world-wide scale with Spain, France, and Holland for the establishment of a colonial empire; its colonial policy toward America was one link in an English foreign policy which rested on mercantilism. We must therefore ask what kind of role the American colonies played in this English mercantile system, and, conversely, what was the significance of the mother country's mercantile policy for the colonies.

If we consider the economic relationship, we can say that the American colonies, in accordance with the Navigation Acts, were made a supply center of raw materials and foodstuffs for the mother country and thus supported one flank of the English mercantile system. The Navigation Acts listed "enumerated articles" which could be exported only to England. The same law stipulated that, in the interests of the expansion of the English commercial empire and the development of the merchant marine, trade between the mother country and the colonies could be conducted only in English ships. In order to protect English industrial capital, an oppressive policy was followed toward manufacturing industries in the colonies. The Wool Act (1699), for example, was enacted explicitly in order to prevent the growth of the infant wool-manufacturing industries in the American colonies; the Hat Act (1732) and the Iron Acts (1750 and 1757) were similarly motivated.

As a governing mechanism which would guarantee the economic subordination of the American colonies to the mother country, the Board of Trade was established in 1696. This supervisory organ of colonial administration had the power to recommend that the Privy Council not sanction any law enacted by the colonial legislatures which the board judged detrimental to the interest of England. The board was also authorized to give various directives to the colonial governors who represented the home government. The nature of the mother country's colonial policy can be also perceived in the series of royalization policies which, under various pretexts, turned the self-governing and proprietary colonies into royal colonies and placed them under the direct control of the home government. By 1752, nine of the thirteen colonies had become royal colonies, and only two, Connecticut and Rhode Island, remained self-governing. Thus, in order to promote English mercantile policy, the mother country gradually intensified its control of the colonies during the century and a half of the colonial period.

However, we must also note that despite the policy of firm colonial control, self-government within the colonies was rather extensively recognized. Although they were dissatisfied with the restrictions of the mercantile policy, the colonies were also beneficiaries of English mercantilism. For example, the southern planters, whose staple product, tobacco, was designated an enumerated article, had to export it exclusively to England. However, because the cultivation of tobacco was prohibited in England and Ireland and because heavy duties were levied on foreign tobacco, American-grown tobacco enjoyed a monopoly in the English market. Also, as we have seen, trade between the colonies and the mother country was permitted only on English vessels. However, since vessels of the American colonies were also recognized as English vessels, here again the colonies benefited from this monopolistic policy, which aided the development of the shipping and shipbuilding industries in New England, New York, and Pennsylvania.

We must also note that when the mother country's policies seriously threatened their interests, the colonists often boldly defied its authority. The most conspicuous example of this was the extensive smuggling that was carried on in Boston and New York in defiance of London's regulations. For example, when the Molasses Act (1733) was passed in order to protect the sugar planters of the British West Indies, the New England merchants carried on a remarkable amount of smuggling in violation of the act. At that time England was preoccupied with a foreign war and could not spare its naval force for the control of smuggling. In addition, customs officials in America were weak and extremely corrupt. Thus, having no ability to suppress it effectively, England had to give the semi-open smuggling its tacit approval.

Again, because of the sheer size of the American continent, England was unable to effectively enforce its measures suppressing manufacturing industries in the colonies in order to protect its own industrial capital. Consequently, in spite of English mercantile policy, by the middle of the eighteenth century American commerce and manufacturing industries, albeit still infantile, were developing steadily.

These positive aspects of their position may have helped for a time to dissuade the colonists from turning their antipathy toward the mother country's control into open defiance. A more important deterrent, however, was the military situation. The struggles among the powers on the European continent re-emerged as power struggles among the various European colonies in the Western hemisphere. The presence of France and Spain on the American continent compelled the English colonies to rely heavily on the protection of the military power of their mother country. The French colony in Canada in particular, with its powerfully unified military force, immediately threatened the English colonies. One might say that the fear of a dangerous neighbor prevented the dissolution of the ties between England

and the colonies. In addition, we must remember that the English colonists relied heavily on the military power of the mother country as they continued to drive the indigenous Indians from their land.

The power relationships between the mother country and its colonies in the colonial era can be succinctly summarized as follows. First, as long as the colonies remained colonies, they were, needless to say, under the control of the mother country. As long as the mother country maintained a mercantile policy, the colonies were controlled, and often victimized, by the policy. On the other hand, the young English colonies on the American continent often relied on the mother country economically and militarily. In this sense, they also benefited from being one link in the English empire.

It was fortunate for the colonies that, preoccupied with foreign wars, England failed to effectively tighten its controls over the colonies. One might also add that the 3,000 miles of ocean separating the colonies from the mother country often prevented the effective exercise of the latter's authority. In any case, Adam Smith, although with some exaggeration, described accurately the power relationship between England and its colonies in America in those days when he wrote in *The Wealth of Nations*: "In everything, except their foreign trade, the liberty of English colonists to manage their own affairs their own way is complete" (Book IV, Ch. 7, part 2). In terms of actual political practice, the mother country and the colonies shared some degree of power and thus maintained a certain equilibrium between them. While England held military and diplomatic power and the right to regulate trade, the colonial legislatures controlled the powers of internal administration, budget, and taxation. Thus, in substance, something akin to a federal system was created. The mother country and the colonies inherently had mutually conflicting interests and political aspirations, but against the background of the world-wide struggles which engulfed the American continent as well, they maintained a certain balance of power and mutual interests. In this sense, the American colonies remained loyal to the mother country and the monarch and were satisfied to be a part of the British Empire.

Power Relations Within the Colonies

The seats of final authority over the colonies were located in England: the monarch, the Privy Council, the Board of Trade, and Parliament. As their subsidiary organs in the colonies, there were governors appointed by the monarch, their advisory organs, the councils, and the rest of the colonial bureaucratic agencies. The governor, in addition to the right to govern following the orders of the monarch, exercised the right to veto any legislation of the colonial legislatures. The members of the councils were in many cases appointed by the monarch through the recommendation of the governors, and many came from the upper classes of the colonies.

In contrast to these organs of control by the mother country, each colony, beginning with Virginia in 1619, established a colonial legislature based on election by the colonists.

One of the functions of these legislatures was to elicit the colonists' agreement to the control of the mother country. At the same time, these colonial legislatures gradually expanded their roles as organs of self-government, and eventually became the centers of resistance to the ruling class in the mother country and to its representatives in the colonies. However, before the colonial legislatures could function as organs of self-government or resistance for all the colonists, they had to establish a broad representation. Suffrage in America, as in England, often required the possession of fifty acres of land or that the voter be a landowner with an income of forty shillings. Needless to say, this restriction alienated many people from political participation; but one can say that in America, where land was then abundant compared to England, political participation was relatively easy. While in England the "enclosures" kept reducing open land, in America the supply of open land was continuously expanding. This meant that even though the formal prerequisites of political participation were the same, actual political participation in America was much more widespread.

Rather than on the right to vote, political disputes in America centered on the issue of regional underrepresentation. The electoral district allotment of many of the colonial legislatures had been fixed at a time when the eastern coastal regions had been brought under cultivation; even after the western regions had been opened up and settled, the regional appointment of legislative members remained almost unchanged. Consequently, the number of elected representatives from the western regions was extremely low compared to that of those from the east. This did not result in a merely regional inequality. In the southern colonies, for example, many of the residents of the western regions were small planters, independents, or poor farmers, as opposed to the large planters of the eastern regions. Thus, the regional imbalance simultaneously implied a class differentiation.

In addition, despite this inequality of representation, taxes were apportioned uniformly for all regions. As a result, the western residents' antagonism toward the eastern ruling class sometimes turned into rebellion. Bacon's Rebellion, which occurred in Virginia in 1676, was the first and the most famous uprising. The western farmers, led by the small planter Nathaniel Bacon, temporarily occupied the legislative chamber in the Virginia capital, Jamestown, but soon were suppressed. This incident is notable in American colonial history because it reveals that the regional imbalance of political participation in American society of those days was simultaneously a sort of class conflict.

The colonial legislatures were often perceived by the colonists as self-governing mechanisms and agents of resistance to the mother country rather than as control mechanisms in the colonies. This was due not only to the wide political participation but also to the colonies' remoteness from the mother country. The home government 3,000 miles away was perceived strictly as authority and the state. The colonies, in contrast, were regarded as their own communities or societies. In a schematic sense, in Europe, state and society existed within the same space one on top of the other. To the colonies, state and society existed separately in different spaces. In American society the sense of of distance from political power tended to be proportionate to the sense of physical distance. In other words, space acted as a determinant of the colonists' sense of distance from political power.

The colonists' view of their own society as non-authoritarian was not necessarily a total illusion. We cannot overlook the fact that the formation of colonial communities in the wilderness required the full cooperation of the residents. In order to achieve this, the direct participation of all the citizens in decision-making, as symbolized by town meetings, was considered necessary and expected. Although, as we know, in practice participation was extremely selective, at least in principle participation in decision-making was one of the responsibilities of constituent members of the community. Consequently, when the representative system was adopted in establishing a legislature, it was perceived as a convenient substitute for direct democracy. In America the concept of representation was rather close to that of proxy, and generally had different connotations from the idea of national representation in England.[3]

In sum, the English-ruled American colonies developed as one link in the British Empire. The colonists perceived their political relationship with the home government in terms of both the mercantile policy and the physical distance that separated them from the mother country. In some ways the colonies were the beneficiaries of the British imperial system and of the mother country's so-called "salutary neglect." For these reasons, in practice, a sort of federal system was developed and maintained between the mother country and the colonies. On the other hand, within the colonies, conflicts of regional interests and of class interests were intertwined and gradually gave rise to internal dissension. However, these conflicts within the colonies were overshadowed by the larger conflict with the mother country, and the colonists were not clearly aware of the internal dissension. Thus, a fairly stable relationship continued to exist both between the colonies and the mother country and among the colonies themselves.

However, the drastic change in the international environment which accompanied the end of the Seven Years' War inevitably changed the relations between the mother country and the colonies. As the mother country tightened its centripetal control over the colonies, the colonies intensified their centrifugal tendencies, and the once stable relationship collapsed.

[3] The principle of participation by all members in decision-making during the period of the founding of settlements in the wilderness, and the concept of a system of representation as a convenient substitute for participation by all members, were discussed vividly by Thomas Paine. Thomas Paine, *Common Sense*, 1776, Modern Library edition, 1943, pp. 6–11 (Japanese translation, 1953).

Documents

Mayflower Compact, November 11, 1620

In the Name of God, Amen. We, whose names are underwritten, the Loyal Subjects of our dread Sovereign Lord King *James*, by the Grace of God, of *Great Britain*, *France*, and *Ireland*, King, *Defender of the Faith*, &c. Having undertaken for the Glory of God, and Advancement of the Christian Faith, and the Honour of our King and Country, a Voyage to plant the first colony in the northern Parts of Virginia; Do by these Presents, solemnly and mutually in the Presence of God and one another, covenant and combine ourselves together into a civil Body Politick, for our better Ordering and Preservation, and Furtherance of the Ends aforesaid; And by Virtue hereof do enact, constitute, and frame, such just and equal Laws, Ordinances, Acts, Constitutions, and Offices, from time to time, as shall be thought most meet and convenient for the general Good of the Colony; unto which we promise all due Submission and Obedience. In WITNESS whereof we have hereunto subscribed our names at *Cape Cod* the eleventh of *November*, in the Reign of our Sovereign Lord *King James* of *England*, *France*, and *Ireland*, the eighteenth and of *Scotland*, the fifty-fourth. *Anno Domini*, 1620.

William Bradford, *History of the Plymouth Plantation*

. . . After this they chose, or rather confirmed, Mr. John Carver (a man godly and well approved amongst them) their governor for that year. And after they had provided a place for their goods, or common store (which were long in unlading for want of boats, foulness of the winter weather and sickness of divers) and begun some small cottages for their habitation; as time would admit, they met and consulted of laws and orders, both for their civil and military government as the necessity of their condition did require, still adding thereunto as urgent occasion in several times, and as cases did require.

In these hard and difficult beginnings they found some discontents and murmurings arise amongst some, and mutinous speeches and carriages in other; but they were soon quelled and overcome by the wisdom, patience, and just and equal carriage of things, by the governor and better part, which clave faithfully together in the main. . . .

But that which was most sad and lamentable was, that in two or three months' time half of their company died, especially in January and February, being the depth of winter, and wanting houses and other comforts; being infected with the scurvy and other diseases which this long voyage and their inaccommodate condition had brought upon them. So as there died some times two or three of a day in the foresaid time, that of 100 and odd persons, scarce fifty remained. And of these, in the time of most distress, there was but six or seven sound persons who to their great commendations, be it spoken, spared no pains night nor day, but with abundance of toil and hazard of their own health, fetched them wood, made them fires, dressed them meat, made their beds, washed their loathsome clothes, clothed and unclothed them. In a word, did all the homely and necessary offices for them which dainty and queasy stomachs cannot endure to hear named; and all this willingly and cheerfully, without any grudging in the least, showing herein their true love unto their friends and brethren; a rare example and worthy to be remembered. Two of these seven were Mr. William Brewster, their reverend Elder, and Myles Standish, their Captain and military commander, unto whom myself and many others were much beholden in our low and sick condition. And yet the Lord so upheld these persons as in this general calamity they were not at all infected either with sickness or lameness. And what I have said of these I may say of many others who died in this general visitation, and others yet living; that whilst they had health, yea, or any strength continuing, they were not wanting to any that had need of them. And I doubt not but their recompense is with the Lord. . . .

St. John Crèvecoeur, *Letters from an American Farmer*, 1782

. . . What attachment can a poor European emigrant have for a country where he had nothing? The knowledge of the language, the love of a few kindred as poor as himself, were the only cords that tied him: his country is now that which gives him land, bread, protection, and consequence: *Ubi panis ibi patria*, is the motto of all emigrants. What then is the American, this new man? He is either an European, or the descendant of an European, hence that strange mixture of blood, which you will find in no other country. I could point out to you a family whose grandfather was an Englishman, whose wife was Dutch, whose son married a French woman, and whose present four sons have now four wives of different nations. *He* is an American, who, leaving behind him all his ancient prejudices and manners, receives new ones from the new mode of life he has embraced, the new government he obeys, and the new rank he holds. He becomes an American by being received in the broad lap of our great *Alma Mater*. Here individuals of all nations are melted into a new race of men, whose labours and posterity will one day cause great changes in the world. Americans are the western pilgrims, who are carrying along with them that great mass of arts, sciences, vigour, and industry which began long since in the east; they will finish the great circle. The Americans were once scattered all over Europe; here they are incorporated into one of the finest systems of population which has ever appeared, and which will hereafter become distinct by the power of the different climates they inhabit. The American ought therefore to love this country much better than that wherein either he or his forefathers were born. Here the rewards of his industry follow with equal steps the progress of his labour; his labour is founded on the basis of nature, *self-interest;* can it want a stronger allurement? Wives and children, who before in vain demanded of him a morsel of bread, now, fat and frolicsome, gladly help their father to clear those fields whence exuberant crops are to arise to feed and to clothe them all; without any part being claimed, either by a despotic prince, a rich abbot, or a mighty lord. Here religion demands but little of him; a small voluntary salary to the minister, and gratitude to God; can he refuse these? The American is a new man, who acts upon new principles; he must therefore entertain new ideas, and form new opinions. From involuntary idleness, servile dependence, penury, and useless labour, he has passed to toils of a very different nature, rewarded by ample subsistence.—This is an American. . . .

2

Independence and Revolution

"The American Revolution" is often translated in Japan as "the independence revolution." One could say that this translation unintentionally expresses simultaneously two aspects of the American Revolution: the winning of political independence for the English colonies in America from the mother country, and, at the same time, a revolution within the American society. Historical interpretations of the American Revolution can, broadly speaking, be divided into those which emphasize the aspect of political independence and those which emphasize the aspect of social revolution. Here, while noting these two aspects, I also want to consider an often neglected aspect of this Revolution: its role in the international struggle between England and the other European powers.

The term "American" Revolution generally refers to the approximately twenty-year period from 1763, when the Seven Years' War ended, to 1783, when America's independence was recognized by England. During this period the tensions created by the strengthening of the mother country's control over the American colonies and the resistance of the colonies to it, although lightened by occasional periods of compromise, finally led to armed conflict in 1775 and the historic Declaration of Independence of 1776. With independence America established its own political structure and began a new phase as the United States of America. In this chapter, while outlining the development of the opposition to England, I also want to consider the political and constitutional theory which was invoked to justify this resistance, because this theory came to be institutionalized when America established its own political structure.

The Strengthening of Control over the Colonies and the Resistance to England

The conflicts among the European powers in the eighteenth century, which centered on the establishment of world empires, induced conflicts among the colonies on the American continent as well. The Seven Years' War between England and France which began in 1756 unfolded on the American continent as the "French and Indian War." By defeating France, England succeeded in establishing a world empire "on which the sun never sets." On the American continent England added Canada and the vast French territory reaching from west of the Appalachian Mountains to the Mississippi River to the original thirteen colonies on the eastern coast. Along with its vast new dominion, the mother country faced the problem of how to govern the expanded empire.

The keynote of the colonial policy which the English government adopted was the renunciation of its former "salutary neglect" in favor of tighter controls. The end of the Seven Years' War enabled England to employ its military force as a powerful means of intensifying control over the colonies.

At the same time, however, with the end of the war the necessity for the colonies to depend on England's military power declined. Until then, the French colonies and the Indians who cooperated with the French had obstructed the westward expansion of the English-dominated Americans. At the end of the Seven Years' War, with the elimination of the French colonies and the weakening of the Indians, the American colonists naturally had strong hopes of land speculation, trade with the Indians in furs and other items, and establishing farming communities on the land which had now become English territory.

However, the British government had other plans, and as they unfolded, England and its colonies, which had cooperated in fighting a common enemy, gradually awoke to the conflicts and contradictions in their relationship. As the first concrete example, one can cite the conflict over the so-called Royal Proclamation of 1763, which was promulgated immediately after the end of the Seven Years' War. This proclamation, which was planned by

English Prime Minister George Grenville, made the new territory west of the Allegheny Mountains an Indian reservation and forbade the colonists' migration into the region. This denied the Southern planters both a source of the fertile land which was always needed for a plantation system and the opportunity for land speculation which could help them defray their expenses. Thus, despite their English gentry mentality, the southern planters were given grounds for opposition and resistance to the English government.

The plan of the mother country, on the pretext of defending colonial territory, to permanently station 10,000 English regular army troops in the colonies and to make the colonies bear the expenses also aroused the opposition of the colonies. London justified the apportionment of the expenses for maintaining the army as follows: first, because of successive foreign wars, an expenditure greater than the present one was impossible for the mother country to bear; second, the Seven Years' War had, in no small measure, advanced the interests of the colonies themselves. However, not only did the colonists fail to perceive the necessity for the permanent stationing of the regular army at a time when the threat from the French colonies had passed; they also regarded the regular army, not as a means of resisting a foreign threat, but as a powerful tool of control over the colonies. England sought to impose a tax on the colonies to defray the expenses of the retention of the army; this tax was first levied in the Sugar Act of 1764, which differed from previous commercial laws levying customs in order to regulate trade: it represented the imposition of customs in order to raise revenue for the national treasury. At the same time, the home government strengthened and expanded the admiralty courts, increased the number of customs officers, and intensified control over the smuggling which formerly it had almost tacitly approved. This inevitably dealt a serious blow to the merchants of the northeastern colonies, who accumulated some of their capital by smuggling, and fostered resistance to the English government among the merchants, shippers, and manufacturers of the New England region.

Up to this point it was only limited regional and class interests, such as those of the southern planters and the northeastern merchants, which were affronted by the mother country's new policy, and the colonies' resistance to the mother country was correspond-ingly limited. It was the enactment of the Stamp Act of 1765 which generalized this partial resistance and spread it among all the American colonists. This law required the affixing of stamps to all kinds of vouchers, and documents, newspapers, pamphlets, etc., within the colonies; like the Sugar Act, it was to raise revenue for the national treasury. The act applied not only in coastal areas but also inland, stipulating an imposition of taxes across the entire land. Because the colonists who felt the economic impact of the law were the so-called opinion leaders such as newspapermen, lawyers, and ministers, who occupied important positions in co-lonial society, the anti-English feeling of the colonists was effec-tively and rapidly expanded and amplified in the reaction to the Stamp Act.

The resistance to England which was thus ignited occasionally took the form of attacking the sellers of the stamps and burning their wares; but as a more effective form of struggle, boycotts of English merchandise were often carried out. Since without the cooperation of the entire colonial society the effect of a boycott was weak, the boycott movement encouraged the development of organizations dedicated to coordinating resistance to the English government. As examples of such organizations, one can cite the Sons of Liberty, which was formed around 1765 as a secret organization in several communities; the Committee of Cor-respondence, an organization which linked the communities; and the Stamp Act Congress of 1765, which was held in order to strengthen solidarity among the colonies.

The boycott of English manufactured goods which was sup-ported by these organizations was effective; the result was that the London merchants petitioned Parliament to repeal the Stamp Act. Seeing that policies such as the Sugar Act and the Stamp Act, whose primary goal was to increase revenue, did not bring substantial results, Parliament decided in 1766 to repeal the Stamp Act and reduce the tax rates of the Sugar Act.

The financial crisis in England, however, made demands for further financial levies on the colonies inevitable. Thus, in 1767 Parliament enacted the so-called Townshend Acts, named after Chancellor of the Exchequer Charles Townshend, which aimed at increasing customs revenues. This law fundamentally broadened the Sugar Act, strengthening it and extending it to include other goods. Further, it included a plan to apply the income received from the taxes to the salaries of colonial officials from governor on down, thereby making them economically independent of the colonial legislatures. The law aroused the violent opposition of the colonists, who, rallying around the merchants, again organized a boycott of English goods; this boycott also succeeded, and Parliament in 1770 was forced to rescind the Townshend Acts except for the tax on tea.

If one investigates schematically the various reactions to the mother country which the colonists were displaying at this time, they can be seen to form a pattern. One type of reaction was that of the group called "Loyalists," in the sense that they pledged their loyalty to the mother country. The main members of this group, who were also called "Tories," were such people as the governors appointed by the king and the officials beneath them; merchants who imported and sold goods from England; ministers of the Church of England; colonists who had recently emigrated from England; and people such as the "poor whites" of southern Appalachia who, because of their intense animosity toward the colonial ruling class, hoped for its suppression by the mother country.

The group called "Patriots," on the other hand, were more or less adamantly opposed to the policies of the mother country. The members of this group, who were also called "Whigs," can be divided into "moderates" and "radicals." The demands of the moderates expressed their concrete dissatisfaction with certain individual policies and sought their abolition, but they did not seek a fundamental change in the colonies' relationship with the mother country. The radicals demanded, not the mere abolition of the causes of individual discontent, but an overall revolution in the relationship with the mother country and ultimately in colonial society itself. The people in this group were the first to demand independence from England.

As moderates, one may cite the southern planters and the merchants, wealthy lawyers, and ministers of New England and the middle colonies. As radicals one may cite lawyers and journalists such as Patrick Henry of Virginia and Samuel Adams of Massachusetts as leaders, and the small farmers of the west and the artisans of the east as supporters. However, I must point out that the above classification is only one scheme, one level of analysis. There were often cases in which the same person on one occasion belonged to the Loyalists, on the next occasion belonged to the moderate group of the Patriots, and again switched to the radical group. Also, there are not a few cases in which it is difficult to determine whether the same person should be classified as a moderate or a radical, or in which there were both Loyalists and Patriots within a single family. In brief, one must bear in mind that the above type of classification is only one way of understanding the dynamics of the anti-England movement.

What this classification implicitly suggests is that, as mentioned above, the politics of American colonial society at that time included both the power relationship between the mother country and the colonies and the power relationships within American society. The American Revolution was a movement which occurred on both levels of this dual relationship. Consequently, the "Patriots" who cooperated in the anti-England movement could often be opposed to one another in the power politics within the colonies; in fact, this very internal conflict among the Patriots was one basic prototype for the dynamics of American political history after the American Revolution.

Now, let us return again to the English policies and the colonies' reaction to them. In 1773, England, in order to solve the financial crisis of the East India Company, decided to export the company's large stockpiles of tea to the American market at low prices. This policy was embodied in the Tea Act of 1773. The American merchants who had monopolized the sale of tea in the colonies, sometimes by smuggling, received a blow. Moreover, there was no guarantee that what had occurred for tea would not occur for other goods. The struggle against England was revived on the basis of cooperation between the merchants and the Radicals, culminating in the so-called "Boston Tea Party" of 1773. Because this incident overtly defied the authority of the English government, that government retaliated against the colony of Massachusetts with the series of punitive laws usually called the "Coercive Acts." From the closing of Boston harbor to the strengthened royalization of Massachusetts colony, they included measures such as the virtual abolition of the jury system and the compulsory quartering of the English army in private houses. General Thomas Gage, the commander-in-chief of all the British troops in North America, was made governor of Massachusetts.

Shortly thereafter England established a permanent Canadian government by the Quebec Act of 1774, and closed the northwest to the American colonists. As a result, the southern colonies also became increasingly firm in their opposition to the home country, and a resistance movement could again be organized on a continental scale. Illegal organs of administration by the colonists themselves began to appear in place of the former legal organs of administration. Their names and forms differed from colony to colony, but they included conventions to function in place of the legislatures, colonial militia which opposed the regular army of the mother country and Committees of Safety to supervise them, and strengthened Committees of Correspondence, which were liaisons between various communities and among all the colonies. Finally, in 1774, a meeting of representatives of all the colonies— the Continental Congress—was called to coordinate the colonies' struggle against England; in the same year, the Continental Association, which organized a unified boycott of English goods, was formed.

In response to this kind of extreme reaction by the colonies, the mother country was forced to prepare for a certain degree of compromise. However, before its compromise plan reached America, in April 1775, an armed encounter between the English regular army and the American colonial militia occurred in a suburb of Boston, and Ralph Waldo Emerson's famous "shot heard around the world" announced the beginning of the War for Independence. The conflict between the mother country and the colonies had entered the stage of armed clash. The colonies opened the Second Continental Congress in May 1775 and, appointing George Washington supreme commander of the colonial army, strengthened their determination to begin a full-scale military conflict with England. One must note, however, that even this anti-English conflict by means of military might did not itself inevitably imply political independence from the mother country.

The Philosophy of the Anti-England Movement

The theory which the colonies adopted concerning their opposition and resistance to England in order to legitimize their own position was not merely a rationalization and legitimation of this conflict, but a philosophy which would later crystallize into the American political system.

The fundamental characteristic of the colonists' anti-English attitude was that it began as the self-assertion of the colonies within the limits of the English constitutional system. The logical basis of the colonial opposition rested originally on the fact that the colonies regarded the British Empire as a "unitary empire" to which they themselves belonged, and they based their actions on the premise that they were under the control of the mother country's legislature. But that legislature was likewise under the restrictions of the English constitution, and consequently its authority was not unlimited and unrestricted. Thus, the colonies, depending on the English constitutional theory which stipulated "no taxation without representation," argued that since the American colonies did not send a representative to Parliament, England could not impose taxes on the colonies without the colonists' consent. In other words, the Sugar Act of 1764, by imposing taxes on the colonists without their consent, violated the English constitution. The resolutions of the Stamp Act Congress logically and persuasively elucidated this rationale of the colonies' opposition.[1]

[1] Resolutions of the Stamp Act Congress, October 19, 1765, III–V (appended to this chapter).

To comprehend the rationale of the legitimization of the Revolution, we must, after all, directly examine the original documents and know their nuances. The era of the American Revolution and the enactment of the Constitution was a period in which ideas in the form of resolutions, proclamations, debates, and statutes were brilliantly and effectively made public, and many of these were later institutionalized. There are many selections of these documents, such as Samuel Eliot Morison, ed., *Sources and Documents Illustrating the American Revolution, 1764–1788* (2nd ed., 1929); Merrill Jensen, ed., *Tracts of the American Revolution* (1967); and Bernard Bailyn, ed., *Pamphlets of the American Revolution, 1750–1776*, vol. I (1965). Some selections of documents are also available in Japanese translation from a number of sources, including *Genten Amerika Shi* (*A Documentary History of the American People*), edited by the Japanese Association American Studies, vol. II (in 7 vols., Iwanami Shoten, 1951) and *Amerika Kakumei* (*The American Revolution*), edited and translated by myself with the help of Takeshi Igarashi (Kenkyusha, 1978). Paine's *Common Sense*, Jefferson's *Notes on Virginia*, *The Federalist* (abridged), and Burke's *Speeches and Letters on American Affairs* are also available in Japanese versions.

In contrast to the colonists' assertion of "no taxation without representation," or "proxy representation," however, in England at that time the concept of "virtual representation" was already dominant. According to this concept, regions within England such as Birmingham which did not actually send a representative to Parliament were regarded theoretically as represented in Parliament, and the same theory was applied to the American colonies. The assertion of the American colonies, although based on the logic which the Whigs employed against the Tories in England in the seventeenth century, had already lost its effectiveness in England of the eighteenth century, where the concept of parliamentary sovereignty had become institutionalized.

The colonies were forced to shift the argument to another constitutional theory. Rather than a "unitary empire," they now called the British Empire a "compound empire." They argued that the English Parliament was the parliament only of the realm of the mother country, and that in each dominion the colonial legislature had the authority to determine policy, at least concerning domestic affairs. According to this interpretation, the mother country's parliament and the colonial legislatures were equal organs under the constitution of the British Empire. Only concerning matters such as foreign wars, diplomacy, and the regulation of commerce, which had bearing on the interests of the entire British Empire, did the English Parliament have jurisdiction over the dominion legislatures, based on voluntary mutual consent and in light of the mutual interests of the mother country and the colonies. Under this constitutional theory, the colonies held that they would submit to tariff measures as a means of regulating the commerce of the entire British Empire, but it was not their duty to submit to taxes such as those under the Sugar Act and the Stamp Act, which aimed at raising revenues within the colonies and violated the constitution of the British Empire. This constitutional theory was outlined in the declaration and resolutions of the Continental Congress in 1774, and became a major weapon in the anti-England struggle.

It is worth mentioning again that this logic denied the decision-making power of the English Parliament over the colonies but did not deny the fact that the American colonies were one link in the British Empire. At least up to this point, the argument of the colonies was still based, at least logically, on the intention of being loyal to the British constitution or the British imperial system. In this sense, the position of the colonies can be seen as more traditional, more adherent to the established order, and more conservative than that of the mother country. It is extremely symbolic that Edmund Burke, who is often regarded as a spokesman for English conservatism, in a speech in Parliament recognized the claims of the American colonies (aside from their legal, theoretical foundation) as loyal to the tradition of the British constitutional system, and criticized English policies toward the colonies as innovations opposed to this tradition.

The leadership of the colonies in the early days of the struggle aimed not at the creation of a new relationship with the mother country but rather at the restoration of the conditions of self-government prior to 1763. Even after April 1775, when armed conflict began, the colonists were not thinking of independence from England, but continued to hope for a restoration of their rights as one member of the British Empire. However, the reality of armed conflict gradually changed the relationship between mother country and colonies, and a new attitude emerged which groped for independence from England.

The so-called War for Independence was of course primarily a colonial war, between England and its colonies. However, in terms of world history this war for independence was fought against a background of long-term conflict among the European powers over the establishment of world empires, especially between England and France, whose hostility continued long after the Seven Years' War. Therefore it necessarily took on some of the features of an international war. France, which hoped for a decline in the international position of England, regarded the revolt of the American colonies against their mother country as a welcome development. The colonies, which were in a fragile position both militarily and financially compared to England, would inevitably require the assistance of foreign countries. Here the common interest between France and the American colonies was born, and an agreement of financial assistance from France to the American colonies was drawn up. The war within the empire—a civil war—was to be escalated into an international war.

However, loyalty to the king or a feeling of affinity to the

English people was for a long time a major psychological obstacle
to independence. The famous pamphlet *Common Sense*, written by
Thomas Paine in 1776, played a major role in skillfully curtailing
this loyalty and sense of affinity. Paine succinctly asserted the
meaninglessness of America's status as a colony, and called its
separation from the British empire natural and "common sense."
(See the excerpt appended to this chapter.) Of course, one cannot
state that this pamphlet alone launched the American colonists'
struggle for independence, but at the same time one cannot deny
that it greatly advanced the cause of the independence movement.
Because *Common Sense* overtly denied the legitimacy of the monarchy, it suggested that political independence signified not only
separation from the British Empire but also the shift from a
monarchical to a republican system. Here again the war against
England can be seen in terms of both political independence from
England and ideological separation from the old European system.

In May 1776 the Continental Congress recommended that each
colony establish its own independent governmental framework.
In June of that year Virginia, the largest colony at that time,
declared its own independence and issued a Bill of Rights (see
text appended to this chapter), and the other colonies began to
follow suit. The Declaration of Independence promulgated in
July by the Continental Congress was the announcement to the
world, broadly and publicly, of this determination of the English
colonies to gain independence.

The Declaration of Independence, which, as is well known,
was drafted chiefly by Thomas Jefferson, was more than a declaration of the actual fact of independence: it was also a statement of the reasons for independence. In addition to criticizing
the arbitrary, tyrannical government of George III of England,
which had become the direct motive force for independence, it
proclaimed the establishment of a new political system based on
the principle of sovereignty of the people. Although fundamentally
the independence philosophy was indebted to the rationale which
had once been used by John Locke in order to legitimize the
Glorious Revolution, the determination of the American independence movement to disassociate itself from the old European system is shown in the fact that it implemented its rationale as the
foundation of its political institutions. In this sense the American

Revolution signified the beginning of the bourgeois revolutions which took place in various Western countries from the end of the eighteenth century on.

The American Revolution, rather than simply marking the extinction of an old system and the establishment of a new one within American society, can be more directly perceived as a severance of American society from the old system in Europe, from which it was separated by the Atlantic Ocean. Speaking metaphorically, one can say that the American Revolution, rather than embodying a separation from the old system within the same space, was a spatial separation from the old system.

The Establishment of a Political Structure

Independence, while it freed American society from the rule of the English state, created the new problem of how to establish an independent state. The initial reaction of Americans to this problem was to deny the necessity of a state. Their distrust of the home government had created a distrust of powerful central government in general. However, the organized military actions of the war inevitably demanded the establishment of an organ of authority. Resolving this paradox was the first problem of the independent Americans.

In speaking of the establishment of organs of authority, one must naturally distinguish between the establishment of individual state governments and the establishment of a government for the entire continent. The state governments presented few problems; in most cases they were formed by continuation or alteration of the political bodies which had existed in the colonial era. As executives, state governors succeeded the royal governors of the colonial era; state legislatures were composed of upper houses (which corresponded to the colonial councils) and lower houses (which corresponded to the colonial legislatures). The court system of the colonial period was adopted almost without change. Thus, the system of the separation of the three powers, executive, legislative, and judicial, was carried over for the most part. However, because in the colonial period the royal governors had been representatives of the authority of the home government and resistance against this authority had been a major cause of the Revolutionary War, in the new state governmental structures the power of the governor was relatively weakened. Thus, in contrast to the separation of powers in the colonial era, which was a balance based on the dominance of the executive branch, after independence the various states adopted a system of separation of powers and balance of authority in which the legislative branch was strongest.

Furthermore, in the struggle with the mother country, the colonists had come to feel keenly the need for protection of basic human rights, and in the new political system they opened the way for the institutional guarantee of basic human rights by means of a written constitution and a Bill of Rights. Written constitutions took precedence over the laws of the legislatures and became the legal foundation which guaranteed basic human rights and restricted the exercise of governmental power.

After the governmental organs of the various states were established, the question of how to construct an American continental government (which had in a sense to correspond to a London government) became an urgent problem. The Articles of Confederation (1781) was the first institutional solution to this problem. Although the first article stipulated that "the style of this confederacy shall be 'The United States of America,'" this "style" did not signify a single centralized state, but a confederation of states in which the several states, retaining their "sovereignty, freedom, and independence," entered "into a firm league of friendship with each other." In other words, it was strictly an alliance of mutually independent states. Thus, for example, according to the Articles of Confederation, Congress held both the legislative and executive power in the Confederation, and so in a sense it was the organ which held the reins of central government. In Congress, however, each state had one vote, and concerning important matters such as war, foreign treaties, and the minting of currency, the consent of nine state, rather than of a simple majority, was required. Moreover, Congress lacked not only the authority to enforce on the states that which it had resolved, but also the right of taxation, which had become a major issue in the conflict with the mother country, and the right to regulate commerce. Consequently, even when incurring military expenses in order to conduct a war, Congress was given authority only to requistion from each state; where a state failed to respond, Congress did not have a method of enforcing procurement. As a result, the United States had to depend on domestic and foreign public loans and the random issuing of paper currency to meet war expenses, and this caused financial confusion.

However weak a union it may have been, a confederation of thirteen states was actually formed; and, because this confederation had already shared the historical experience of fighting a war against England, gradually a common consciousness of being one American people emerged among the residents of the various states. While they were still primarily conscious of themselves as Virginians, or New Yorkers, at the same time they were beginning to be conscious of themselves as Americans.

Now we must turn our attention to the question of who controlled these thirteen independent power structures and the central power structure, and what type of policy decisions were made as a result. I have previously mentioned the dispute between the moderates and the radicals in the independence movement; after independence, the conflict between these two groups became a struggle for influence in each state and in the Confederation government. The Loyalists, who in general formed the upper class in colonial society, with independence lost their status, and the American Revolution entered a new stage in which conflict centered around the domestic policies of the two Patriot factions, the moderates and the radicals.

How much internal change did American society experience in the revolutionary era? Historians are greatly divided on this question. The interpretation of the so-called "Internal Revolution School" exaggerates the scale of change, while the interpretation of the "Neoconservative School" underestimates it. It is probably true that since American society was characterized by far fewer status and class distinctions than European society at that time, drastic change was not necessary and did not occur. On the other hand, a certain degree of social change did inevitably occur during the era of the Revolution. One can point to the abolition of quitrents, primogeniture, and entail; the confiscation and redistribution of large estates owned by former Loyalists; the abolition of the established Church in Virginia and the institutionalization of freedom of religion which accompanied it.[2]

In order to understand the trends in American society after independence, we must emphasize, in addition to these various legislative reforms, the problem of the increased issue of paper currency as a bone of contention in domestic politics. Economic development in in the latter part of the colonial period created a division of interests within American society between creditors and debtors, which was intertwined with regional conflicts of interests and with the political dissension between Moderates and Radicals. There was sharp conflict, over the continuous issues of paper currency and over the declaration of debt moratoria, between the planters and merchants of the eastern seaboard, who stood in the position of creditors, and the small farming class of the western hinterlands, who were in the position of debtors. In several states, a Paper Money Party had emerged and effected inflationary policies. During the brief period when these policies were in the ascendancy, with their favorable results for debtors, we can say that the political structure in many states was being transferred from the planters and larger merchants into the hands of the small farmers—from the moderates to the radicals.

How was the war itself progressing during this time? At first the American army, which was inferior in military and financial strength, was naturally at a disadvantage, and found it necessary

[2] The American Revolution is a period in American historiography for which interpretations are extremely divergent. Along with the Patriotic explanation of the first half of the nineteenth century and the development of the Positivist school of history in the second half of the nineteenth century, there is the "Imperial school," which emphasized the relationship within the British Empire, *i.e.*, the aspect of independence; the twentieth-century Progressive school, which emphasized the revolutionary nature of American society; the postwar Neoconservative school, which called into question the revolutionary character of the Revolution; the New Left school, which again noted its revolutionary character; and the Atlantic Revolution theory, which tried to consider it a forerunner of the European bourgeois revolutions; and many other kinds of interpretations. My own interpretation, in brief, as I have already suggested in the text, is as follows. The European system was transplanted to America, but altered under the American conditions and climate and in the late eighteenth century was actually already in the process of becoming a new society different from that of Europe. The American Revolution first emerged as an attempt to "conserve" this new society and its independence from Great Britain; the revolution confirmed the establishment of this new society both theoretically and institutionally. In this regard, its revolutionary nature lies in the flow of a long revolutionary movement for independence, rather than in individual, tangible reforms.

to rely on foreign officers such as the Marquis de La Fayette and Baron Friedrich Wilhelm von Steuben and to solicit financial assistence from France and other countries. On the other hand, however, the American continent's distance from Europe and its vast expanse of territory made movement very difficult for the English regular army, which was unfamiliar with this kind of land and battle form, and gave a great advantage to the American troops, both militia and regular Continental Army. One must also point out that this war against the American colonies was extremely unpopular in England, and the home government was unable to obtain the unified support of the people for its war policies.

Finally, the international aspects of the war were particularly significant. After the conclusion of a Franco-American alliance in 1778, French military and financial aid to America contributed significantly to the outcome of the war, which ended for all practical purposes in October 1781, when the British army under the command of General Charles Cornwallis was defeated at Yorktown by the American army under Washington, with the help of the French army and navy. Fearing further involvement in a war with France, England gave up fighting this futile war and took steps toward recognizing the independence of the American colonies. Peace negotiations were conducted secretly in Paris, and finally, in September 1783, the Paris Peace Treaty between England and the United States of America was formally signed.

In this treaty, the English government, in addition to recognizing the independence of the United States of America (Article I), transferred to the new nation ownership of the vast territory from the Appalachian Mountains west to the Mississippi River (Article II) and recognized American fishing rights in the North Atlantic (Article III). The American government promised to pay the debts which Americans owed English merchants (Article IV) and to recommend to the legislatures of the several states that they enact laws requiring the restitution of, or compensation for, estates confiscated from the Loyalists during the war (Article V). The treaty was favorable to the United States, and consequently it had a very bad reputation in England. The English government, however, reluctant to continue the war in view of the involvement of its longstanding enemy, France, was determined to conclude a treaty. The American diplomatic delegation, beginning with Franklin, was well acquainted with the intricate interests of the powers; undoubtedly making free use of European Machiavellian diplomacy, they concluded a treaty favorable to their country.

With the end of the War for Independence, a substantial part of the vast British Empire was dismantled; after this bitter experience, England resolved on a reorganization of the empire. With its final victory in the Napoleonic Wars, the so-called "Pax Britannica," based on England's overwhelming naval power and economic strength, was instituted.

The United States, which had achieved independence, had to work hard to maintain it in a world where it was just one among other feeble nations. Separated from the British empire, America now confronted the new problem of its own unification.

Documents

Resolutions of the Stamp Act Congress, October 19, 1765

The members of this Congress, sincerely devoted with the warmest sentiments of affection and duty to His Majesty's person and Government, inviolably attached to the present happy establishment of the Protestant succession, and with minds deeply impressed by a sense of the present and impending misfortunes of the British colonies on this continent; having considered as maturely as time will permit the circumstances of the said colonies, esteem it our indispensable duty to make the following declarations of our humble opinion respecting the most essential rights and liberties of the colonists, and of the grievances under which they labour, by reason of several late Acts of Parliament.

I. That His Majesty's subjects in these colonies owe the same allegiance to the Crown of Great Britain that is owing from his subjects born within the realm, and all due subordination to that august body the Parliament of Great Britain.

II. That His Majesty's liege subjects in these colonies are intitled to all the inherent rights and liberties of his natural born subjects within the kingdom of Great Britain.

III. That it is inseparably essential to the freedom of a people, and the undoubted right of Englishmen, that no taxes be imposed on them but with their own consent, given personally or by their representatives.

IV. That the people of these colonies are not, and from their local circumstances cannot be, represented in the House of Commons in Great Britain.

V. That the only representatives of the people of these colonies are persons chosen therein by themselves, and that no taxes ever have been, or can be constitutionally imposed on them, but by their respective legislatures.

VI. That all supplies to the Crown being free gifts of the people, it is unreasonable and inconsistent with the principles and spirit of the British Constitution, for the people of Great Britain to grant to His Majesty the property of the colonists. . . .

Declaration of the Causes and Necessity of Taking Up Arms, July 6, 1775

. . . Lest this declaration should disquiet the minds of our friends and fellow-subjects in any part of the empire, we assure them that we mean not to dissolve that union which has so long and so happily subsisted between us, and which we sincerely wish to see restored.—Necessity has not yet driven us into that desperate measure, or induced us to excite any other nation to war against them.—We have not raised armies with ambitious designs of separating from Great-Britain, and establishing independent states. We fight not for glory or for conquest. We exhibit to mankind the remarkable spectacle of a people attacked by unprovoked enemies, without any imputation or even suspicion of offence. They boast of their privileges and civilization, and yet proffer no milder conditions than servitude or death.

In our own native land, in defence of the freedom that is our birthright, and which we ever enjoyed till the late violation of it—for the protection of our property, acquired solely by the honest industry of our fore-fathers and ourselves, against violence actually offered, we have taken up arms. We shall lay them down when hostilities shall cease on the part of the aggressors, and all danger of their being renewed shall be removed, and not before.

With an humble confidence in the mercies of the supreme and impartial Judge and Ruler of the Universe, we most devoutly implore his divine goodness to protect us happily through this great conflict, to dispose our adversaries to reconciliation on reasonable terms, and thereby to relieve the empire from the calamities of civil war.

Thomas Paine, *Common Sense,* 1776

Of the Origin and Design of Government in General

Some writers have so confounded society with government as to leave little or no distinction between them, whereas they are not only different but have different origins. Society is produced by our wants, and government by our wickedness; the former promotes our happiness *positively* by uniting our affections, the latter *negatively* by restraining our vices. The one encourages intercourse, the other creates distinctions. The first is a patron, the last a punisher.

Society in every state is a blessing, but government even in its best state is but a necessary evil, in its worst state an intolerable one; for when we suffer or are exposed to the same miseries *by a government* which we might expect in a country *without government,* our calamity is heightened by reflecting that we furnish the means by which we suffer. Government, like dress, is the badge of lost innocence; the palaces of kings are built on the ruins of the bowers of paradise. For were the impulses of conscience clear, uniform, and irresistibly obeyed, man would need no other lawgiver; but that not being the case, he finds it necessary to surrender up a part of his property to furnish means for the protection of the rest, and this he is induced to do by the same prudence which in every other case advises him out of two evils to choose the least. Wherefore, security being the true design and end of government, it unanswerably follows that whatever form thereof appears most likely to ensure it to us, with the least expense and greatest benefit, is preferable to all others.

In order to gain a clear and just idea of the design and end of government, let us suppose a small number of persons settled in some sequestered part of the earth, unconnected with the rest; they will then represent the first peopling of any country, or of the world. In this state of natural liberty, society will be their first thought. A thousand motives will excite them thereto; the strength of one man is so unequal to his wants and his mind so unfitted for perpetual solitude that he is soon obliged to seek assistance and relief of another, who in his turn requires the same. Four or five united would be able to raise a tolerable dwelling in the midst of a wilderness, but one man might labor out the common period of life without accomplishing anything; when he had felled his timber, he could not remove it, nor erect it after it was removed; hunger in the meantime would urge him from his work and every different want call him a different way. Disease, nay even misfortune, would be death; for though neither might be mortal, yet either would disable him from living and reduce him to a state in which he might rather be said to perish than to die.

Thus necessity, like a gravitating power, would soon form our newly arrived emigrants into society, the reciprocal blessings of which would supersede and render the obligations of law and government unnecessary while they remained perfectly just to each other; but as nothing but Heaven is impregnable to vice, it will unavoidably happen that in proportion as they surmount the first difficulties of emigration, which bound them together in a common cause, they will begin to relax in their duty and attachment to each other, and this remissness will point out the necessity of establishing some form of government to supply the defect of moral virtue . . . .

Virginia Bill of Rights, June 12, 1776

A *declaration of rights made by the representatives of the good people of Virginia, assembled in full and free convention; which rights do pertain to them and their posterity, as the basis and foundation of government.*

1. That all men are by nature equally free and independent, and have certain inherent rights, of which, when they enter into a state of society, they cannot by any compact deprive or divest their posterity; namely, the enjoyment of life and liberty, with the means of acquiring and possessing property, and pursuing and obtaining happiness and safety.

2. That all power is vested in, and consequently derived from, the people; that magistrates are their trustees and servants, and at all times amenable to them.

3. That government is, or ought to be instituted for the common benefit, protection, and security of the people, nation, or community; of all the various modes and forms of government, that is best which is capable of producing the greatest degree of happiness and safety, and is most effectually secured against the danger of maladministration; and that when any government shall be found inadequate or contrary to these purposes, a majority of the community hath an indubitable, unalienable and indefeasible right to reform, alter or abolish it, in such manner as shall be judged most conducive to the public weal.

4. That no man, or set of men, are entitled to exclusive or separate emoluments or privileges from the community, but in consideration of publick services which, not being descendible, neither ought the offices of magistrate, legislator or judge to be hereditary.

5. That the legislative and executive powers of the state should be separate and distinct from the judiciary; and that the members of the two first may be restrained from oppression, by feeling and participating the burthens of the people, they should, at fixed periods, be reduced to a private station, return into that body from which they were originally taken, and the vacancies be supplied by frequent, certain, and regular elections, in which all, or any part of the former members to be again eligible or ineligible, as the laws shall direct.

6. That elections of members to serve as representatives of the people in assembly, ought to be free; and that all men having sufficient evidence of permanent common interest with, and attachement to the community, have the right of suffrage, and cannot be taxed or deprived of their property for publick uses, without their own consent, or that of their representatives so elected, nor bound by any law to which they have not, in like manner, assented for the public good.

7. That all power of suspending laws, or the execution of laws, by any authority without consent of the representatives of the people, is injurious to their rights, and ought not to be exercised.

8. That in all capital or criminal prosecutions a man hath a right to demand the cause and nature of his accusation, to be confronted with the accusers and witnesses, to call for evidence in his favour, and to a speedy trial by an impartial jury of his vicinage, without whose unanimous consent he cannot be found guilty; nor can he be compelled to give evidence against himself; that no man be deprived of his liberty, except by the law of the land or the judgment of his peers.

9. That excessive bail ought not to be required, nor excessive fines imposed, nor cruel and unusual punishments inflicted.

10. That general warrants, whereby an officer or messenger may be commanded to search suspected places without evidence of a fact committed, or to

seize any person or persons not named, or whose offence is not particularly described and supported by evidence, are grievous and oppressive, and ought not to be granted.

11. That in controversies respecting property, and in suits between man and man, the ancient trial by jury is preferable to any other, and ought to be held sacred.

12. That the freedom of the press is one of the great bulwarks of liberty, and can never be restrained but by despotick governments.

13. That a well-regulated militia, composed of the body of the people trained to arms, is the proper, natural and safe defence of a free state; that standing armies in time of peace should be avoided as dangerous to liberty; and that in all cases the military should be under strict subordination to, and governed by, the civil power.

14. That the people have a right to uniform government; and, therefore, that no government separate from, or independent of the government of Virginia, ought to be erected or established within the limits thereof.

15. That no free government, or the blessings of liberty, can be preserved to any people, but by a firm adherence to justice, moderation, temperance, frugality and virtue, and by frequent recurrence to fundamental principles.

16. That religion, or the duty which we owe to our Creator, and the manner of discharging it, can be directed only by reason and conviction, not by force or violence; and therefore all men are equally entitled to the free exercise of religion, according to the dictates of conscience; and that it is the mutual duty of all to practise Christian forbearance, love, and charity towards each other.

Articles of Confederation, November 15, 1777

Art. I. The Stile of this confederacy shall be "The United States of America."

Art. II. Each state retains its sovereignty, freedom and independence, and every Power, Jurisdiction and right, which is not by this confederation expressly delegated to the United States, in Congress assembled.

Art. III. The said states hereby severally enter into a firm league of friendship with each other, for their common defence, the security of their Liberties, and their mutual and general welfare, binding themselves to assist each other, against all force offered to, or attacks made upon them, or any of them, on account of religion, sovereignty, trade, or any other pretence whatever. . . .

CHAPTER

3

The Framing of the Constitution and the Federalists

The end of the War for Independence signified, on the one hand, the stabilization of the United States by the elimination of an external threat. At the same time, this elimination of the threat from without weakened the momentum for unification within. The antagonisms among many states and sections and the conflict between the radical and the moderate groups, all of which had been more or less subsumed in the common purpose of executing the war, threatened to reemerge with the end of the war.

Thus beset with internal tensions, the newly established, feeble United States also faced the necessity of preserving its political and economic independence in the midst of a complex international environment. It had to claim its own right of independent government on the American continent, where the European powers were engaged in bitter rivalry. Under these conditions, the establishment of a central government and the formation of a unified nation was demanded, and American politics moved toward making a constitution. We must, however, note that the drafting of a constitution was not considered to be the process of founding a single unified state. The constitution makers attempted to accomplish the task of unification by creating a "more perfect union" in the form of a federal state.

The Demand for the Formation of a Nation

The primary factors which caused American society to proceed toward the formation of a nation were the many diplomatic and economic disadvantages to which the United States of America was subjected because it was not a unified country. Individual states were often unwilling to be bound by the peace treaty with England and tried to evade the treaty's obligations; England also frequently ignored the treaty so long as the United States did not function as a unified nation. The other European countries which had colonies on the American continent viewed the rise of a republican nation with suspicion. As a result, even on the American continent the position of the United States was not secure enough.

With independence America had left the protection of the English mercantile system and entered into a conflictive and competitive trade relationship with England. Creation of a protective system for its own trade became an urgent task for the new nation, but it lacked the means to enforce its own protective trade regulations, and efforts to conclude a commercial treaty with England were unsuccessful.

The War for Independence itself had in a sense acted as a protective tariff, but with the end of the war English manufactured goods again flooded the American market, impeding the development of the infant native manufacturing industries. Moreover, each state independently established tariffs to protect its own economy; these tariff barriers divided the United States, as a market, into small parts and severely damaged the economic interests of the nation as a whole. Also, because the United States lacked the power to tax, and the states often failed to make their allocated contributions to the Continental Congress, the nation's finances steadily deteriorated.

Pressure for the establishment of a central government was also coming out of the whirlpool of political disputes within the country. The power struggle between the moderates and radicals continued in each state. Growing opportunities for the western farming class to participate in politics tended to increase the influence of the radical group. Consequently, political power in many states in many cases was held by the radicals, and laws favorable to debtors were repeatedly enacted. Aspiring to restrict the radicals' power indirectly through a strong national government, the moderates undertook the formation of a central government and the concomitant restriction of state government power.

The problem of administering the United States's vast land holdings must be considered one of the major factors in the creation of a unified nation. Under the terms of the Peace Treaty of 1783, the vast territories extending west of the Appalachian Mountains to the Mississippi River were transferred from England to the United States. However, struggles over the possession and management of these territories emerged among the various states and between Congress and the states. The central question was whether the vast space extending west of the thirteen states should belong to each state, or to the United States. After complex and tangled negotiations it was decided that the western lands should be directly owned by the United States, and Thomas Jefferson and others proceeded with plans to determine the method of control and jurisdiction over these territories. The Northwest Ordinance of 1787 stipulated that the western lands, rather than remaining in effect perpetual colonial territories under the control of the central government, would be admitted into the United States as individual states, with the same rights as the original thirteen states, after reaching a certain population and following certain steps. This measure, while preserving the principle of the republican system, made territorial expansion possible.

Fueled by the realities of external relations and shifts in domestic power relations, the pressure to transform the United States into a single nation gradually grew stronger. On the other hand, the vast American continent with its great regional variation tended to weaken the shared feeling of being Americans, and many colonists who had so recently fought against domination by one sovereign state were reluctant to create another. The demand for the creation of a unified nation and the sentiment against it maintained a balance of strength in public sentiment during this period.

Shays's Rebellion, which erupted in Massachusetts in August 1786, upset this balance in favor of the pressure for formation of a strong unified nation. Its origin lay in the depression in which American agriculture found itself following independence. With the end of hostilities, there was surplus production of agricultural products, and prices declined. The prices of the goods which farmers bought, however, did not decline, widening the price differential between agricultural goods and other products. Consequently, the western farmers could not pay their debts; many lost their farms, which had been mortgaged, and some were even imprisoned for debt. In many states these farmers pressed for relief in the form of legislation, and strove to restore their own economic position. In Massachusetts, however, the conservatives controlled the legislature, and the farmers could not win enactment of measures which had been carried out in other states. The farmers in western Massachusetts, under the leadership of Daniel Shays, a captain in the Continental Army during the Revolutionary War, resorted to an armed uprising. The rebellion was finally suppressed in February 1787 by the state government in Boston, but details of the incident were widely reported in all the American states, and the demand for a strong central government was revitalized.

By 1787 attempts to revise the Articles of Confederation in order to give Congress the power to tax and regulate trade had been repeatedly made. Because revision of the Articles of Confederation required the consent of all thirteen states, these efforts had never been successful. With a view to bypassing the Articles with their self-circumscribed nature, leaders in several states began advocating the establishment of a new national constitution in place of the Articles of Confederation. Shays's Rebellion added momentum to this constitutional movement. In May 1787, a special convention was to be opened by representatives from the states; on the convention's agenda was revision of the Articles of Confederation.

The Drafting and Ratification of the Federal Constitution

Rhode Island, where the power of the radicals was strong, did not send representatives to the Federal Convention in Philadelphia. Seventy-four representatives were chosen from twelve states, and fifty-five actually attended. The majority of those fifty-five were men who had belonged to the moderate group in the revolutionary period.

The convention delegates gave much adroit consideration to the rules and procedures for framing the constitution. First, they elected George Washington as president of the convention. Washington had gained national fame as the supreme commander of the Continental Army in the War for Independence, and because of his personal integrity he enjoyed the confidence of the people. The naming of Washington, who was in a sense a symbol of the independence and unity of the United States, as president heightened the dignity of the entire convention and greatly increased respect for the constitution. A second major step was making the convention a secret conference. While the antipathy of the anti-constitutional forces swirled outside, this secrecy made it possible for the Federal Convention to carry out free discussion isolated from external influences, and made it possible to announce the constitution to the outside only after it had been drawn up.[1]

Consideration was also given to the skillful avoidance of all legal and procedural obstacles to the revision of the Articles of Confederation. No revision of the Articles could be carried out without the agreement of the legislatures of all thirteen states; as several of the state legislatures were controlled by the radicals, unanimous consent for a complete revision would have been impossible to obtain. The Federal Convention decided, therefore, to entrust the ratification of the draft constitution to the deliberation, not of the state legislatures, but of constitutional conventions to be specially convened in each state. In addition, ratification by nine states, rather than all thirteen, was made sufficient for the adoption of the constitution.

Many of the delegates participated in the Federal Convention with a national perspective. At the same time, each delegate represented the interests of his home state or section, and these interests were often in conflict. The conflict between large and small states and the antagonism between the southern and the northern states, in particular, were pronounced. As a result of these frequent clashes, the constitution became known as a

[1] Partly becaue it was a secret conference, the official minutes of the convention are extremely brief, and it is impossible to discern from them the full extent of the debates. Fortunately for historians, however, several of the delegates to the convention left behind notes on the proceedings. In particular, James Madison, who was an advocate of the enactment of the constitution and was later called "the father of the Constitution," kept a detailed record of the daily proceedings. This record was published in 1840, four years after his death, and here for the first time the full story was made public. Later, the formal minutes and these private minutes were combined and edited by Yale University professor Max Farrand and published in four volumes, the last of which appeared in 1937. This material is invaluable not only for the insight it gives into the process of the enacting of the constitution, but also for the glimpses it gives us of the political thought of the leaders of the time.

"bundle of compromises." However, along with the disagreements among the delegates, there was a fundamental consensus on certain major points. First, as the convention minutes show clearly, many delegates shared misgivings about an "excess of democracy," as one of them, Elbridge Gerry of Massachussetts, termed it. (See the minutes of the May 31, 1787, debates appended to this chapter.) Second, most delegates agreed that in order to prevent such excesses it was necessary to strengthen the central government. However, this consensus did not lead the convention to a rejection of a democratic political system or to the establishment of a powerful centralized state. With very few exceptions the delegates did not completely reject either popular sovereignty or the spirit of local autonomy, both fundamental principles of the revolution.

On the basis of their fundamental consensus, the delegates to the Federal Convention continually juggled the various interests which they represented, and drafted a constitution. First, the Virginia Plan, which had been principally drafted by James Madison, was presented to the convention. This proposal clearly advocated the creation of three national powers: legislative, executive, and judiciary. It recommended that each state, rather than uniformly sending an equal number of representatives to the central legislature, send a number of representatives which would correspond either to the state's financial contribution to the federal government or to its proportion of the population. This plan urged the adoption of a completely new constitution and the recognition of the United States as a unified nation. In contrast, the plan which was later presented by New Jersey, as a sort of counterproposal, represented the viewpoint of the smaller states. While recognizing the necessity of strengthening the Articles of Confederation, this plan opposed changing their fundamental nature. It proposed that the representatives to the central legislature not be proportional to population, but be elected in equal numbers by each state. Thus, the United States would not ultimately be reorganized as a single state, but would exist as a federation among independent states, with the smaller states having the same representation as the larger.

The conflict between the large and small states, which focused on the disagreement over the number of representatives to the central legislature, was resolved by a compromise which stipulated that the House representatives would be elected in proportion to population, and the Senators would be elected in equal numbers by each state. The conflict between the interest of the southern and the northern states came to a head over the question of whether to include slaves in computing the adult population of each state. This issue was finally settled by a compromise which calculated one slave as three-fifths of a person. North and south were also in conflict over the regulation of foreign trade. This dispute was also settled by a compromise which required the consent of a two-thirds majority rather than a simple majority in the Senate for the conclusion of a treaty with a foreign country.

Without going into more detail here on its specific provisions, I want to summarize the fundamental characteristics of the constitution which was signed in September of 1787.

First, the constitution took the form of a written document, and it presented itself as the highest law of the land, controlling and restricting the power which all organs of authority, including the legislature, were to exercise. The powers of the federal government were clearly limited by the constitution to "delegated and enumerated powers," and actions or laws which transcended them would be invalidated as unconstitutional. The source of this characteristic of the constitution can probably be sought in the experience of the struggle with England during the revolutionary period. Both the principle of popular sovereignty, which was basic to the revolution, and the idea that the people possess the power to enact a constitution were made basic premises.

The second fundamental characteristic of the constitution lies in that although it aimed at the reorganization of the United States as a unified state, it did not deny the independent authority of the states. The constitution recognized a division of authority between the central government and the state governments, and aimed to establish an intermediate form between the single centralized state and the confederation of independent states. It set up a federal system rather than consolidation or confederation, in the words of that time. This characteristic of the constitution was also based on the experience of the colonial and revolutionary eras, and one can probably say that the demands for centralization and the insistence on local autonomy were harmonized.

As its third fundamental characteristic, the constitution adopted the system of separation of the three powers which had already been effected in each state, and in this sense also can be said to have been based on the experience of the colonial and revolutionary eras. However, one must note that the separation of the three powers in the federal constitution differed from that in the state constitutions, where the separation of powers was meant to limit the executive branch. In the federal system, the executive and judiciary branches were meant to control the legislature. Although both systems established separation of powers, they were responses to different political conditions.

The constitution was publicly announced and submitted to the state ratification conventions, and the issues it presented were debated fiercely in each state. Perhaps the most important issue was the question of whether this constitution would fundamentally alter the nature of the United States as defined by the Articles of Confederation. In answer to the defenders of the confederate system, the supporters of the constitution replied that it would define the United States as a federal state, rather than a single nation-state, and they called themselves Federalists rather than Nationalists. The anti-constitution faction came to be called Anti-Federalists, which term placed them in a passive position. By their adroit use of terminology, the pro-constitution faction had seized the initiative in the struggle for the adoption of the constitution. Eight-five essays in defense of the constitution appeared under a pseudonym in New York newspapers during the struggle over ratification; they were actually written by Alexander Hamilton, John Jay, and James Madison, and later were published in book form under the title *The Federalist*. This work was written by practical politicians, but it was more than just an attempt to justify the constitution. As a work which, through debates on the constitution, expounded political thoughts transcending the immediate points at issue, it occupies a position of great importance in the history of American political thought. (See the excerpt appended to this chapter.)

A second point of contention was the omission of a Bill of Rights from the original constitution. The pro-constitution people argued that because the constitution defined the federal government as a limited government which could enact only certain types of measures, it was not necessary to attach to it a Bill of Rights. Certainly, this argument was logical. However, to many Americans of those days the concept of a constitution was linked indivisibly with that of a Bill of Rights which would guarantee the protection of human rights against authority; thus this constitution which lacked a Bill of Rights gave many Americans the impression that it ignored the rights of the people. In fact, many of the state conventions ratified the constitution only on the condition that a Bill of Rights be appended later.

The anti-constitution group also frequently pointed out that this constitution would protect the interests of the wealthy classes and would sacrifice the interests of the lower classes—that its provisions were more advantageous for merchants, who were owners of personal property, than for the small farmers of the west.

Centering on these issues, a fierce debate between the Federalists and Anti-Federalists raged at the state conventions. The radical groups, which had been insufficiently represented at the Federal Convention, developed a powerful opposition movement aimed at the obstruction of ratification in the individual state conventions. One can cite, for example, the activities of men like Patrick Henry in Virginia, a hero of the revolutionary period, in the opposition movement. By 1788, however, eleven states had ratified the constitution, and it went into effect as the Constitution of the United States.

The ratification itself did not signify unanimity. In New York, for example, which was the eleventh state to ratify, there were thirty votes for and twenty-seven against, so the Constitution was ratified by the small margin of three votes. In the eleven states as a whole, there were 844 votes, or 64.4 percent, in favor, and 467 votes, or 35.6 percent, against. In other words, approximately one-third of the votes were in opposition to ratification. These negative votes were more numerous in the west; the small farming class still harbored a distrust of the merchants and the planters, the elite of the east coast, who constituted the political leadership and supported the Federalist movement. Thus, in the process of enactment, the grounds for conflict between moderates and radicals, Federalists and Anti-Federalists, the eastern elite and the western farmers, were clearly identified. These conflicts over the enactment of the Constitution would evolve into conflicts centering on the national power structure established by the Constitution.[2]

The Federalist Administration

With the ratification and enactment of the Constitution, the United States of America was restructured as a nation with a federal government which had direct law enforcement power over the individual citizen. However, the question of who was to control this governing organ became an urgent political issue. The men who were most active in the movement to create and enact the Constitution—namely, the Federalists—were of course interested not only in establishing a central government but also in taking control of that government in opposition to the radicals who held power in many of the individual states. Control of the executive branch became the first objective. As the first president, the Federalists endorsed George Washington, who not only was popular and respected but also was considered to be independent of factional squabbles. On April 6, 1789, the presidential electors unanimously elected Washington, and the first presidential inaugural ceremony of the United States of America was held in New York on April 30. John Adams of New England was elected Vice-President, and the renowned drafter of the Declaration of Independence, Thomas Jefferson, who was then in Europe, was appointed Secretary of State. The young Alexander Hamilton was appointed Secretary of the Treasury, and it was he who was the central pillar of the Federalist regime. Hamilton likened his own position to that of the English First Lord of the Treasury (prime

[2] Among the interpretations of the history of the enactment of the Constitution, the one which regards its enactment as distinct from the Revolution and another which views it as a continuation of the Revolution are, at least theoretically, sharply opposed. This dispute is closely connected to the question of whether the Revolution itself was a break with the colonial era (an affirmation of its revolutionary character) or a continuation of the colonial era (a denial of its revolutionary character). I for one should like to emphasize that throughout the colonial period, the revolutionary period, and the enactment of the Constitution there was both a continuity within American society and a separation from European society: American history was characterized by continuity in time and discontinuity in space.

minister), and he energetically promoted Federalist policies. Members of the pro-Constitution faction occupied a majority of the seats in Congress, and James Madison held the position of leadership there. John Jay was Chief Justice of the Supreme Court, and justices connected with the Federalists were in the majority. The occupation of the pivotal positions in the executive, legislative, and judicial branches by the three authors of *The Federalist*, Hamilton, Madison, and Jay, in itself symbolized the hold of the Federalists on the new government.

Americans at that time held two mutually opposing visions of the future. One was what may be termed agrarianism. It held that American society was fortunately separated from Europe by the Atlantic Ocean, and that America, therefore, could and should develop a new society which would be structurally different from European society, utilizing its abundant natural spaces to grow as an agricultural society—a nation of farmers. This vision was held by, among others, the planter Jefferson. The opposing vision may be called commercialism. It looked to European society as a model, and held that in order to catch up with and overtake Europe— and in particular England, the most advanced commercial and industrial nation—America must bend its efforts to the development of commerce and industry. This vision was naturally supported by the merchants and industrialists of the cities along the eastern seaboard, and their representative in the government was Secretary of the Treasury Hamilton.[3] By installing Washington, a planter, as President, and Jefferson, another planter, as Secretary of State, and then appointing Hamilton Secretary of the Treasury, the Federalists attempted to balance within the national government the mutually opposing interests of agriculture on the one hand and commerce and industry on the other. However, because Hamilton was in charge of economic policies, the interests of the merchants and industrialists tended to be promoted. Hamilton dealt with all the major economic and financial issues of the time—the public debt, taxation, currency, banking, and manufacturing—

---

[3] These two visions of the future were also reflected in differences over America's foreign policy. Agrarians aimed at separation from Europe's power politics (isolationism) and the creation of an empire on the American continent. Commercialists and industrialists intended to give due consideration to Europe's power politics, and wished to create a maritime empire based primarily on commerce. Ideologically as well, the former rejected the European system and made the American system their ideal, while the latter perceived America broadly as one link in a Western system.

and did so from the perspective of commercialism. The public debt policy which was announced in his "Report on the Public Credit" in 1790 aroused much controversy. The United States, in addition to its debt to France and Holland of over ten million dollars, had a domestic debt of over forty million dollars, in the form of bond issues which had been floated during the War for Independence. Hamilton proposed the redemption of all outstanding bonds at face value. In addition he urged that the federal government bear responsibility for the debts which the individual states had incurred during the war. Although Hamilton's public debt policy was primarily intended to restore confidence in the United States at home and abroad, it also protected the interests of the relatively wealthy commercial and industrial classes of the eastern seaboard, who were at that time the government's major creditors, and hurt the many debtors and farmers who had already had to sell their bonds at less than face value. Consequently, Hamilton's policy intensified the conflict between the interests of commerce and industry and the interests of agriculture.

The federal assumption of the public debt of all the states gave rise to a conflict between the northern states which held large debts and the several southern states which had already repaid their public debts on their own. In addition, Hamilton sought to finance the redemption of the bonds through the sale of government-owned land, a plan which further exacerbated the class and regional conflicts. The sale of public land to raise revenue for the federal government antagonized farmers and other landed interests, who had expected that the vast public lands would eventually be distributed among them for cultivation, and the policy for the disposition of public lands remained a major issue in American politics throughout the first half of the nineteenth century.

The federal government also contemplated taxation as a means of securing revenue for the execution of its public debt policy. As a first step, Hamilton instituted a system of moderately protective tariffs on imports. Second, a series of domestic excise taxes were enacted. Among these, the whiskey tax in particular incurred the marked hostility of the farmers of the western heartland, many of whom relied for their cash income on the sale of homemade whiskey.

Hamilton outlined the new government's monetary policies in his "Report on a National Bank" of December 1790. In order to remedy the defects of the United States monetary system, stabilize public credit, and promote various industries, Hamilton stressed, it was necessary to create a central bank like the Bank of England. He also proposed abolishing the wartime inconvertible paper currency, and unifying the currency system under the control of the central bank. The Bank of the United States was founded in Philadephia in December 1791. A bitter controversy over the constitutionality of the federal government's establishing such a bank attended its founding. Jefferson, a "strict constructionist" who interpreted the constitution narrowly as giving the federal government authority only in those areas specifically mentioned, judged the activity unconstitutional; to Hamilton, a "liberal constructionist" who interpreted the constitution broadly, it was a permissible function of the federal government.

Accompanying the financial and monetary policies was Hamilton's desire to protect and nurture the infant American manufacturing industries in order to catch up with and overtake England. This aspiration was vividly evident in the "Report on Manufactures" which Hamilton submitted to Congress in December 1791. In the report Hamilton described the factors impeding the development of American industry, and proposed the means to overcome them. These included the encouragement of immigration, the recruitment of women and children to provide inexpensive labor power in factories, and the establishment of a protective tariff policy in order to safeguard domestic industry. However, in those days, farmers were in the overwhelming majority in American society. Hamilton's plan for the development of industry failed to secure broad support, and ultimately was defeated in Congress.

As we have seen, Hamilton's economic policies would have neglected the interests of the farmers in favor of commercial and industrial development. Naturally, they gave rise to a major political dispute. The western farmers' opposition to the Federalist policies was especially intense, and at times reached the point of rebellion. In particular, the so-called Whiskey Rebellion, which broke out in the interior of Pennsylvania in July 1794 against the excise tax on whiskey, alarmed the Federalists.

The rebellion was suppressed within the year by state militia called out by President Washington. The western farmers, however, remained distrustful and resentful of the Federalist government.

Even more disturbing to the Federalists than the opposition of the western farmers, however, was that of the southern planters to Hamilton's fiscal and monetary policies. The planters had cooperated with the northern merchants in the creation of a strong central government, but the two groups became bitterly opposed on policy questions. Their estrangement resulted in a split in the Federalist party which extended all the way up to the leadership. The discord between Jefferson and Hamilton, which began over the establishment of a central bank, was complicated by personal emotional factors and grew worse. Finally, Jefferson resigned the office of Secretary of State. Madison, as spokesman for several southern states on the question of the federal assumption of the states' debts, opposed Hamilton and allied himself with Jefferson. This estrangement was further aggravated by the three men's positions on the revolution which had broken out in France. Hamilton feared that the influence of the revolution would spread to America, while Jefferson admired its republican ideals. Calling themselves the Republicans, Jefferson and his supporters formed a rival political organization.

In 1796 the presidential election pitted the Federalists, with the former vice-president, John Adams, as their candidate, against the Anti-Federalists, or Republicans, backing Thomas Jefferson. It was in a sense a presidential election fought along political party lines. Adams won by a margin of three electoral votes, and the Federalist government continued for the next four years. However, compared with their first administration, the Federalists operated the government in a distinctly partisan way. This was directly symbolized by the Alien and Sedition Acts of 1798, which were enacted in order to ward off the influence of the French Revolution and to suppress domestic criticism of the Federalist administration. However, the policy of strengthening political power through such authoritarian measures resulted in encouraging the opposition under Jefferson, who criticized the Federalists' oppressive measures as unconstitutional.

In the election of 1800 the Federalists were defeated by the Republicans, who were to remain in power for more than half a century. After the election of 1816 the Federalists disbanded, and the Federalist era came to an end in both name and fact.

There were many reasons why the Federalist regime held office for such a relatively short period. Hamilton's concept of industrialization was premature in the American society of that time, in which farmers constituted the overwhelming majority of the population and sufficient land was available for development. Hamilton's plans were realized only after the conclusion of the Civil War, over half a century after the Federalist administration, when the prerequisite social and economic conditions had finally developed. One can say that Hamilton, who is often called a realist, was, in this sense, an idealist. In contrast, Jefferson, who is often said to have been an idealist, perceived more accurately the social conditions of America just after independence, and in this sense was eminently realistic.

The Federalists also had the problem of political organization. After the enactment of the Constitution, the Federalists presented themselves as the representatives of the entire nation, rather than as a party—that is, as one of the parts which constituted the body politic. By styling themselves as a "transcendental" government which was above partisanship, they neglected the fundamental function of modern party politics—the creation of a majority through the organization of votes. The Republicans, as an opposition group, were strongly motivated by the desire to form a majority. In this respect too, we may say that Jefferson was the more pragmatic politician.

Documents

The Federal Convention, Debates, May 31, 1787

Mr. SHERMAN [Conn.] opposed the election by the people, insisting that it ought to be by the State Legislatures. The people, he said, immediately should have as little to do as may be about the government. They want information, and are constantly liable to be misled.

Mr. GERRY [Mass.]. The evils we experience flow from the excess of democracy. The people do not want virtue, but are the dupes of pretended patriots. In Massachusetts it had been fully confirmed by experience that they are daily misled into the most baneful measures and opinions by the false reports circulated by designing men, and which no one on the spot can refute. One principal evil arises from the want of due provision for those employed in the administration of government. It would seem to be a maxim of democracy to starve the public servants. He mentioned the popular clamour in Massachusetts for the reduction of salaries and the attack made on that of the Governor, though secured by the spirit of the Constitution itself. He had he said been too republican heretofore: he was still however republican, but had been taught by experience the danger of the levilling spirit.

Mr. MASON [Va.] argued strongly for an election of the larger branch by the people. It was to be the grand depository of the democratic principle of the Government. It was, so to speak, to be our House of Commons. It ought to know and sympathise with every part of the community; and ought therefore to be taken not only from different parts of the whole republic, but also from different districts of the larger members of it, which had in several instances, particularly in Virginia, different interests and views arising from difference of produce, of habits, etc., etc. He admitted that we had been too democratic, but was afraid we should incautiously run into the opposite extreme. We ought to attend to the rights of every class of the people. He had often wondered at the indifference of the superior classes of society to this dictate of humanity and policy; considering that however affluent their circumstances, or elevated their situations might be, the course of a few years not only might but certainly would distribute their posterity throughout the lowest classes of society. Every selfish motive, therefore, every family attachment, ought to recommend such a system of policy as would provide no less carefully for the rights and happiness of lowest than of the highest orders of citizens.

Mr. WILSON [Penn.] contended strenuously for drawing the most numerous branch of the Legislature immediately from the people. He was for raising the federal pyramid to a considerable altitude, and for that reason wished to give it as broad a basis as possible. No government could long subsist without the confidence of the people. In a republican government this confidence was peculiarly essential. He also thought it wrong to increase the weight of the State Legislatures by making them the electors of the National Legislature. All interference between the general and local governments should be obviated as much as possible. On examination it would be found that the opposition of States to federal measures had proceded much more from the officers of the States, than from the people at large.

Mr. MADISON considered the popular election of one branch of the National Legislature as essential to every plan of free government. He observed that in some of the States one branch of the Legislature was composed of men already removed from the people by an intervening body of electors. That if the first branch of the general legislature should be elected by the State Legislatures, the second branch elected by the first, the Executive by the second together with the first; and other appointments again made for subordinate purposes by the Executive, the people would be lost sight of altogether; and the necessary sympathy between them and their rulers and officers, too little left. He was an advocate for the policy of refining the popular appointments by successive filtrations, but thought it might be pushed too far. He wished the expedient to be resorted to only in the appointment of the second branch of the Legislature, and in the executive and judiciary branches of the government. He thought, too, that the great fabric to be raised would be more stable and durable, if it should rest on the solid foundation of the people themselves, than if it should stand merely on the pillars of the Legislatures.

Mr. GERRY did not like the election by the people. The maxims taken from the British Constitution were often fallacious when applied to our situation which was extremely different. Experience he said had shewn that the State legislatures drawn immediately from the people did not always possess their confidence. He had no objection, however, to an election by the people, if it were so qualified that men of honor and character might not be unwilling to be joined in the appointments. He seemed to think the people might nominate a certain number out of which the State legislatures should be bound to choose.

Mr. BUTLER [S. C.] thought an election by the people an impracticable mode.

On the question for an election of the first branch of the National Legislature by the people:

Mass. ay. Conn. div. N.Y. ay. N.J. no. Penn. ay. Del. div. Va. ay. N. C. ay. S.C. no. Geo. ay.

The Federalist, No. 51 (Madison), 1788

To the People of the State of New York:

. . . But the great security against a gradual concentration of the several powers in the same department, consists in giving to those who administer each department the necessary constitutional means and personal motives to resist encroachments of the others. The provision for defence must in this, as in all other cases, be made commensurate to the danger of attack. Ambition must be made to counteract ambition. The interest of the man must be connected with the constitutional rights of the place. It may be a reflection on human nature, that such devices should be necessary to control the abuses of government. But what is government itself, but the greatest of all reflections on human nature? If men were angels, no government would be necessary. If angels were to govern men, neither external nor internal controls on government would be necessary. In framing a government which is to be administered by men over men, the great difficulty lies in this: you must first enable the government to control the governed; and in the next place oblige it to control itself. A dependence on the people is, no doubt, the primary control on the government; but experience has taught mankind the necessity of auxiliary precautions.

This policy of supplying, by opposite and rival interests, the defect of better motives, might be traced through the whole system of human affairs, private as well as public. We see it particularly displayed in all the subordinate distributions of power, where the constant aim is to divide and arrange the

several offices in such a manner as that each may be a check on the other—
that the private interest of every individual may be a sentinel over the public
rights. These inventions of prudence cannot be less requisite in the distribution
of the supreme powers of the State.

But it is not possible to give to each department an equal power of self-
defence. In republican government, the legislative authority necessarily pre-
dominates. The remedy for this inconveniency is to divide the legislature into
different branches; and to render them, by different modes of election and different principles of action, as little connected with each other as the nature of
their common functions and their common dependence on the society will
admit. It may even be necessary to guard against dangerous encroachments
by still further precautions. As the weight of the legislative authority requires
that it should be thus divided, the weakness of the executive may require, on the
other hand, that it should be fortified. An absolute negative on the legislature
appears, at first view, to be the natural defence with which the executive magistrate should be armed. But perhaps it would be neither altogether safe nor
alone sufficient. On ordinary occasions it might not be exerted with the requisite firmness, and on extraordinary occasions it might be perfidiously abused.
May not this defect of an absolute negative be supplied by some qualified connection between this weaker department and the weaker branch of the stronger
department, by which the latter may be led to support the constitutional rights
of the former, without being too much detached from the rights of its own
department?

If the principles on which these observations are founded be just, as I per-
suade myself they are, and they be applied as a criterion to the several State
constitutions, and to the federal Constitution, it will be found that if the latter
does not perfectly correspond with them, the former are infinitely less able to
bear such a test.

There are, moreover, two considerations particularly applicable to the
federal system of America, which place that system in a very interesting point
of view.

First. In a single republic, all the power surrendered by the people is submitted to the administration of a single government; and the usurpations are
guarded against by a division of the government into distinct and separate departments. In the compound republic of America, the power surrendered by
the people is first divided between two distinct governments, and then the
portion allotted to each subdivided among distinct and separate departments.
Hence a double security arises to the rights of the people. The different governments will control each other, at the same time that each will be controlled
by itself.

Second. It is of great importance in a republic not only to guard the society
against the oppression of its rulers, but to guard one part of the society against
the injustice of the other part. Different interests necessarily exist in different
classes of citizens. If a majority be united by a common interest, the rights of
the minority will be insecure. There are but two methods of providing against
this evil: the one by creating a will in the community independent of the ma-

jority—that is, of the society itself; the other, by comprehending in the society so many separate descriptions of citizens as will render an unjust combination of a majority of the whole very improbable, if not impracticable. The first method prevails in all governments possessing an hereditary or self-appointed authority. This, at best, is but a precarious security; because a power independent of the society may as well espouse the unjust views of the major, as the rightful interests of the minor party, and may possibly be turned against both parties. The second method will be exemplified in the federal republic of the United States. Whilst all authority in it will be derived from and dependent on the society, the society itself will be broken into so many parts, interests and classes of citizens, that the rights of individuals, or of the minority, will be in little danger from interested combinations of the majority. . . .   Publius

From the New York Packet, Friday, February 8, 1788

George Washington, Farewell Address, 1794

. . . Europe has a set of primary interests which to us have none or a very remote relation. Hence she must be engaged in frequent controversies, the causes of which are essentially foreign to our concerns. Hence, therefore, it must be unwise in us to implicate ourselves by artificial ties in the ordinary vicissitudes of her politics or the ordinary combinations and collisions of her friendships or enmities.

Our detached and distant situation invites and enables us to pursue a different course. If we remain one people, under an efficient government, the period is not far off when we may defy material injury from external annoyance; when we may take such an attitude as will cause the neutrality we may at any time resolve upon to be scrupulously respected; when belligerent nations, under the impossibility of making acquisitions upon us, will not lightly hazard the giving us provocation; when we may choose peace or war, as our interest, guided by justice, shall counsel.

Why forego the advantages of so peculiar a situation? Why quit our own to stand upon foreign ground? Why, by interweaving our destiny with that of any part of Europe, entangle our peace and prosperity in the toils of European ambition, rivalship, interest, humor, or caprice?

It is our true policy to steer clear of permanent alliances with any portion of the foreign world, so far, I mean, as we are now at liberty to do it; for let me not be understood as capable of patronizing infidelity to existing engagements. I hold the maxim no less applicable to public than to private affairs that honesty is always the best policy. I repeat, therefore, let those engagements be observed in their genuine sense. But in my opinion it is unnecessary and would be unwise to extend them.

4

Agrarian Democracy and a Continental Empire

Following the victory of Thomas Jefferson in the election of 1800, the Republican (later the Democratic) Party remained in power most of the time until 1861. This government of the Democratic-Republicans was primarily supported by the southern planters and the western farming class. It represented primarily agricultural interests.

During this period, having consciously excluded the influence of the European powers and acquired a vast territory on the continent, America established a continental empire. The opportunity for the masses to participate in politics also expanded, and democracy spread across the American continent. Today we regard the United States as an industrial country and a world maritime power, but we must remember that before it became an industrial country or a maritime power, it was a continental empire in which agriculture was the major form of production.

While the nation was growing as a continental agricultural empire, Americans were envisioning a unique American civilization different from Europe's, and American nationalism, or Americanism, was born. At the same time, this immense nation inevitably harbored many conflicts and differences. Of the numerous conflicts which grew increasingly conspicuous in the early nineteenth century, the sectional conflict between the south and the north was most serious. In due time it would result in an armed encounter, the Civil War.

Republican Victory and Agricultural Interests

In the presidential election of 1800 Thomas Jefferson was again

61

the Republicans' candidate. Jefferson, who enjoyed a national reputation as the drafter of the Declaration of Independence, was widely respected as a defender of the farmers' interests. Though he was a southern planter, he showed deep sympathy for the independent farmers of the western hinterlands. He also showed his willingness to adopt a realistic election strategy by selecting his antithesis, the New York City politician Aaron Burr, as his running mate in order to solicit votes from such groups as the artisans of the northeast.

Jefferson received seventy-three electoral votes and defeated, by a small margin, the Federalists' John Adams, who received sixty-five. The Republicans also won a majority of seats in both the Senate and the House. The main campaign issues included the Alien and Sedition Acts, the rising taxes which had accompanied the expansion of government expenditures, and the Federalists' pro-English foreign policy; all of these were reflections of the conflict between the agricultural interests and the commercial-industrial interests—or, to use the contemporary jargon, between the landed interests and the moneyed interests. The very fact that Jefferson won this election signaled the ascendancy of the agricultural interests.

The Federalists, after their defeat in both the presidential and congressional elections, strove, during the remaining months of Adams's term of office, to entrench their influence through the judicial branch. Secretary of State John Marshall was appointed Chief Justice of the Supreme Court, and on the day before Jefferson's presidential inauguration many Federalist judges were sent to the federal courts in so-called "midnight appointments." Certainly, these political appointments prolonged the Federalist influence in the judicial branch, and they sowed the seeds of later conflict between the judicial branch and the legislative and executive branches. Specifically, in the Marbury v. Madison decision of 1803, Marshall asserted and established the right of judicial review of the constitutionality of Congressional acts. During the thirty-four years he served as Chief Justice, Marshall endeavored to strengthen the Union.

In March 1801, Jefferson was inaugurated as president in Washington, D.C., which had officially become the capital in the summer of the preceding year. In his inaugural address, Jefferson stated, "We are all Republicans, we are all Federalists," emphasizing reconciliation, homogeneity, and continuity. Jefferson later referred to his election as the "revolution of 1800." In the sense that the outcome of the election was to redirect basic policy orientation from an emphasis on commerce and industry to an emphasis on agriculture, which had the support of the majority of the people, it might be termed "revolutionary." However, the Republican administration also was supported by many prominent and wealthy citizens. The Republican presidents after Jefferson, such as James Madison and James Monroe, were all illustrious planters from Virginia, and their successive administrations were called the "Virginia dynasty."

In terms of concrete policies, the Republican administration began both negatively, through abolition of some Federalist policies, and positively, by enacting new policies protecting and aiding the agricultural interests. Having inherited the public debt which was central to Federalist financial policies, Albert Gallatin, Secretary of the Treasury, took steps to repay it as rapidly as possible. During Jefferson's administration, from 1801 to 1809, the balance of unpaid public debt actually decreased from $83,000,000 to $57,000,000. The Federalist tax policies, which had been especially unpopular among farmers, were revised on a wide scale, and taxes such as the excise tax on whiskey were abolished. Asserting that a good government is "a wise and frugal government," Jefferson effected a simplification of the government structure, which had begun to expand greatly under the Federalist administrations. When the charter of the Bank of the United States expired, the Republican administration dissolved this institution which, established during the Federalist era, had caused a violent constitutional debate. The Alien and Sedition Acts, which the Federalists had frequently used to suppress opposition, were abolished immediately upon their expiration, and those imprisoned under them were released.

In addition to these revisions of Federalist policies, the Republicans also took steps to protect agricultural interests. First came improvements in the means of domestic communication and transportation. On this immense continent such improvements were essential if American agriculture, which was at that time evolving from a self-sufficiency basis to a commercial basis, was to convert its products more effectively into merchandise. The western farmers strongly demanded that the federal government take positive steps to open up an east-west transportation route. The Republican administration began planning a network of toll roads and canals. Construction of a national road, the Cumberland Road, from the vicinity of the capital, Washington, over the Appalachian Mountains to the Ohio valley, was begun in 1807. These improvements signified not only the development of the east as a market for agricultural products, but also the growth of the western market for the products of the eastern industries.

Second, the Republican administration gradually revised the system of management of public lands, which had been considered an important source of revenue for the national treasury. It decided to promote the sale of these lands in small units at low prices to small and medium-sized farmers. Originally, the minimum area for the sale of public land had been 640 acres, but in May of 1800 this was reduced by half, to 320 acres. During the Republican administration, it became considerably easier for small farmers to acquire land. However, the farmers' original demand that public lands be given free to those who would cultivate them remained unsatisfied, and the disposal of public lands remained a major political issue.

A third policy change involved the expansion of the land space itself. The government determined to incorporate into the nation's territory as new agricultural land the vast territory to the west of the Mississippi River. In October 1800, France had succeeded, by secret treaty with Spain, in recovering as its own territory the Louisiana region west of the Mississippi River. Napoleon Bonaparte planned to reestablish a French colonial empire on the North American continent. In due time this secret treaty became known to Jefferson. He feared that if the port of New Orleans, at the mouth of the Mississippi River, became French territory, it would be closed to Americans. New Orleans was the port from which agricultural goods from the Mississippi River basin were forwarded to eastern markets; in this sense, it was a vital link in the western agricultural system. Therefore, Jefferson sent a mission to Paris to negotiate with the French government for the purchase of New Orleans. By that time, France was faced with a slave rebellion in its Haitian colony, as well as a war in Europe, and was therefore driven to abandon the scheme to build a colonial empire on the American continent. Consequently, in 1803, the United States succeeded in purchasing, at an extremely low price, not only New Orleans, but also a vast territory west of the Mississippi River, the so-called Louisiana Territory. As a result, the nation's territory was almost doubled, and its position of dominance on the American continent was firmly established. Even prior to the purchase of this territory, Jefferson had planned the exploration and opening up of the region west of the Mississippi, and he sent the expedition of Meriwether Lewis and William Clark (1803–6) to the western interior to explore a transportation route to the Pacific coast.

By means of such policies, the United States began, under the Jefferson administration, to establish the foundation upon which it would develop as an agricultural nation. The fortuitous expansion of the nation's territory made possible simultaneously the expansion of the slavery-based plantation system, with its inherent need for new, fertile land, and the development of the independent western farmers. This ability to please both the southern planters and the western farmers, two groups whose interests were contradictory, was the fundamental basis of the stability of the Republican administration.[1]

Nationalism and Sectionalism

American independence would not have been possible without the international power struggle in Europe which centered on England and France. In order to maintain its independence once it had been achieved, it was necessary for the United States, as a backward and relatively minor nation, to isolate itself from the struggles among the various European powers.

---

[1] The acquisition of this immense expanse of land and the promotion of agricultural interests meant that for a long time the majority of the total population had to be farmers. As a result the belief that farmers were the nucleus of American society was firmly established. Long ago Jefferson said, "We have an immensity of land courting the industry of the husbandman. . . . Those who labour in the earth are the chosen people of God, if ever he had a chosen people" (Thomas Jefferson, "Notes on Virginia," 1787, in *The Life and Selected Writings of Thomas Jefferson* [Modern Library edition], 1944, p. 280). (See excerpt appended to this chapter.)

The Hamiltonian vision of a commercial maritime empire and the Jeffersonian vision of a continental agricultural empire agreed on this point. Despite this, however, the impact of the French Revolution and the accompanying conflict between England and France extended even to America, and inevitably exerted a major influence on American foreign policy. The government was faced with the decision of whether to side with France on the basis of the Franco-American alliance during the War for Independence, or to maintain neutrality on the basis of the principle of non-involvement in European affairs. The English blockade against France was also damaging to American trade and had more than a minor effect on the American economy.

In this situation, pro-French, anti-British feeling was strong in American society, and in one sector there was even pressure for war with England. The incumbent Federalist administration, however, chose to protect trade by accommodation with England. In 1794 Washington sent Chief Justice John Jay to England as special envoy, and Jay's Treaty, as it is commonly known, was concluded. This treaty stipulated the withdrawal of English troops from the northern part of America and the protection of American trade and fishing interests. However, because it recognized debts to England incurred prior to the War for Independence and pledged their payment, it was criticized not only by the Republicans, but even by some industrialists and Federalists. Nonetheless, due to the vigorous lobbying of Hamilton and others, it was approved by the Senate the next year and ratified. It was a domestically unpopular treaty, but it enabled the United States to remain outside the European conflict for the time being.

Before leaving office as president in 1796, Washington delivered a farewell address in which he emphasized that, due to its geographical isolation from Europe, it was possible for America to follow a path different from that of Europe, and he urged his nation not to be engulfed in European conflicts involving interests unrelated to America. (See the excerpt appended to Chapter 3.) In view of the international political situation at the time and the fragile national power of America, this concept of "non-alliance" was extremely practical. It could also be said to have been the most suitable from the perspective of power politics.

Jefferson also, in his presidential inaugural address, as one of his basic policies, promised "peace, commerce, and honest friendship with all nations, entangling alliances with none." However, in his case the concept of non-involvement was mingled with an ideological orientation which asserted that American society must develop in a direction essentially different from that of European society.

Under the Jefferson administration, the basic policy of maintaining neutrality from Europe was so thorough that it resulted in the promulgation of the Embargo Act of 1807, which actually caused the interruption of commercial relations between America and many European countries and evoked intense criticism from the industrialists and merchants of New England. The immediate cause of the enactment of this law was an incident in which the English navy by force of arms seized the American ship *Chesapeake* just off Norfolk, Virginia, alleging that some British deserters were among its crew. The incident, which was not the first of its kind, reawakened anti-British sentiment among Americans, and stimulated feelings of nationalism. During 1810 and 1811, supported by these anti-British and nationalist feelings, a group called the "war hawks" became influential in Congress. Led by such men as Henry Clay of Kentucky and John C. Calhoun of South Carolina, they were mostly from the west or the south and represented the agricultural interests of those sections, and they strongly urged war with England. Those from the northwest, who were continually warring with the Indians, demanded eradication of the British power behind those Indians, and also wanted to obtain possession of Canada. The southerners wanted to gain possession of Florida, which belonged to Spain. Finally, in June 1812, under the fourth president, James Madison, the United States declared war on England.

This war, often called the "Second War for Independence," came to an inconclusive end in 1815 because, among other things, England was fighting Napoleon and America was internally split, with strong opposition to the war coming from the northeast's commercial interests. The war, which ended without a definite victory for either England or the United States, in the end brought no benefit to America. It was not, however, insignificant in American history. First, by means of this war the identity of the American people was expanded and strengthened. Second, the embargo on British goods which accompanied the war actually functioned as a protective tariff for the United States, which had depended on British industry for many of its consumer goods, and presented a great opportunity for the development of American domestic manufacturing industries. In other words, this war was extremely important in that it aided the growth of both national consciousness and economic independence, and in this dual sense truly functioned as a second War for Independence. Also, with the end of the war there emerged a stability in the relations between Europe and America. Due to the balance of power on the European continent, none of the European powers had the capacity to interfere in North America, and so it was possible for America to isolate itself from Europe, enjoying "free security," and give exclusive attention to the development of the interior of the American continent. In this sense as well, one could say that this war guaranteed America's independence from Europe.

The American nationalism strengthened by this isolation from Europe and by the expansion into the interior of the American continent was proclaimed in the so-called Monroe Doctrine of 1823. This doctrine was conceived during James Monroe's presidency by the then Secretary of State, John Quincy Adams. Its immediate objective was the suppression of the advances of the Russian empire, which had begun to encroach upon the Pacific Coast. The doctrine extolled the "principle of anti-colonization," asserting that henceforth the American continent could not be the object of European colonization. It also took cognizance of events to the south of the United States. During the Napoleonic Wars, many colonies in Central and South America had achieved independence. With the end of the wars, however, the old regimes were restored under the Holy Alliance among the European powers. The Monroe Doctrine stated American opposition to the restoration of the old regime in Latin America on the "principle of non-interventionism," which excluded the interference of Europe from America or the Western Hemisphere. In a third point, which was the reverse aspect of the second, the doctrine stated that neither would the United States interfere in the affairs of Europe. (See the excerpt appended to this chapter.)

The Monroe Doctrine, which focused on these three points, is important as a reflection of America's growing power and self-confidence with respect to Europe during the first half of the nineteenth century. It could be said, however, that what actually guaranteed the provisions of the declaration was the 3,000-mile expanse of the Atlantic Ocean, the existence of a balance of power among the European nations, and the British fleet as the guarantor of that balance of power. In this way the United States attained hegemony on the North American continent and in the Western Hemisphere. Here, however, we must note that this hegemony was not merely the result of contemporary power politics, but also grew from an ideological orientation that fostered on the American continent a political and social system different from that of Europe. In this respect it is not difficult to perceive in the Monroe Doctrine itself images which contrasted the old world, the old regime, the Holy Alliance, and despotism with the new world, a new regime, and freedom. This line of thinking eventually evolved into the later concept of "manifest destiny."[2]

American nationalism, which aspired to create a unique American culture and civilization distinct from that of Europe, demanded the creation of a so-called American national literature. Emerson's 1837 lecture, "The American Scholar"—in which he declared, "Our day of dependence, our long apprenticeship to the learning of other lands, draws to a close"—was one example of the effort to develop independent American forms of art and science. In this same spirit, Noah Webster drew attention to the development of an American language which differed from English, and compiled a dictionary of American-English.

After the war of 1812, the rivalries among political factions

[2] The creation of the United States of America's hegemony on the American continent, even if not accompanied by a territorial advance toward Central and South America, signified the emergence of a new threat to those countries soon after their independence. Indeed, in due time, the existence of the United States of America, the "Giant of the North," became both an economic and a cultural threat. The Latin American nations had inherited from Spain and Portugal a Latin culture quite different from Anglo-Saxon culture; religiously, they were Catholic. Rather than perceiving North and South America as a single entity, as North Americans often did, they saw them as two very different continents. This explains why Latin America later regarded the Monroe Doctrine as sowing the seeds of "American imperialism."

virtually disappeared. Monroe's reelection in 1820 signaled the dissolution of the Federalists; the American political system had in effect become a one-party system. The frequent use of the term "Era of Good Feelings" to refer to this period indicates its relatively stable atmosphere. However, beneath the surface of this external unity vis-à-vis Europe and the apparent domestic unity which accompanied the disappearance of political partisanship, America of the 1820s in reality continued to be rife with internal sectional conflict, or "sectionalism," as differences in economic structure among the sections, due to divergent climate and topography, became increasingly conspicuous. Antagonism between north and south had existed as early as the period of the Revolutionary War. With the opening up and development of the west, its position as an independent section became stronger, and henceforth the sectional conflict among north and south, east and west took on major significance in American politics.

The concept of "the West" is peculiar to American history; in addition to its geographical connotation, it is also, as Frederick Jackson Turner indicated, an eminently social term. Rather than denoting a single, fixed region, it literally moved westward with history. In the first half of the nineteenth century "the West" generally referred to the region west of the Appalachian Mountains and east of the Mississippi River. Stimulated by policies such as internal improvements and sale of public lands, the number of migrants to the west increased year by year, and with it the relative importance of the west in the Union. The population west of the Appalachians, which in 1800 was 570,000 or approximately one-tenth of the total population of the Union, rose in 1820 to 2,300,000 or one-fourth of the total population, and in 1830 reached 3,600,000 or one-third of the total population. By 1821 ten new states had entered the Union from the west. This naturally meant an expansion of the influence of the west in Congress and in presidential elections.

Compared to the rigid society of the east, western society was relatively fluid; it lacked divisions by social status, and equality of opportunity was more real than in eastern society. In the new states of the west the right of universal suffrage for white males was almost taken for granted, and a system of rotation of office was also generally practiced. This was perhaps due more to the special circumstances of frontier life than to political principle; creating a new community in the west required the labor and money of the residents, and in order to obtain their full cooperation, it was necessary to grant them meaningful political participation. In any event, democracy was actually more widely practiced in western society than in the east. As the west gradually developed in this manner and expanded its influence in the Union, it sought, as its own political demand, an expansion of popular political participation on a national level. In the economic sphere, the west demanded further improvement of the means of transportation and communication with the east and the distribution of public land to cultivators at low prices or, better yet, free. It also sought the expansion of landed space for agricultural cultivation and further expansion toward the west.

The south, although centered like the west around agricultural and landed interests, exhibited a rather different developmental pattern. Since I will discuss the south again in the next chapter, here I shall merely touch on it briefly. Southern society began to develop through tobacco cultivation based on the slave system. By the time of the Revolutionary War, this system of plantation agriculture had proven economically unprofitable, and it was therefore thought that the eventual disappearance of slavery itself was a matter of time. In this sense, by the time of the War for Independence the south did not consider itself a peculiar region based on the "peculiar institution" of slavery. However, the invention of the cotton gin by Eli Whitney in 1793 simplified the removal of cotton seeds, and the production of raw cotton in the south rapidly increased. At the same time, the English cotton cloth industry centered in Manchester was developing rapidly, and the demand for raw cotton grew apace. Thus the cultivation of cotton expanded rapidly in the beginning of the nineteenth century, especially in the western part of the original southern states and in the new southern states. As a result, the south came to have major world importance in cotton production. The slavery system reestablished itself in the section, and a positive rationale in defense of slavery emerged.

Thus in the 1820s the south began to make the following three political demands: the positive maintenance of the slavery system which supported the cultivation of cotton; the acquisition of new, fertile territory to cope with the rapid devastation of land by the system of plantation agriculture; and the strengthening of the policy of free trade in order to guarantee the export of raw cotton to, and the purchase of cheap manufactured goods from, England. The southern planters felt that it was necessary to grasp power on a national level in order to protect their special interests and to enact their own policies. Their pursuit of national power and advancement of their own interests deepened the conflict between the south and the other sections, and in due time culminated in the Civil War.

The northeast, as we have already seen, accumulated capital via shipping, commerce, and some manufacturing. In federal politics Hamilton's concept of industrialism had collapsed as premature, and for some time thereafter the Republicans stressed agricultural interests. However, the War of 1812 dealt an enormous blow to American shipping and commerce. Capital which until then had been invested in commerce was now invested in manufacturing, and the American manufacturing industries began to develop.

A modern integrated cotton-spinning factory was built at Waltham, Massachusetts, in 1813 by Francis C. Lowell. Thenceforth, the cotton textile industry developed rapidly and vigorously in the northeast. Entrepreneurs accumulated capital by forming joint-stock companies, and depended for labor power on the cheap labor force of local women and immigrants. To run the machines they used the water power of New England; for raw material, needless to say, they used the cotton of the south; and for a market they had the American west, which had gradually been opened up. Consequently, the northeast began to shift its political pressure from free trade to a protective tariff which would work in favor of the manufacturing industries. Further, it stressed the encouragement of immigration in order to guarantee a labor force and the improvement of transportation in order to expand the market.

Conflicts of interest among the different sectional economic structures inevitably came to be reflected in American politics. By the time of the election of 1824, in which the Republicans were still the sole political party, the "Era of Good Feelings" had already passed. Each section began to put forth politicians who would speak for its interests. Daniel Webster represented the northeast, and John C. Calhoun represented the south; in the west there were Henry Clay and Andrew Jackson speaking for the southwest. Ultimately, the presidential election was fought by four candidates: John Quincy Adams representing the northeast, Henry Clay and Andrew Jackson from the southwest, and William H. Crawford representing the old south. Jackson received the highest number of both electoral and popular votes, but because he did not command a majority of electoral votes, in accordance with the stipulations of the Constitution, a final vote was held in the House of Representatives. In this vote Adams defeated Jackson and was elected the sixth president. He was inaugurated in 1825.

John Quincy Adams was the son of the second president, John Adams, and was from an old family of Massachusetts. A capable politician of long experience, he had served as Secretary of State under President Monroe. His administration's policies, as might be expected given his background, had a more or less Federalist tinge. In particular, under the Adams administration the policy of internal improvement, which aimed at the expansion and unification of the domestic market, was stressed. An expansion of the navy was planned in order to expand and protect foreign trade, and Adams also adopted a protective tariff policy in order to nurture northern industrial capital. This series of Federalist-oriented policies, especially the tariff policy, began to incur strong opposition from the southern planters.

The Adams administration had been created by the vote of the House of Representatives and lacked the support of the majority of the people from the beginning. Its policies further estranged it from the farmers of the west and the south. Consequently, one could say that regardless of the intelligence and capability of Adams as an individual, his administration was extremely unstable. Supported by the dissatisfaction of the farming class, the Republican left wing, which centered around Andrew Jackson, quickly began a campaign looking toward the election of 1828, which indeed was contested by Jackson and Adams. In this election Jackson and his supporters called themselves Democrats, and the Adams faction took the name of National Republicans.

The election resulted in a victory for Jackson by such a wide margin that he had 178 electoral votes to Adams's 83. For the first time in American history a westerner was elected president.

Jacksonian Democracy

Andrew Jackson was born in Waxhaw, South Carolina. Early orphaned, he roamed around the south and west, receiving virtually no formal education. Eventually he emerged as a leader in Tennessee. After serving in the House of Representatives and the Senate and in such important public offices as chief justice of the Tennessee Supreme Court, he rose socially as well and became a slave-owning planter. In the course of his colorful career, he was decisively promoted to the status of a national figure when, in 1815, at the end of the War of 1812, he led the militia which defeated the British regular army at New Orleans. This battle was actually fought after the treaty had been signed at Ghent and the war had formally ended, and thus did not directly affect the course of the war. However, as the leader in the only brilliant victory on the side of the United States in this unpopular war, Jackson became a national hero. As one can also surmise from his career, Jackson differed from the earlier presidents in that he was a typical western "self-made man."

One must also note that while Jackson was the idol of the small "common man" farmers of the west, he himself was a planter, and showed a certain degree of class affinity with the southern planters. This affinity was clearly revealed in the fact that Calhoun, political representative of the south, supported Jackson and became his running mate in the election of 1828. Cooperation in wooing votes is after all a fundamental principle of American party politics. In this connection, it is significant that Jackson joined forces with New York machine politician Martin Van Buren and received the support of New York's newly rising artisan class. Here, in the cooperation between the southern planters and the machine politicians of the northern cities, one can already discern the outlines of the constituency of the later Democratic Party.

Jackson was inaugurated as president in 1829. The so-called

"era of Jacksonian Democracy" included his two terms in office and the succeeding administration of Martin Van Buren. Jacksonian democracy originated in the trends which accompanied the development of the west after 1800, and Jackson himself was a living symbol of these trends.[3]

First, this era attempted to institute on a national scale that equality of the opportunity to participate in politics which had, until then, been a special sectional characteristic of western society. The westerners had challenged the existing monopolization of political power at the federal level by the elite of the eastern seaboard. One of the means of achieving this equality of opportunity was the "spoils system." (The name derives from the expression, "To the victor belong the spoils.") Based on the principle that the lengthy retention of a political office by a single person would cause the monopolization and corruption of power, the system set fixed terms of office and required rotation in office. After the introduction of this system, a change in administration after an election occasioned the distribution of many offices among supporters as the "spoils" for the victor in the election. Today, "spoils system" has become a synonym for corrupt politics, but one should remember that, at least initially, this system was a challenge to the monopolization of offices by an elite. (See the excerpt from Jackson's first annual message, 1829, appended to this chapter.)

A second element which contributed to the expansion of political participation was the nation-wide extension of male suffrage. In the west, universal suffrage had been assumed from an early date. With the advent of the Jacksonian era, the artisan and working classes of the eastern states as well demanded universal suffrage for white adult males. By the 1830s this was nearly

[3] Alexis de Tocqueville, in the introduction to his *Democracy in America*, which is regarded as the classic treatise on America by a foreigner, wrote: "Among the novel objects that attracted my attention during my stay in the United States, nothing struck me more forcibly than the general equality of condition among the people" (Alexis de Tocqueville, *Democracy in America, 1835–40*, Vintage edition, 1900, vol. 1., p. 3). Tocqueville visited America for about nine months beginning in April 1831, and his stay corresponded to the period of the Jackson administration. When he said "the general equality of condition among the people," he clearly referred to Jacksonian Democracy, and he perceived in it both the benefits and the dangers of democracy. (See excerpt appended to this chapter.) Incidentally, *Democracy in America* was translated into Japanese in 1873 in an abridged edition and in a more complete form in 1883 under the title *The Principle of Freedom* [*Jiyu genron*].

attained. The number of votes in the election of 1828 was three times that in 1824. The expansion of the electorate stimulated the development of the local organizations and substructures of political parties as vote-getting machines. American political parties are generally said to be coalitions of local organizations, and this characteristic dates from the Jacksonian era, when the local organizations came to occupy a more important position in the party power structure.

This democratization of political party organization led to demands for reform in the system of nominating party electoral candidates, so that not just a few party leaders but all party members could participate. Up to this time a presidential candidate was nominated at a party caucus—a general meeting of the Congressional members of each political party; but in the 1830s the method of nomination by party conventions was gradually adopted. This change clearly indicated a shift in the nature of a political party from an organization under the leadership of a small group of men to a coalition of local substructures. This structure was markedly different from those in the European countries.

With the expansion of the electorate and the development of local organizations, the style of election campaigns also began to change conspicuously. Previously, campaigns had often relied on the circulation of letters among influential persons. Now campaign speeches and eye-catching symbols began to be widely employed as means of mass persuasion. The election campaign, with its torchlight parades, "apple cider" parties, and so forth, became a sort of boisterous festival, and was designed to appeal to the emotions, rather than the reason, of the electorate. The candidates strained themselves to emphasize their homogeneity with the voters. For example, in the west a candiate's roots in the farming class, which constituted the majority of the electorate, would be avidly capitalized upon for soliciting votes: every candidate was "born in a log cabin."

Equality of opportunity in economic gains also came to be emphasized in the era of Jacksonian Democracy. One incident which symbolized this trend was Jackson's exercise of veto power with regard to the Bank of the United States. The Bank, which had been temporarily abolished in Jefferson's era, only to be reestablished when the government needed funds for the War of 1812, pursued a basically deflationary policy. Consequently, the farmers, who, as debtors, had consistently demanded an inflationary policy, generally regarded the Bank with the strongest suspicion. Indeed, there were many farmers who, unable to pay their debts to the banks, lost their mortgaged farmland. Because the Bank's charter was to expire in 1836, the Bank question became a major issue for Jackson's administration. The president of the Bank, Nicholas Biddle, originally a Federalist, felt greatly threatened by the emergence of Jackson's faction. Even before the 1832 election, supporters of the Bank, led by Biddle, had begun to lobby in Congress, and achieved passage of a bill extending the term of the Bank's charter. President Jackson, however, claimed that the Bank was an institution which benefited the privileged, and he vetoed the bill. (The veto power was one of the presidential powers recognized in the Constitution, but it had never actually been used politically.)

This veto increased Jackson's popularity even further, and he was reelected in 1832 by an overwhelming majority. Like other powerful presidents in American history, Jackson succeeded in identifying himself with the people; he understood that the president was the direct representative of the whole people, while the members of Congress, in contrast, were a collection of representatives of minority interests. This characterization of the presidency resulted in the expansion and strengthening of the power of the presidency relative to that of Congress.

Although the Jackson administration took a decisive position on the Bank question, it had to be more subtle on the issue of tariffs in order to mediate between the south and the north. The southern planters fiercely opposed the tariff enacted in 1832, which was somewhat milder than that of 1828 (the "Tariff of Abominations") but still retained the protective principle. Jackson, however, stressing the need for the unity of the nation and showing his willingness to use force if necessary, firmly suppressed the opposition to the tariffs.

Equality of economic opportunity and free competition also came to be legitimized by the judiciary. For example, one can cite the Charles River Bridge Co. *v.* Warren Bridge Co.

decision (1837) under Chief Justice Roger Brooke Taney, whom Jackson appointed following Marshall's death. The decision rejected the right of vested interests and confirmed the principle of competition.

It was during the Jacksonian era that the people began to demand equality of educational opportunity as a requisite for social equality of opportunity. Various states, beginning with Massachusetts, successively responded to this demand by establishing so-called "free schools" systems. The first workers' party in American history was founded in 1828 as a local party in Philadelphia, and its platform included equal opportunity in education.

However, as Jackson indicated in his message explaining his veto of the Bank of the United States (see excerpt appended to this chapter), the contemporary demand for equalization did not seek absolute equality among individuals. It was instead premised on inherent differences among individual human beings. Based on this premise, the demand for equalization essentially sought to allow individuals (as long as they were white and male) to give full play to their inherent abilities with equal and free opportunity for competition. The principles of equal opportunity and free competition had originated as the creed of the independent farmer. In due time, when America had achieved rapid and vigorous industrialization, these independent farmers' values were adopted by the industrial society as the so-called "spirit of capitalism." In this sense, regardless of his personal intentions, Jackson was a spokesman not only for the values of American agrarianism, but also for the spirit of American capitalism. In other words, he was, above all, an eminent symbol of American democracy. However, the expansion of political participation and Jacksonian Democracy encountered one major stumbling block—slavery and the southern plantation system based upon it.

Documents

Thomas Jefferson, *Notes on Virginia,* **1784**

. . . The political economists of Europe have established it as a principle that every state should endeavor to manufacture for itself; and this principle, like many others, we transfer to America, without calculating the difference of of circumstance which should often produce a difference of result. In Europe the lands are either cultivated, or locked up against the cultivator. Manufacture must therefore be resorted to of necessity, not of choice, to support the surplus of their people. But we have an immensity of land courting the industry of the husbandman. Is it best then that all our citizens should be employed in its improvement, or that one half should be called off from that to exercise manufactures and handicraft arts for the other? Those who labor in the earth are the chosen people of God, if he ever had a chosen people, whose breasts he has made his peculiar deposit for substantial and genuine virtue. It is the focus in which he keeps alive that sacred fire, which otherwise might escape from the face of the earth. Corruption of morals in the mass of cultivators is a phenomenon of which no age nor nation has furnished an example. It is the mark set on those who, not looking up to heaven, to their own soil and industry, as does the husbandmen, for their subsistence, depend for it on the casualties and caprice of customers. Dependence begets subservience and venality, suffocates the germ of virtue, and prepares fit tools for the designs of ambition. This, the natural progress and consequence of the arts, has sometimes perhaps been retarded by accidental circumstances; but, generally speaking, the proportion which the aggregate of the other classes of citizens bears in any state to that of its husbandmen is the proportion of its unsound to its healthy parts, and is a good enough barometer whereby to measure its degree of corruption. While we have land to labor then, let us never wish to see our citizens occupied at a workbench, or twirling a distaff. Carpenters, masons, smiths, are wanting in husbandry; but, for the general operations of manufacture, let our workshops remain in Europe. It is better to carry provisions and materials to workmen there than bring them to the provisions and materials, and with them their manners and principles. The loss by the transportation of commodities across the Atlantic will be made up in happiness and permanence of government. The mobs of great cities add just so much to the support of pure government, as sores do to the strength of the human body. It is the manners and spirit of a people which preserve a republic in vigor. A degeneracy in these is a canker which soon eats to the heart of its laws and constitution. . . .

James Monroe, Seventh Annual Message to Congress, December 2, 1823

. . . The citizens of the United States cherish sentiments the most friendly in favor of the liberty and happiness of their fellow-men on that side of the Atlantic. In the wars of the European powers in matters relating to themselves we have never taken any part, nor does it comport with our policy so to do. It is only when our rights are invaded or seriously menaced that we resent injuries or make preparation for our defense. With the movements in this hemisphere we are of necessity more immediately connected, and by causes which must be obvious to all enlightened and impartial observers. The political system of the allied powers is essentially different in this respect from that of America. This difference proceeds from that which exists in their respective Governments; and to the defense of our own, which has been achieved by the loss of so much blood and treasure, and matured by the wisdom of their most enlightened citizens, and under which we have enjoyed unexampled felicity, this whole nation is devoted. We owe it, therefore, to candor and to the amicable relations existing between the United States and those powers to declare that we should consider any attempt on their part to extend their system to any portion of this hemisphere as dangerous to our peace and safety. With the existing colonies or dependencies of any European power we have not interfered and shall not interfere. But with the Governments who have declared their independence and maintained it, and whose independence we have, on great consideration and on just principles, acknowledged, we could not view any interposition for the purpose of oppressing them, or controlling in any other manner their destiny, by any European power in any other light than as the manifestation of an unfriendly disposition toward the United States. In the war between those new Governments and Spain we declared our neutrality at the time of their recognition, and to this we have adhered, and shall continue to adhere, provided no change shall occur which, in the judgment of the competent authorities of this Government, shall make a corresponding change on the part of the United States indispensable to their security. . . .

Andrew Jackson, First Annual Message, 1829

. . . There are, perhaps, few men who can for any great length of time enjoy office and power without being more or less under the influence of feelings unfavorable to the faithful discharge of their public duties. Their integrity may be proof against improper considerations immediately addressed to themselves, but they are apt to acquire a habit of looking with indifference upon the public interests and of tolerating conduct from which an unpracticed man would revolt. Office is considered as a species of property, and government rather as a means of promoting individual interests than as an instrument created solely for the service of the people. Corruption in some and in others a perversion of correct feelings and principles divert government from its legitimate ends and make it an engine for the support of the few at the expense of the many. The duties of all public officers are, or at least admit of being made, so plain and simple that men of intelligence may readily qualify themselves for their performance; and I can not but believe that more is lost by the long continuance of men in office than is generally to be gained by their experience. I submit, therefore, to your consideration whether the efficiency of the Government would not be promoted and official industry and integrity better secured by a general extension of the law which limits appointments to four years. . . .

Andrew Jackson, Veto of the Bank Renewal Bill, 1832

. . . It is to be regretted that the rich and powerful too often bend the acts of government to their selfish purposes. Distinctions in society will always exist under every just government. Equality of talents, of education, or of wealth can not be produced by human institutions. In the full enjoyment of the gifts of Heaven and the fruits of superior industry, economy, and virtue, every man is equally entitled to protection by law; but when the laws undertake to add to these natural and just advantages artificial distinctions, to grant titles, gratuities, and exclusive privileges, to make the rich richer and the potent more powerful, the humble members of society—the farmers, mechanics, and laborers—who have neither the time nor the means of securing like favors to themselves, have a right to complain of the injustice of their Government. There are no necessary evils in government. Its evils exist only in its abuses. If it would confine itself to equal protection, and, as Heaven does its rains, shower its favors alike on the high and the low, the rich and the poor, it would be an unqualified blessing. In the act before me there seems to be a wide and unnecessary departure from these just principles. . . .

Alexis de Tocqueville, *Democracy in America,* 1836

Among the novel objects that attracted my attention during my stay in the United States, nothing stuck me more forcibly than the general equality of condition among the people. I readily discovered the prodigious influence that this primary fact exercises on the whole course of society; it gives a peculiar direction to public opinion and a peculiar tenor to the laws; it imparts new maxims to the governing authorities and peculiar habits to the governed.

I soon perceived that the influence of this fact extends far beyond the political character and the laws of the country, and that it has no less effect on civil society than on the government; it creates opinions, gives birth to new sentiments, founds novel customs, and modifies whatever it does not produce. The more I advanced in the study of American society, the more I perceived that this equality of condition is the fundamental fact from which all others seem to be derived and the central point at which all my observations constantly terminated.

I then turned my thoughts to our own hemisphere, and thought that I discerned there something analogous to the spectacle which the New Would presented to me. I observed that equality of condition, though it has not there reached the extreme limit which it seems to have attained in the United States, is constantly approaching it; and that the democracy which governs the American communities appears to be rapidly rising into power in Europe.

Hence I conceived the idea of the book that is now before the reader.

It is evident to all alike that a great democratic revolution is going on among us, but all do not look at it in the same light. To some it appears to be novel but accidental, and, as such, they hope it may still be checked; to others it seems irresistible, because it is the most uniform, the most ancient, and the most permanent tendency that is to be found in history. . . .

There is one country in the world where the great social revolution that I am speaking of seems to have nearly reached its natural limits. It has been effected with ease and simplicity; say rather that this country is reaping the fruits of the democratic revolution which we are undergoing, without having had the revolution itself.

The emigrants who colonized the shores of America in the beginning of the seventeenth century somehow separated the democratic principle from all the principles that it had to contend with in the old communities of Europe, and transplanted it alone to the New World. It has there been able to spread in perfect freedom and peaceably to determine the character of the laws by influencing the manners of the country.

It appears to me beyond a doubt that, sooner or later, we shall arrive, like the Americans, at an almost complete equality of condition. But I do not conclude from this that we shall ever be necessarily led to draw the same political consequences which the Americans have derived from a similar social organization. I am far from supposing that they have chosen the only form of government which a democracy may adopt; but as the generating cause of laws and manners in the two countries is the same, it is of immense interest for us to know what it has produced in each of them.

It is not, then, merely to satisfy a curiosity, however legitimate, that I have examined America; my wish has been to find there instruction by which we may ourselves profit. Whoever should imagine that I have intended to write a panegyric would be strangely mistaken, and on reading this book he will perceive that such was not my design; nor has it been my object to advocate any form of government in particular, for I am of the opinion that absolute perfection is rarely to be found in any system of laws. I have not even pretended to judge whether the social revolution, which I believe to be irresistible, is advantageous or prejudicial to mankind. I have acknowledged this revolution as a fact already accomplished, or on the eve of its accomplishment; and I have selected the nation, from among those which have undergone it, in which its development has been the most peaceful and the most complete, in order to discern its natural consequences and to find out, if possible, the means of rendering it profitable to mankind. I confess that in America I saw more than America; I sought there the image of democracy itself, with its inclinations, its character, its prejudices, and its passions, in order to learn what we have to fear or to hope from its progress. . . .

CHAPTER
5

Slavery and the Civil War

As we have seen, the Democratic-Republican administrations succeeded, in the first half of the nineteenth century, in creating a majority party through the promotion of landed interests and the values of agrarianism. The slave-owning planters of the south were a minority not only nationally but even within southern society. Nevertheless, by controlling the Democratic Party, they were able to hold national political power and tenaciously defend their interests. However, the rapid industrialization in the northeast had a strong impact on agrarian America. Further, the conflicts among the farmers themselves, between the southern planters and the western farmers, grew steadily during the first half of the nineteenth century. The anti-planter forces joined together to form the Republican Party, and with the election of the Republican candidate, Abraham Lincoln, in the presidential election of 1860, the southern planters were finally driven from the national seat of power.

In the Civil War which followed, the southern planters were decisively defeated and were forced to renounce the hope of holding political power on a national level. During the postwar "reconstruction" which aimed at a reform of southern society itself, the planters endeavored to reestablish in the south the hegemony which they had lost on the national level.

Slavery and Planter Oligarchy

The more or less monocultural plantation system, while it was facilitated by the climate and topography of the south, required a vast amount of cheap labor power. At first indentured servants were utilized. But they were not invariably a cheap labor force, and their terms of employment were limited. Hence, the planters turned their attention to a labor force composed of slaves, and slavery was introduced on a wide scale. The first Negro slave was brought to America in 1619, and in 1661 slavery was formally established by law in the colony of Virginia. During the colonial period the principal crop of the plantation system was tobacco. In due time, because tobacco consumption reached its limit and because its cultivation devastated the land, the plantation system, and the slavery which supported it, seemed to be headed for extinction.

However, the invention of the cotton gin and the advance of the industrial revolution in England in the late eighteenth century caused a marked increase in both the demand for and the supply of raw cotton, and the plantation system based on slavery gained a new lease on life. In the years between 1819 and 1860, total cotton production increased over thirtyfold, and between 1810 and 1856 the amount exported increased about fivefold; cotton came to represent 54 percent of the total value of American exports. As revealed in the expression "Cotton is King," the southern economy was reorganizing to focus on cotton cultivation. The planters not only reinforced their dominance in southern society, but also strengthened their position in national politics on the basis of the importance of cotton production in the national economy.

The actual number of planters was extremely small, not only nationally but within southern society itself. In 1850, of the total slave states' white population of about six million, about 350,000 were members of slave-holding families, and no more than approximately 8,000 families owned more than fifty slaves and could truly be called planters. This extremely small group was able to maintain their overwhelmingly powerful position in the southern states because they were at the top of a rigid hierarchical society created in the south. Below them were the independent farmers who owned few or no slaves; beneath them were the so-called "poor whites," who were in a sense social bankrupts; and the lowest class were the black slaves who numbered as many as 3,250,000. The poor whites and the independent, non-slave-owning farmers constituted a numerical majority in southern society, but they were completely cut of off by institutional and social barriers from the black slaves who constituted over one-third of the population. Thus the ruling power of the planters was guaranteed in southern society, in spite of their numerical inferiority.

In order to maintain a grasp on political power beyond the south, however, the planters needed a political strategy on the national level. As a symbolic maneuver, they emphasized their own identification with the farming class which constituted the majority in contemporary American society, and supported the Democratic Party. The Democratic administrations, beginning with that of Jackson, continued to expand the opportunity for political participation. The southern planters, who were a minority, skillfully capitalized upon this expansion of political participation and advanced their own interests from positions of power within the Democratic Party.[1]

What policies were followed by the Democratic administrations during this period? Dominated by the planters and their interests, they promoted the system of free trade. Through several reforms, the tariff rate imposed by the Tariff Act of 1832 was lowered; with the Revenue Act of 1846 the system of protective tariffs was essentially dissolved. Finally in 1857 trade became virtually un-restricted. The Democratic administrations also embarked on a program of territorial expansion.

After the Louisiana Purchase, the urge to expand westward was strong among the southern planters. Around 1830, many Ameri-cans moved into Texas to build plantations. Texas was then a territory of Mexico, which had achieved independence from Spain in 1821. The United States immediately recognized Texas when it became independent of Mexico in 1836. Soon a movement to annex the independent Republic of Texas gained momentum,

[1] The fact that the southern planters were at the nucleus of political power did not necessarily mean that they directly occupied such offices as the presidency. That would have identified the Democratic Party with a minority and would have contradicted the logic of a political party as an instrument for the formation of a majority. Consequent-ly, national war heroes, westerners, or northerners were nominated as Democratic presidential candidates. The southern planters, like Calhoun, however, held real power in the Senate. The nomination of a planter as a presidential candidate in 1860 came, paradoxically, when the planters' influence in national politics was on the wane.

although the northern states opposed it. Following its initial rejection by the Senate, the treaty to annex Texas was approved by a joint resolution of Congress in 1845, and a vast territory which included the present state of Texas was annexed to the United States.

In 1846 a war with Mexico broke out over a border dispute, and one of its outcomes was that in 1848 the U.S. acquired from Mexico a vast territory which included the present states of California, New Mexico, and Arizona. In 1846, the border between the northwest Oregon territory and British Columbia was established along the 49th parallel. Thus, by 1850 the territory of the present continental United States of America was nearly complete.

The purpose of this expansion was to obtain agricultural land. However, precisely because it was based on the demands of the agricultural or landed interests, it could not occur without arousing the strong opposition of the northeast, where development was based on commerce and industry and where the moral legitimacy of expansionism was questioned. The doctrine of "Manifest Destiny" was presented as a solution to this problem. It legitimized the expansion of Americans on the American continent both morally and providentially. This doctrine argued that Americans possessed a mission to extend freedom on the American continent, and that expansion was the means of realizing that mission. This logic was an extension of the peculiarly American world view, previously implied by the Monroe Doctrine in 1823, which emphasized the severance of the American from the European continent and the construction of a new type of civilization on the American continent.

This rapid expansion, however, could not take place without conflict among the north, the south, and the west over the distribution of new territories. The issue was, when the new territories were eventually incorporated into the union as states, whether they should be "free states" which recognized no slavery or "slave states" which approved it. This question had tremendous bearing on the maintenance of the sectional balance of power in the federal government, especially in Congress. Consequently, the principle was established that whenever a slave state was incorporated, a free state would also be added. For example, in 1820, when Missouri was admitted to the union as a slave state, the north had Maine admitted as a new state, and thus the balance of twelve "free states" versus twelve "slave states" was maintained. At the same time Congress passed a resolution prohibiting slavery in the Louisiana Territory north of 36° 30' north latitude, thus in effect making the 36° 30' parallel a boundary dividing the south and the north, or the "slave states" and the "free states." These two actions were collectively called the Missouri Compromise. In a similar spirit, in 1850 when California wanted to enter the Union as a free state, the planters, fearing that the balance between south and north would be broken, decided to enact a strong Fugitive Slave Act as a countermeasure in exchange for recognizing California as a free state. This was the Compromise of 1850.

The planters went on the offensive. In 1854, when Kansas was organized as a territory, they planned to have it as a future slave state, although the Missouri Compromise clearly designated it a free state by virtue of its latitude. The planters used the theory of "squatter sovereignty" or "popular sovereignty" in arguments presented in Congress by Senator Stephen A. Douglas, a Democratic leader from the midwest. They asserted that when Kansas and Nebraska became states, the question of whether they should be "slave states" or "free states" should be decided by the will of the residents of those states. Their claim, further compounded by such factors as railroad construction, ultimately prevailed. In 1854 the famed Kansas-Nebraska Act put the slave-or-free decision in the hands of the peoples of these territories. The ensuing violent struggles between the factions in Kansas gave the territory the name "Bleeding Kansas." By 1856 a battle was being fought which presaged, on a small scale, the impending Civil War.

The Kansas-Nebraska Act repealed the earlier Missouri Compromise, and it was given judicial sanction by the famous Dred Scott decision of the Supreme Court in 1857 (see the excerpt from the decision appended to to this chapter). The decision on the case written by Chief Justice Taney stated that slaves were property, and property rights were guaranteed by the Constitution. Wherever in the United States a slave might be, it did not alter the fact that he was property; even if he happened to be in a territory which Congress declared to be "free," he did not lose his status as a slave. Therefore, "The Act of Congress which prohibited a citizen from holding and owning property of this kind in the territory of the United States north of the line therein mentioned, is not warranted by the Constitution, and is therefore void." The Missouri Compromise which prohibited slavery in the territory north of the 36°30′ parallel was judged unconstitutional. Slavery, as judicially sanctioned by this decision, might have spread throughout the territories. However, the expansion of the special interests of the slave owners during the Democratic administration had inevitably been subject to bitter criticism from many quarters. The forces opposed to the expansion of slavery, while they included various opposing interests and elements, in due course came to rise above their differences and form a national political party.

The Anti-Planter Forces and the Civil War

Opposition to the southern planters and the policies they were able to enact at the national level was a major order of business for the leaders of the northeast. The free trade system which had been enacted at a time when America was beginning to compete as a capitalistic nation with the advanced nation of England was extremely disadvantageous for the manufacturing industry of the northeast, which had been developing rapidly since the 1820s and whose interest lay in protecting and expanding the domestic market. Moreover, the plantation system and slavery required a large amount of capital for their operation, and so the southern planters competed with northeastern industrial capitalists who from the start had suffered from shortage of capital.

In addition to economic factors there was growing opposition to slavery on moral grounds, particularly among a group of New England intellectuals. In 1831 William Lloyd Garrison began publishing a magazine called *The Liberator* which demanded the immediate abolition of slavery. Intellectuals like Henry David Thoreau, author of *Walden, or Life in the Woods*, and the poet Henry Wadsworth Longfellow also participated actively in this movement. The abolition of slavery in Mexico in 1828 made a strong impression on the abolitionists. In 1833 the national American Anti-Slavery Society was formed. In 1852 Harriet Beecher Stowe published the popular novel *Uncle Tom's Cabin*, which made a broad appeal to the American populace by painting a poignant picture of the wretched fate of blacks under slavery. It is said that at publication nearly 300,000 copies of this novel were sold. Thus the abolitionist movement, centering around New England intellectuals, became active in the north, but one must remember that it was never a movement which reflected the sentiments of the northern people as a whole. The possession of slaves as property was still protected by the Constitution, and even among northerners there was more than a little opposition to abolitionism from the perspective of the protection of private property.

Under these conditions, opposition to the further expansion of slavery became a more viable position and had broader support than arguing for its immediate abolition. This opposition to expansion gradually spread among the small farmers of the west, who, although supporters of the same Democratic Party, had interests quite different from those of the southern planters. They aligned themselves with the southerners in pressing for territorial expansion. However, their interests with regard to the disposition of the land which was thus acquired often differed from those of the southern planters. The fundamental demand of the westerners was the enactment of the Homestead Act, which provided that the public lands in the west be given free to the farmers who actually cultivated them. The western farmers came to oppose violently the inroads into the west of the southern planters who, backed by large capital holdings, extended plantations by large-scale land speculation and thus limited the possibilities for expansion of independent farms. Again, in spite of the fact that the western farmers were in great need of improved transportation facilities in order to effectively market their products, the southerners were, as a rule, opposed to such improvements. At the same time, the development of manufacturing in the northeast suggested that in due time the northeast would become a large-scale consumers' market for western agricultural products. Thus, the west weakened its ties to the southern market to which it was linked by a river system centering on the Mississippi and gradually strengthened its ties with the northeast through the improvement and development of roads, rivers linked by canals, and railroads, which had spread rapidly after the 1830s.

In this way the movement to expand the plantation system, and with it slavery, eventually resulted in an internal split within the Democratic Party. The western farmers within the party were gradually forced to choose between continuing to cooperate with the planters and cooperating with eastern capital in the formation of a new political party. This latter possibility was symbolically expressed by the formation of the Free Soil Party, which opposed the expansion of slavery and advocated the enactment of the Homestead Act. Employing the slogan "Free soil, free speech, free labor, and free men," it ran an independent presidential candidate in 1848. The party itself had no broad base of support, had only a short life, and arose in New England rather than in the west; still, one must give it serious consideration as a movement which, in its aspirations, already suggested the future cooperation between the northeast and the west, between industrial capital and western farmers.[2]

At the same time, an anti-planter trend, although weak, was emerging even within the south itself. Fearing the emergence of rebel leaders, the planters forbade the slaves of that time, except for ministers, to receive education. Despite this, small-scale, desperate rebellions often broke out among the oppressed Negro slaves, and many ran away. In many cases those rebels and fugitives who had been caught received extremely cruel punishment in order to intimidate the others. The Nat Turner Insurrection was the most famous among such rebellions. This rebellion, which occurred in Virginia in 1831, led by the black minister Nat Turner,

[2] It is necessary to say a word here about the lineage of American political parties. After the election of 1816 the Federalists did not run a presidential candidate and essentially dissolved, and one-party rule by the Republicans emerged. However, in the election of 1824 the Republicans began to split internally; in the election of 1828 the faction of J. Q. Adams was called the National Republicans, and Jackson's faction was called the Democratic Republicans. From about 1832 on, the latter were called the Democratic Party; formally, this was the origin of the present-day Democratic Party. On the other hand, the National Republicans, following their defeat in the election of 1832, likened Jackson to a despotic monarch; choosing the name of an English party opposed to despotic monarchy, they began to call themselves Whigs. The Whigs lasted until the election of 1856; they were the successors of the Federalists and the National Republicans, and made the northeast and the northwest their territorial bases and such men as Webster and Clay their representative leaders. Twice, in 1840 and 1848, they nominated popular victorious generals as presidential candidates and gained political power, but their policies were Federalist and resembled those of J. Q. Adams. (Incidentally, it was during the Whig administration that Commodore Perry was sent to Japan.) In 1856 the Republican Party held a national convention and emerged as a national party; formally, this was the origin of the present-day Republican Party. The election of 1856 was fought among the Democrats, Whigs, and Republicans, but afterwards the Whigs disbanded, many of them being absorbed into the Republican Party.

was extensive: fifty-seven whites, including women and children, were killed by the rebels. In retaliation, over one hundred Negroes were slaughtered without trial, and twenty were sentenced after trial to capital punishment.

In the 1840s an underground organization which systematically aided black slaves in escaping to the northern states and further to Canada was established; it is said that ultimately it brought about the escape of as many as 50,000 slaves. Some Negroes themselves played important roles in this "underground railroad"; among these was Harriet Tubman, who was called a "black Moses." She herself had been a slave, but had escaped via this organization, and afterwards she returned to the slave states illegally many times and helped other slaves to escape. A freed Negro journalist in the north, Frederick Douglass, actively opposed slavery. Viewed as a whole, however, the number of free Negroes was very small, and the vast majority of Negroes remained bound in shackles.

The large majority of those southern whites who owned no slaves, in particular the poor whites, were dominated by the planters. Often they lived as parasites on the plantations. Appeals to racial unity effectively suppressed economic class divisions among white southerners. Consequently, even among those totally estranged from the plantation system, only an exceptional few opposed the planter oligarchy and urged the abolition of slavery. Hinton Rowan Helper was one of them. The south gradually became isolated, politically and socially, as it tried to defend its system of slavery, not as a necessary evil, but as a positive good, morally, religiously, and sociologically

The slavery issue eventually caused the realignment of the American political party organizations. In the northwestern states, conventions of the "Republican Party" were held during the spring and summer of 1854, and in many areas the Kansas-Nebraska Act was violently criticized. Then, in June prior to the presidential election of 1856, the Republican Party formally held a national convention in Philadelphia. The various groups which opposed the further expansion of the planters' power—the Free Soil Party, the Whig Party, and breakaway elements among the Democrats who opposed the planters—united. The national convention adopted opposition to the expansion of slavery as the common campaign slogan, and nominated John Charles Fremont as the party's presidential candidate. The Republicans received 1,340,000 votes, or one-third of the total number cast in the election, and thus indicated that they would become a major force in the future. Prior to the election of 1860 the members of the new party began a vigorous movement to overthrow the control of the southern planters. In October 1859, the abolitionist John Brown, who had for some time asserted that rebellion by the slaves themselves was necessary in order to overthrow slavery, attacked the federal arsenal at Harper's Ferry, Virginia, and attempted to start a slave insurrection. His slave uprising failed to occur; the rebellion was suppressed in two days, and Brown was hanged. This attempted rebellion, however, greatly shocked the southern planters, and they made a serious issue of it as a slave insurrection instigated by the north. They disseminated propaganda asserting that it was not merely the action of an abolitionist, but had the "Black Republicans" behind it. As the 1860 election approached, the Democrats' internal split worsened. In opposition to the northwestern Democratic leaders who supported Stephen Douglas as their presidential candidate, the southern planters, now clearly a minority faction, split from the party mainstream and nominated John C. Breckenridge of Kentucky as their independent candidate. In addition, some southern Democratic Party leaders who disagreed with this extreme action and one part of the remnants of the Whig Party formed the Constitutional Union Party and nominated John Bell of Tennessee as their presidential candidate; they hoped to appeal to voters in the border states.

During this time of dissension among the Democrats, the Republican Party was trying to built an organization from diverse elements. They required a leader and candidate who could mediate between and unite, on the one hand, those radicals who argued for the immediate abolition of slavery and, on the other hand, the conservative industrialists of the northeast. Abraham Lincoln was chosen for his appeal to the northeastern capitalists, the abolitionists, and the party's largest group of potential supporters, the western farmers.

Lincoln had emerged in 1858 as a national politician with his "A house divided against itself cannot stand" speech (see the excerpt appended to this chapter). His position on slavery, however, was not clear. He was never an abolitionist, and he was extremely critical of Brown's rebellion. Certainly, with his western-farmer background Lincoln symbolized American social mobility in the "from a log cabin to the White House" sense. His image in the northeast as a "rustic westerner" was swept away by the rational, logical approach which he showed in his Cooper Union speech in New York, and his abilities came to be esteemed highly by the easterners as well. In the election of 1860 Lincoln did not receive a majority of the popular vote, but he was elected president with a majority of the electoral votes. Stephen Douglas received approximately 30 percent of the popular vote, indicating that the mainstream of the Democratic Party still could not be ignored. Breckenridge's vote was almost entirely restricted to the south, and he received less than 20 percent of the total popular vote. It was now obvious that the planters were in a minority position in national politics.

One important reason for Lincoln's victory was that, while opposing slavery, he did not explicitly advocate its immediate abolition. Nevertheless, his victory expressed the people's desire to prevent the expansion of slavery. As such, it was an immense blow to the south. As a result of this election, the southern planters lost their grasp on national political power. They were driven to a choice between remaining in the United States of America as a permanent minority or seceding from the Union and forming a separate nation. The planters saw very little choice. In order to maintain their hegemony, at least in southern society, they had to clearly draw a boundary between the south and the rest of the nation and emphasize the internal unity of the south.

Thus, southern sectionalism changed into southern nationalism. The south attempted by seceding from the Union to maintain its own unity.[3] The Confederate States of America was formed in

[3] From the point of view of the south, secession was neither a simple, *de facto* act nor an illegal and rebellious act: rather, it was an act based on a legal right. The southern leaders regarded the Constitution as a contract among the states and held that, as a contracting party, each state had the right freely to secede from the United States. This is analogous to the invocation of constitutional theory by the American colonists during the American Revolution, and can be said to indicate the importance of constitutional controversies in American political history.

The formation of the United States of America by the Constitution of 1787 as a federal system made the relationship between the central government and the indi-

February 1861. At this time, seven states seceded from the Union; later four more joined to form an eleven-member "Southern Confederacy." Four states which recognized slavery did not join the Confederacy. The attitude of these "border states," Maryland, Delaware, Kentucky, and Missouri, would be of major significance in determining the outcome of the war between the north and the south.

The unity of the south itself was not necessarily so stable as to warrant speaking of the "solid south." The resolutions of the southern state conventions to secede from the Union received a rather large number of negative votes. For example, in Alabama, the resolution to secede was passed by a vote of fifty-four to forty-five. In Virginia, the anti-secession faction itself seceded from the state and established West Virginia as a separate state, loyal to the Union. Because of this "south divided" character, and because its claims were based on the states' rights principle, the Confederacy was organized as a confederation of states, not as a single integrated nation, and it was faced with major institutional difficulties in policy implementation and leadership within itself.

After secession, the southern states anticipated a war with the north. They began war preparations by such means as the seizure of Union arsenals and the transfer of their arms and ammunition to the south, and by having commissioned officers

vidual states an important and complex point of dispute in American history. This meant that the Supreme Court, which possessed the right of judicial review, had in reality to play a political role whether or not it wished to. Historically, the authority of the federal government has been greatly expanded by a broad interpretation of the Constitution. On the other hand there has always been a movement to limit by a strict interpretation the power of the federal government. For example, beginning with the Kentucky Resolution (1798) and the Virginia Resolution (1799), which declared invalid the Alien and Sedition Acts enforced by the Federalist administration, there were a series of state resolutions, such as those of the Hartford Convention, which opposed the Republicans' Embargo Act and the War of 1812. These resolutions defended the authority of the individual state on the basis of the logic of a federal system, and limited the authority of the federal government. Broadly, they were known as "states' rights theory." Another conspicuous example was South Carolina's announcement of the nullification of the Tariff Act of 1832. This position eventually developed into a secession theory. As a result of the Civil War, both nullification theory and secession theory were discredited, but states' rights theory continued to be used frequently, sometimes legally, sometimes politically. States' rights theory was one basis of the Supreme Court's decision on the unconstitutionality of New Deal legislation in the 1930s, and provided a rationale for the south's resistance to the abolition of racial discrimination in the 1950s and 1960s.

from the south resign from the U.S. army to be commissioned in the southern army. These acts intimated that an armed encounter between south and north was not far off, though Lincoln tried to prevent it. In March, he emphasized in his inaugural speech that he and his Republican Party recognized slavery in the south itself, and he strongly urged the southern states to return to the Union (see the excerpt appended to this chapter).

However, with the southern army's attack on Fort Sumter on April 12, 1861, the Civil War began. The Confederacy was composed of eleven states and had a population of approximately nine million, of which one-third were slaves. In contrast, the north contained twenty-three states with a total population of twenty-two million. Although the south had many well-trained officers, its war potential in terms of ability to recruit troops, level of industrialization, and maneuverability (as shown in the relative underdevelopment of its railroads) was markedly inferior to that of the north. Its decision to embark on war under such conditions was not due to a regional warlike spirit or the predominance of violent elements; nor was it merely a desperate choice made in fear that the south would otherwise have to abandon its way of life. Knowing that their abundant supply of raw cotton was indispensable to the cotton industries in England, the southern states expected economic and military aid from abroad, and hoped to turn the war to its advantage by escalating it from a mere civil war to an international conflict. Indeed, the English government and the industrialists of Manchester did adopt a position sympathetic to the south. However, partly under pressure from the working classes, which opposed slavery on moral grounds, the government in the end decided not to interfere in the American conflict, and the Confederacy was left to rely on its own devices.

The north, as Lincoln repeatedly emphasized, fought neither to abolish slavery nor to preserve it, but to save the Union. Northern public opinion was united in its opposition to the expansion of slavery. However, except for the abolitionists, the majority regarded slaves as private property, and was rather unenthusiastic about embarking on a campaign to free them. Indeed, because of the need to draw on the cooperation of the border states, which harbored many slave owners, it was rather counterproductive for the north to advocate the abolition of slavery. Moreover, the fact that the war initially developed to the advantage of the south, which had made better preparations for war, made it difficult for the north to adopt an extremely stiff attitude toward slavery.

Lincoln, faced with these complex interests within the northern camp, had to play the role of a mediator or unifier to make them all cooperate in the war. He avoided the appearance of a crusade based on a moralistic view of slavery. As the war continued and the fighting gradually shifted to the advantage of the north, however, the voices of religious and other groups demanding the abolition of slavery as a war aim grew stronger. Many came to expect that the war would establish the moral superiority of the north over the south. In addition, some anticipated that the abolition of slavery would actually pose a military threat to the south. If the abolition of slavery were announced, it was thought, the south would have to divert much of its military strength to preventing the rebellion and escape of slaves within its own camp. Under such conditions, as an effective means of executing the war and achieving victory, the federal government issued the Preliminary Emancipation Proclamation in September 1862. Actually, because this proclamation did not emancipate the slaves of the border states, over which the U.S. government had no authority, it could not advance the goal of emancipation itself. However, inasmuch as it gave the north the goal of emancipation as a definite war aim, and gave great hope to the slaves of the south, it influenced the course of the war.

The longer the war continued, the more advantageous it became to the north, which was superior in mobilization capacity. In particular, the north's blockade of the southern coast prevented the south from importing weapons, ammunition, and foodstuffs, and the south's numerical inferiority gradually became decisive. In desperation, the Confederacy had to plan the mobilization of the slaves for the war, and the southern society which centered on the planter oligarchy approached imminent collapse. On April 9, 1865, General Robert E. Lee, supreme commander of the Confederate army, surrendered to General Ulysses S. Grant, supreme commander of the Union army, and the war between the south and the north came to an end. The preservation of the Union, which Lincoln had consistently made his war aim, was achieved. The urgent question was how to reunite the southern states with the Union, and closely connected with this question was that of how at the same time to reconstruct southern society.

The Civil War lasted five years; the total number of fatalities, more than 600,000 on both sides, was the largest America would incur in any war, including the Second World War. On that account alone it left deep scars in American society. More even than to the casualties, however, the scar which remained should be attributed to the ensuing military administration of the south during the "reconstruction" period.

Reconstruction and Reunion

Confronted with the problem of how to rebuild the south and southern society after the Civil War, the Republican Party divided, broadly speaking, into two factions. One was made up of radicals who asserted that it was necessary not only to drive the planters from the seat of national political power, but also to destroy their dominance in the south. The radical faction itself was not necessarily unified. Within it there was one group which had inherited the tendency of the abolitionists to emphasize the emancipation of slaves from a moralistic viewpoint. Their leaders were such men as Senator Charles Sumner. In contrast, another group sought to destroy the planters and purge them from southern society in order to promote the advance of industrial capital into the south, and on that basis establish their own dominance over the region. Men such as Roscoe Conkling, also a senator, were representative of this group.

The conservatives within the Republican Party, on the other hand, favored the preservation of the status quo in southern society. They argued that treating the south not as a defeated region but as a former compatriot would lead more quickly to its stabilization and would ultimately ease the advance of northern industrial and commercial interests into the south. William Henry Seward, Secretary of State under Lincoln, represented this idea, and Lincoln's own opinion was rather close to that of the conservatives, as he demonstrated in his appeal to the people at the end of his second inaugural address in 1865: "with malice toward none, with charity for all." The preservation of the Union had been the goal of the war, and Lincoln felt that once the south had been defeated, the best way to realize this goal was to allow it to return to the Union as quickly as possible. Consequently, the proposal his administration drew up for the readmission of the southern states was extremely lenient.

However, soon after the conclusion of the Civil War, Lincoln was assassinated. With Vice-President Andrew Johnson's assumption of the presidency, the latent internal conflicts in the Republican Party, which had been suppressed under Lincoln's powerful leadership and the stress of war, were brought into the open. Because of Johnson's background as a member of the south's "poor white" class, he had strongly opposed the planters, and during the war he had belonged to the radical faction. However, with the end of the war, his instincts as a southerner led him to oppose northern interference in the south. He found repulsive the emancipation of the slaves, who were potential competitors with his fellow poor whites. Reflecting this ambivalence, Johnson followed Lincoln's policies and hoped for the quick readmission and reconstruction of the south. However, he lacked Lincoln's ability to mediate, and intense conflict broke out within the Republican Party and within the north.

In these circumstances Congress was convened and began to debate measures for the reconstruction of the south. Ironically, in this Congress the number of members from the south in the House of Representatives increased because the emancipation of the slaves had resulted in the entire black population's being included in the population base for the election of representatives. This raised the possibility that, if the northern Democrats and conservative Republicans united with the southern Democrats, the radicals, despite their victory in the war, might fall into the position of a minority. Fearing this possibility, the radicals barred the southern members from Congress and, forming a Joint Committee of Fifteen, independently began to devise a reconstruction policy.

In 1866 the radicals introduced the Civil Rights Act. This bill sought to give blacks not only the right to vote but also the right of equality with whites as citizens. Johnson vetoed it, but Congress overrode the veto and the bill was enacted. The Freedman's Bureau, established during the war in 1865 as an agency which would give land to blacks, teach them farming skills, and guarantee their economic independence, was expanded and strengthened. Led by the Joint Committee of Fifteen, the radicals also sought to make the granting of civil rights to blacks a permanent provision of the Constitution. They proposed the Fourteenth Amendment, guaranteeing equal protection of the laws. This amendment, after undergoing some revisions due to the strong opposition of the Democrats and conservative Republicans, was passed by Congress in June 1866 and sent to the individual state legislatures for ratification. The Reconstruction Act, enacted in March 1867, placed the southern states under military administration, divided them into five military districts, and appointed army commanders as the military administrators (see the excerpt appended to this chapter). It stipulated that special constitutional conventions held under these military governments would decide on the ratification of the Fourteenth Amendment. This meant that the readmission of the southern states would be recognized only when they ratified the Fourteenth Amendment. The period from 1867 to 1877, during which the south was under military government, is referred to as the Reconstruction Period.

During this period the defeated south was further victimized by the vicious "carpetbaggers" who came from the north and selfishly exploited southern society. Consequently, the south of the era of reconstruction is characterized by such images as occupation, exploitation, corruption, confusion, disorder, and poverty. On the positive side, however, in this period the blacks who had been emancipated from slavery received at least some civil rights, had their right to political participation recognized, and, along with enlightened whites, attempted the reform of the south. For example, in the state of South Carolina, which had a very large black population, 94 of the 124 members of the Lower House, including the Speaker and the Secretary, were blacks, as were all the guards. A system of free-school education was opened for blacks, who until then had been forbidden to go to school, and the number of black school children increased rapidly. Tax reform was carried out, a progressive tax was promulgated, and hospitals and other welfare facilities were established.

However, because in the past political power in the south had been monopolized by a few planters, many of the rising politicians were ignorant of the practical problems of politics. This resulted in many difficulties, both administrative and financial, and in the confusion the former ruling class attempted to restore its hegemony in southern society. This phenomenon was known as "redemption." Concretely, it meant that blacks were again barred from political participation. Secret societies such as the KKK (Ku Klux Klan), created for that purpose, exploited the superstitions of the uneducated blacks, menaced them in mysterious and grotesque ways, sometimes resorted to lynching, and put pressure on whites who were sympathetic to blacks. Their goal was, by cultivating racial prejudice and by asserting white supremacy, to oppose the trend which had emerged in the postwar south toward class identification transcending racial differences, and to reinstate racial identification. They also encouraged a feeling of antagonism toward the outside—toward the north.

On the national level, the conflict within the Republican Party between the radicals, who had a majority in Congress, and President Johnson became increasingly acute. It reached the point where, in 1868, after he dismissed Secretary of War Edwin M. Stanton, Johnson was impeached by the House of Representatives. The Senate acquitted him by a mere one vote short of the two-thirds majority required to impeach, but from then on Congress ignored Johnson, and his authority as president was completely lost.

In the election later that year the Republicans naturally replaced Johnson and ran as their candidate Ulysses S. Grant, the brilliant Civil War general. Despite Grant's mass popularity as a general and champion of the emancipation of the slaves, the Republicans did not achieve a landslide victory. Grant received approximately 3,000,000 votes while Horatio Seymour, the Democratic candidate, received 2,700,000. This slender margin indicated that the radicals had failed to create a stable national majority. The south, under the reconstruction promoted by the radicals, had not returned to stability politically, and consequently could not become a stable market for the industries of the north. In 1876, the Republican presidential candidate, Rutherford B. Hayes, represented the conservative wing of the Republican Party. Advocating a compromise which abolished military rule in the south, Hayes managed to defeat Democrat Samuel J. Tilden. In April 1877, the northern army finally withdrew from the south; the south was again entrusted to the hands of southerners, a coalition of the former planters and a new breed of leaders who would try to industrialize the south in the image of the north—to build the "New South."

Thus the south again fell into the hands of its old ruling class, and the structure of southern society returned to its original form. Slavery was not restored, but a system of segregation which legally defined racial differences was established. Blacks were deprived of the right to vote; their civil rights were violated; and their opportunity for political participation, which had temporarily opened up in the era of reconstruction, was again withdrawn. At the end of the nineteenth century, blacks were almost completely alienated from the political process; the percentage of blacks who were registered to vote dropped to less than 5. Economically as well, blacks were placed in a situation not very different from their prewar status, because of a system of tenancy known as sharecropping, in which the farmer borrowed land, farm tools, etc., from the planters and repaid them with produce.

At the end of the era of reconstruction, the south was reunited with the Union, but its defeat and occupation left the south both economically and spiritually warped. Blacks were placed in the fetters of discrimination, and their true emancipation had to wait another century, for the civil rights movement of the "second reconstruction period."

Documents

Supreme Court Decision, Dred Scott v. Sandford, 1857

TANEY, C. J. . . . . The rights of private property have been guarded with equal care. Thus the rights of property are united with the rights of person, and placed on the same ground by the fifth amendment to the Constitution. . . . An Act of Congress which deprives a person of the United States of his liberty or property merely because he came himself or brought his property into a particular Territory of the United States, and who had committed no offense against the laws, could hardly be dignified with the name of due process of law. . . .

Now . . . the right of property in a slave is distinctly and expressly affirmed in the Constitution. The right to traffic in it, like an ordinary article of merchandise and property, was guaranteed to the citizens of the United States, in every State that might desire it, for twenty years. And the Government in express terms is pledged to protect it in all future time, if the slave escapes from his owner. . . . And no word can be found in the Constitution which gives Congress a greater power over slave property, or which entitles property of that kind to less protection than property of any other description. The only power conferred is the power coupled with the duty of guarding and protecting the owner in his rights.

Upon these considerations, it is the opinion of the court that the Act of Congress which prohibited a citizen from holding and owning property of this kind in the territory of the United States north of the line therein mentioned, is not warranted by the Constitution, and is therefore void; and that neither Dred Scott himself, nor any of his family, were made free by being carried into this territory; even if they had been carried there by the owner, with the intention of becoming a permanent resident. . . .

Abraham Lincoln, House Divided Speech, June 17, 1858

Mr. President and Gentlemen of the Convention: If we could first know where we are, and whither we are tending, we could better judge what to do, and how to do it. We are now far into the fifth year since a policy was initiated with the avowed object and confident promise of putting an end to slavery agitation. Under the operation of that policy, that agitation has not only not ceased, but has constantly augmented. In my opinion, it will not cease until a crisis shall have been reached and passed. "A house divided against itself cannot stand." I believe this government cannot endure permanently half slave and half free. I do not expect the Union to be dissolved; I do not expect the house to fall; but I do expect it will cease to be divided. It will become all one thing, or all the other. Either the opponents of slavery will arrest the further spread of it, and place it where the public mind shall rest in the belief that it is in the course of ultimate extinction, or its advocates will push it forward till it shall become alike lawful in all the States, old as well as new, North as well as South.

Have we no tendency to the latter condition?

Let any one who doubts, carefully contemplate that now almost complete legal combination—piece of machinery, so to speak—compounded of the Nebraska doctrine and the Dred Scott decision. Let him consider, not only what work the machinery is adapted to do, and how well adapted, but also let him study the history of its construction, and trace, if he can, or rather fail, if he can, to trace the evidences of design, and concert of action, among its chief architects from the beginning.

The new year of 1854 found slavery excluded from more than half the States by State Constitutions, and from most of the National territory by Congressional prohibition. Four days later, commenced the struggle which ended in repealing that Congressional prohibition. This opened all the National territory to slavery, and was the first point gained. . . .

Abraham Lincoln, First Inaugural Address, March 4, 1861

. . . Apprehension seems to exist among the people of the Southern States that by the accession of a Republican administration their property and their peace and personal security are to be endangered. There has never been any reasonable cause for such apprehension. Indeed, the most ample evidence to the contrary has all the while existed and been open to their inspection. It is found in nearly all the published speeches of him who now addresses you. I do but quote from one of those speeches when I declare that "I have no purpose, directly or indirectly, to interfere with the institution of slavery in the States where it exists. I believe I have no lawful right to do so, and I have no inclination to do so." . . .

I now reiterate these sentiments, and, in doing so, I only press upon the public attention the most conclusive evidence of which the case is susceptible, that the property, peace and security of no section are to be in any wise endangered by the now incoming administration. I add, too, that all the protection which, consistently with the Constitution and the laws, can be given, will be cheerfully given to all the States when lawfully demanded, for whatever cause—as cheerfully to one section as to another. . . .

A disruption of the Federal Union, heretofore only menaced, is now formidably attempted.—

I hold that, in contemplation of universal law and of the Constitution, the Union of these States is perpetual. Perpetuity is implied, if not expressed, in the fundamental law of all national governments. It is safe to assert that no government proper ever had a provision in its organic law for its own termination. Continue to execute all the express provisions of our national Constitution, and the Union will endure forever—it being impossible to destroy it except by some action not provided for in the instrument itself.

Again, if the United States be not a government proper, but an association of States in the nature of contract merely, can it as a contract be peaceably unmade by less than all the parties who made it? One party to a contract may violate it—break it, so to speak; but does it not require all to lawfully rescind it?

Descending from these general principles, we find the proposition that in legal contemplation the Union is perpetual confirmed by the history of the Union itself. The Union is much older than the Constitution. It was formed, in fact, by the Articles of Association in 1774. It was matured and continued by the Declaration of Independence in 1776. It was further matured, and the faith of all the then thirteen States expressly plighted and engaged that it should be perpetual, by the Articles of Confederation in 1778. And, finally, in 1787 one of the declared objects for ordaining and establishing the Constitution was "to form a more perfect Union."

But if the destruction of the Union by one or by a part only of the States be lawfully possible, the Union is less perfect than before the Constitution, having lost the vital element of perpetuity.

It follows from these views that no State upon its own mere motion can lawfully get out of the Union; that resolves and ordinances to that effect are legally void; and that acts of violence, within any State or States, against the authority of the United States, are insurrectionary or revolutionary, according to circumstances.

I therefore consider that, in view of the Constitution and the laws, the Union is unbroken; and to the extent of my ability I shall take care, as the Constitution itself expressly enjoins upon me, that the laws of the Union be faithfully executed in all the States. Doing this I deem to be only a simple duty on my part; and I shall perform it so far as practicable, unless my rightful masters, the American people, shall withhold the requisite means, or in some authoritative manner direct the contrary. I trust this will not be regarded as a menace, but only as the declared purpose of the Union that it will constitutionally defend and maintain itself. . . .

First Reconstruction Act, March 2, 1867

An Act to provide for the more efficient Government of the Rebel States

Whereas no legal State governments or adequate protection for life or property now exists in the rebel States of Virginia, North Carolina, South Carolina, Georgia, Mississippi, Alabama, Louisiana, Florida, Texas, and Arkansas; and whereas it is necessary that peace and good order should be enforced in said States until loyal and republican State governments can be legally established: Therefore,

Be it enacted, That said rebel States shall be divided into military districts and made subject to the military authority of the United States as hereinafter prescribed, and for that purpose Virginia shall constitute the first district; North Carolina and South Carolina the second district; Georgia, Alabama, and Florida the third district; Mississippi and Arkansas the fourth district; and Louisiana and Texas the fifth district.

Sec. 2. That it shall be the duty of the President to assign to the command of each of said districts an officer of the army, not below the rank of brigadier-general, and to detail a sufficient military force to enable such officer to perform his duties and enforce his authority within the district to which he is assigned. . . .

Sec. 5. That when the people of any one of said rebel States shall have formed a constitution of government in conformity with the Constitution of the United States in all respects, framed by a convention of delegates elected by the male citizens of said State, twenty-one years old and upward, of whatever race, color, or previous condition, who have been resident in said State for one year previous to the day of such election, except such as may be disfranchised for participation in the rebellion or for felony at common law, and when such constitution shall provide that the elective franchise shall be enjoyed by all such persons as have the qualifications herein stated for electors of delegates, and when such constitution shall be ratified by a majority of the persons voting on the question of ratification who are qualified as electors for delegates, and when such constitution shall have been submitted to Congress for examination and approval, and Congress shall have approved the same, and when said State, by a vote of its legislature elected under said constitution, shall have adopted the amendment to the Constitution of the United States, proposed by the Thirty-ninth Congress, and known as article fourteen, and when said article shall have become a part of the Constitution of the United States said State shall be declared entitled to representation in Congress, and senators and representatives shall be admitted therefrom on their taking the oath prescribed by law, and then and thereafter the preceding sections of this act shall be inoperative in said State *Provided*, That no person excluded from the privilege of holding office by said proposed amendment to the Constitution of the United States, shall be eligible to election as a member of the convention to frame a constitution for any of said rebel States, nor shall any such person vote for members of such convention. . .

6

Industrialization and the Reform Movement

During the seventy years from 1861, when Lincoln took office, to 1933, when Franklin Delano Roosevelt became president, the occupants of the White House were all, except for Grover Cleveland and Woodrow Wilson, Republicans. The Civil War formed a line of demarcation. Prior to the war, political power in America lay with a Democratic Party which made the farmers its supporters and the promotion of landed interests its goal. After the war, power shifted to a Republican administration which, focusing on industrial capital and counting as its supporters the western farmers, planned the rapid industrialization of America. By the 1890s the United States had become the greatest industrial nation in the world. During this period, Americans believed in the principles of equality of opportunity and free competition.

At the same time, however, this rapid industrialization contained within it many contradictions. At the end of the nineteenth century the concentration of industrial enterprises increased, dissatisfaction mounted among the farmers and factory workers, and movements to organize them sprang up. In the 1890s America arrived at a major turning point, symbolized by the closing of the frontier. A variety of conflicts, such as those between labor and capital, rural and urban dwellers, and old and new immigrants, intensified, and were often accompanied by violence. In response to this crisis, a reform movement from below sponsored by the Populists, a movement for external expansion through the Spanish-American War, and a movement to maintain the system by reform from above, called progressivism, all took form in the early twentieth century.

The Republican Administration and Industrialization

When Lincoln took office as president in 1861, the immediate problem was the solution of the conflict between the south and the north. In the long run, however, the Republican administration which replaced the rule of the southern planters made its goal the development of America as an industrial nation. However, industrialization in America, with its vast land area, differed from that in England in that it did not mean the abandonment of agriculture. On the contrary, American industrialization had as one of its major objectives the development of the farmers and the west, which would constitute the domestic market for manufactured products. In fact, the rapid expansion of America's industrial production power in the late nineteenth century was accompanied by a remarkable increase in agricultural productivity.

This was the period of *laissez-faire*. In order to guarantee the free operation of the economy, the government refrained from actions which would suppress the development of economic activity. It is indicative of the spirit of the times that after Lincoln, not one president in the nineteenth century left a reputation as a "strong" president. This was a period in which presidential leadership was not essential.[1] Congress, especially the Senate, played the principal role in policy-making, and in a sense the Senate upheld the principle of *laissez-faire* with its power of veto. Although this is called the era of *laissez-faire*, however, many positive policies were adopted which guaranteed and stimulated economic development and activity.

First, there was a policy of positive aid in the consolidation and

---

[1] The Englishman James Bryce, in his classic 1888 book, *The American Commonwealth*, devoted a chapter specifically to "Why Great Men Are Not Chosen Presidents." He cited as the primary reason the fact that in America the economic world attracts the capable people. The scholar E. E. Schattschneider, in his excellent essay on the history of American political parties, notes: "The achievement of the Republican party at the peak of its ascendancy cannot be understood in terms of the legislation enacted by Congress but in terms of *what was prevented*. The accomplishments of the Republican party might be measured more accurately, therefore, by the gap produced between the social legislation of western European countries and that of the United States before 1932. The American lag in social legislation suggests that the Republican party in terms of its own goals (economic *laissez faire*) was a powerful and effective political organization." (E. E. Schattschneider, "United States: The Functional Approach to Party Government," in Sigmund Neuman, ed., *Modern Political Parties: Approaches to Comparative Politics*, 1956, p. 198).

development of transportation networks, especially the railroads, which were necessary in order to tame the vast spaces of the American continent and turn them into a market. In place of the roads, canals, and rivers of the early nineteenth century, the railroads now played the main role in the economic unification of America; during the forty years from 1861 to 1900, railroad mileage increased over sixfold. The completion of the first transcontinental railroad in 1869 was particularly significant. Construction of the Central Pacific R.R. advanced inland from California while the Union Pacific R.R. simultaneously progressed westward from Nebraska. The completion of this transcontinental railroad symbolized the internal development and unification of the continent. However, railroad construction required enormous amounts of capital, and for private enterprise the risk was great, so the Republican administration provided aid. One form of assistance was the grant to railroad companies of wide strips of public land on alternate sides along the roadbed; the companies then were also able to sell this land at a high price. The total area of the land which was granted to the railroads in this way reached 150 million acres—more land than the entire area of Great Britain. At the same time, the government gave enormous subsidies for the construction expenses of building the railroads. This government largesse to the railroads resulted in many scandalous incidents of graft and political corruption. Because the railroads were often essentially monopolistic enterprises, the presidents and directors of railroad companies, such as Leland Stanford, Edward H. Harriman, Collis P. Huntington, and Cornelius Vanderbilt, made their millions before Andrew Carnegie, in steel, or John D. Rockefeller, in petroleum.

The development of the railroads, in addition to providing eastern industry with a vast new domestic market, also stimulated the growth of western agriculture and provided it with an eastern market. Consequently, it contributed to the formation of a mutually complementary market relationship between industry and agriculture. America is often called a "child of the railroads," and certainly this is applicable to America of the late nineteenth century.

The development of western agriculture was aided by the expansion of the railroads, but it was advanced even more effectively by the Homestead Act of 1862. As we have seen, the farmers, or potential farmers who hoped to migrate to the west, had been demanding the free grant of public lands ever since the nation was founded. Their hopes were first realized in 1862, during the Lincoln administration. According to the Homestead Act, those who actually established their own farms and engaged in cultivation for five years after moving to the west would be given 160 acres of land free. It is reported that between 1862 and 1890, two million people (farmers and their families) moved to the west and began farming.

However, precisely how effective a role the Homestead Act actually played is an open question. It has been pointed out that among those who moved west and became farmers, many more bought land from the railroad companies than acquired it under the Homestead Act. In total, far more public land was given to the railroad companies than was given to farmers. One cannot deny, however, that the Homestead Act contributed to a considerable extent to America's image as a society different from that of Europe, as a land of opportunity.

As a means of protecting the vast, newly expanded domestic market from the penetration of foreign industry, especially that of England, the Republican administration adopted a protective tariff. In 1869 the average tariff rate on imported goods reached 47 percent, and with the enactment of the Dingley Tariff Act in 1897, the high rate of 57 percent was established. As is frequently noted, American industry was developed through reliance upon a domestic market, and a protective tariff system was necessary in order to protect this extensive and affluent market. Even after the United States had become the leading industrial nation in the world, it maintained a high tariff in order to protect its monopolistic prices within the country. Even today, the U.S. is very sensitive to the erosion of its domestic market by competition from other countries.

Another policy which must be noted was the effort to secure a cheap labor force for the burgeoning industries. The development of the west signified an expansion of the market for the east, but at the same time it meant the siphoning off to the west of the eastern labor force. Consequently, the cheap labor needed for rapidly developing industries had to be secured through immigration from foreign countries. The creation of the office of Commissioner of Immigration was indicative of the Republican administration's policy of encouraging immigration. In the 1880s, immigration, which had stagnated slightly in the 1860s and 1870s due to the influence of the Civil War and the depression of 1873, increased rapidly; during this decade as many as 500,000 people crossed over to America each year.

One must note that this increase in the numbers of immigrants was at the same time accompanied by a qualitative change. Until this time, immigrants to America had come mainly from northern and western Europe. Now, immigration from the nations of eastern and southern Europe—Italy, Poland, Russia, and Austria-Hungary —increased. While the earlier immigrants were predominantly Protestants, who hoped, after entering the country, to move west and become farmers there, many of the new immigrants were Catholics or Jews, who settled in the large cities of the eastern seaboard and became factory workers or clerks in stores—the urban masses. These religious, cultural, and occupational changes led to serious tensions between the old and the new immigrants, and gave rise to an "ethnic problem" within the national structure of America from the end of the nineteenth century onwards.

Another policy change was the 1863 passage of the National Banking Act. Its immediate objective was to defray the wartime expenses of the federal government, but the revival of the national banking system also guaranteed an abundant supply of capital and sound currency policies. National bank notes secured with government bonds were issued, superceding those which until then had been issued by the individual states. Although the United States monetary system had been based on gold and silver bimetalism, after 1873 the minting of silver coinage was suspended, and in effect the U.S. adopted a gold standard. This change made the free coinage of silver a major issue in the late nineteenth century.

With the support of policies such as these, American industrialization progressed rapidly. The U.S. iron and steel industry, which in 1860 had ranked fourth in size in the world, by 1890 had developed into the world's largest. During the thirty-year period from 1860 to 1890, the total volume of production of manufactured goods increased nearly threefold. This kind of industrial development gave rise to a number of mergers, or "combinations," among enterprises. The process of combination and the emergence of giant enterprises began in the 1870s based on the system of joint-stock companies. In the 1880s, the "trusts" became predominant, and in the 1890s the holding company system began to emerge on a large scale. In each sector of the industrial economy, such as iron and steel, leather, cotton, railroads, petroleum, and sugar, the merger of enterprises continued, and monopolization—or, more precisely, oligopolization—became the rule. An oft-cited typical example was the monopoly which centered on the Standard Oil Company under John D. Rockefeller. The U. S. Steel Corporation, when it was established in 1901, possessed capital of $1,100,000,000 and controlled 60 percent of the total American output of iron and steel; behind it was the finance capital of John Pierpont Morgan. This trend toward industrial mergers and combines gave rise to immense differences among individuals in the possession of wealth. In 1893 over 70 percent of the total wealth of the U. S. was controlled by a minority of 9 percent of the total population.

Rapid industrialization also stimulated urbanization, and the cities along the seacoasts rapidly increased their populations. New large cities such as Chicago also grew up in the midwest. Because of the deficiency of public welfare facilities in the cities, however, this urbanization was often accompanied by the development of slums.

Urbanization and the large-scale influx of new immigrants stimulated the rapid growth of the political machines as sub-structural organizations peculiar to American political parties. The machines wielded enormous influence in city government and local politics by distributing benefits such as help in obtaining citizenship, jobs, and aid for the sick to the large numbers of immigrants who had come to a strange land, and in return receiving their votes. The machines were not a new phenomenon; Tammany Hall, the Democratic machine in New York City, had a history almost as old as that of the Democratic Party itself. However, the votes of the immigrant groups gave them unprecedented power in city government and local politics. Certainly, the machines were often involved in corruption. On the other hand, they functioned as a sort of social security system for the newly arrived immigrants, humanizing the impersonality of a merciless, grim, competitive society.[2]

The rather harsh social character of late-nineteenth-century American society owed much to the widespread acceptance of Social Darwinism. This theory, which attempted to apply the laws of biological evolution—"struggle for existence" and "survival of the fittest"—to human society as well, originated in the work of the Englishman Herbert Spencer, but in its popular form it was disseminated even more widely in America than in England. It was an ideal vehicle for the traditional American virtues of independent enterprise, competition, and, above all, hard work. In presenting success as purely the result of natural competition, it made any intervention in the social system seem useless and unnecessary, and thus was the perfect vehicle for the era's conservative political beliefs. For those who succeeded, it was presented as legitimization of their own success; at the same time, it was presented to the lower classes as scientific evidence for the concept that success was possible through their merits and efforts. The ethos of work and success which was supported by Social Darwinism permeated both the upper and lower classes; it could support and encourage rapid industrialization while at the same time covering up the instability which accompanied it.

Social Darwinism was disseminated from the universities by men such as William Graham Sumner and by published works such as *The Gospel of Wealth* by Andrew Carnegie, himself a millionaire (see the excerpt appended to this chapter), and was often advocated in sermons by ministers like Russell H. Conwell. It was also popularized in the form of the many Horatio Alger "success stories" intended for young boys and girls. However, in an era which legitimized success itself more than work, Social

---

[2] The machine has been described by such foreign scholars of American politics as Moisei Y. Ostrogorsky, James Bryce, and Max Weber. In America as well, both reformers and scholars often equated machines with political corruption. However, if the role of the machine as an agency of social relief is ignored, its longevity cannot be understood. One could say that the machine, as a social institution, should be analyzed in light of the distinctive American milieu, an impersonal, competitive society, where universal suffrage was practiced early and which absorbed large numbers of immigrants. In this respect, the theory of Robert Merton, who was not a political scientist but a sociologist, is suggestive (*Social Theory and Social Structure*, 1949, pp. 71–81). In addition to the assistance given by the machine itself, he emphasizes the social function of humanizing and personalizing the big cities and providing all manner of assistance to those in need.

Darwinism functioned as a doctrine not of the homogenization of society, but of social discrimination, and became a factor which caused divisions in American society.

Discontent and the Reform Movement

To a certain degree all the American people, including the farmers and workers, were the beneficiaries of the rapid economic growth of the late nineteenth century. In the climate of Social Darwinism, farmers and workers came to some extent to identify themselves with the system. However, the impact of rapid industrialization often victimized them. In particular, the waves of depression which attacked every ten years, in 1873, 1883, and 1893, dealt the most severe blows to the farmers and workers.

In response to the mergers of enterprises and the nationalization of the economy, the farmers and workers gradually formed their own special-interest groups. Transmitting their dissatisfaction to the policy-making organs, they attempted to bring about policies which would be beneficial to themselves. Starting at the local level, they also formed third parties separate from the two major parties, and attempted to elect their own candidates to office.

American farmers were reaping both the benefits and the disadvantages of the spectacular growth in the nation's agricultural system. The number of farmers had increased, and the area of cultivated land, which was 400 million acres in the 1860s, had practically doubled to 800 million acres by 1900. These increases in scale, combined with advances in mechanization, such as the tractor and the harvester, and the rationalization of management, brought about a nearly threefold increase in production in the second half of the nineteenth century. At this point American agriculture developed into a modern industry which depended on international as well as domestic markets. At the same time, capitalistic agriculture meant that the impact of economic depressions on agriculture became more serious, and agriculture became subject to business cycles. Depressions caused production surpluses and a drop in the prices of agricultural goods, and the farmers, who, unlike the industrialists, lacked the power to adjust prices, were severely afflicted by the price differential between the manufactured products they had to buy and the prices they received for their produce.

The Republican administration, with its *laissez-faire* principles, did not come to the aid of the farmers during depressions. The farmers themselves therefore organized for their own benefit. The Grange movement was the first of such organizational movements. Originally, the Grange was a completely non-political, farmers' social club for mutual aid: farmers scattered over a wide territory organized voluntarily, with such goals as exchange and cooperation in agricultural techniques. The Grange, which spread rapidly among western farmers after the Civil War, became politicized after the panic of 1873. The farmers, who had been hurt by the fall in the prices of agricultural produce during this panic, were particularly critical of the railroads, which were able to charge virtually monopoly-level prices for the freight transport on which the farmers depended to market their goods. The farmers demanded the regulation of railroad freight charges and of the warehouses, which were often managed simultaneously by the railroads, or the placement of railroads and warehousing businesses under the management of state governments. Individual state laws which were enacted in response to the farmers' demands and which provided for government regulation of freight charges were recognized as constitutional by the Supreme Court in the Munn *v.* Illinois case in 1877. However, the effective regulation of railroad freight charges could not be accomplished at the individual state level. Lobbying at the national level was necessary. The Grange movement, with its basis in local organizations, was not equipped for national activity and began to decline in the 1880s.

One of the policies favored by the farmers, who traditionally were debtors, was an inflationary expansion of the money supply, which they hoped would make the repayment of their debts easier and at the same time cause the prices of agricultural products to rise. This view was a time-honored one; Paper Money parties had been formed in various states during the War for Independence. After the Civil War, however, the Republican administration withdrew from circulation the paper currency ("greenbacks") which had been issued and adopted a deflationary policy, so the farmers who were demanding an inflationary policy started a national third party called the Greenback Party and campaigned in the presidential election of 1876. The principal demand of this party was the increased issue of paper money and the coinage of silver, but its platform also addressed many of the social and economic issues which were to become problems at the end of the nineteenth century: it advocated labor legislation, the exclusion of Chinese immigrants, and the enactment of a graduated income tax. However, this party emerged suddenly as a national party and lacked sufficient local organization; its strength soon peaked and began to wane.

In the 1880s, the Farmers' Alliance appeared in place of the declining Grange. This group also was originally an organization which aimed at fraternity, social intercourse, and vigilance among farmers. But, stimulated by the panic of 1883, it expanded its activities into the economic field as well. It attempted, by means of cooperative associations which managed warehouse businesses, issued insurance policies, and so forth, to eliminate exploitation by intermediaries. Because they had little capital and were inexperienced in management, the farmers were overwhelmed by existing business enterprises and ultimately failed. Nevertheless, the Alliance, supported by farmers who distrusted railroad companies and real estate dealers, gradually grew in size and influence. The movement, which advocated such policies as public ownership of the railroad industry and the creation of financial agencies which would make long-term, low-interest loans to farmers, expanded rapidly in the south as well as the west, as a progressive reform movement. It challenged the dominance of the Democratic Party at the state level, and in individual states began to succeed frequently in electing governors or in dominating the state legislatures. In the final analysis, however, like the Grange movement, its activities seemed limited to the articulation of discontent, the organization of pressure groups, or the acquisition of political power on a purely local level; at a time when the economic structure was being nationalized, it was difficult to achieve the movement's desired goals.

Industrial workers were more successful in organizing to further their own interests. Working conditions in America were relatively favorable for the immigrant workers compared with Europe. However, work weeks still sometimes exceeded sixty hours, wages were low, and the workers had no protection against losing their jobs when business conditions were unfavorable. As a result, the workers organized to demand the improvement of working conditions. Various kinds of local labor organizations already existed prior to the Civil War. However, as the market economy became organized on a national level after the Civil War, the organization of labor was also nationalized. The first national organization of workers, the National Labor Union, was organized by an iron molder, William Sylvis. Under his leadership, this organization advocated an eight-hour day and equal wages for men and women, and in its most active period had over 300,000 members. The cohesion of this organization depended to a large extent on Sylvis's personal leadership, however, and it collapsed rapidly after his death in 1869.

The National Labor Union was succeeded by the Knights of Labor, which aimed at the organization not only of factory workers in the narrow sense but of anyone who was called a worker (see the excerpt from the Knights' constitution appended to this chapter). Membership qualifications made no distinction between skilled and unskilled workers or on the basis of race. The Knights' main demands were an eight-hour work day and fair distribution of the land held by railroad and real estate companies. In 1885, they supported a railroad workers' strike, and the success of the strike raised their stock among workers. In 1886, at the peak of its popularity, the Knights of Labor had nearly 700,000 members. However, precisely because it was an organization which included all types of workers, clashes of interest among its members could not be avoided; as a result, there were constant struggles within the organization.

The dissatisfaction of skilled workers with the principle of equal treatment of unskilled workers caused a split within the movement, and the skilled workers began to organize their own national labor union. In 1886 the American Federation of Labor was organized around Samuel Gompers. The AF of L at first took the form of a loose federation of local craft unions; like these local unions, it was exclusive and tended to be concerned only with achieving immediate economic demands. Until the emergence of the Congress of Industrial Organizations (CIO) after the Great Depression of 1929, the AF of L was the center of the American labor movement. Gompers continued his activities as president of the AF of L until his death in 1924. Membership of the AF of L by that time had reachèd almost 200,000, but because this included only skilled workers, it was less than 10 percent of the total industrial labor force. Other workers' organizations, for example the powerful railroad employees' union, existed and conducted their own activities separately.

Strikes for improvements in working conditions, such as the large-scale railroad strike of 1877, occurred frequently from the 1870s on. In particular, the national general strike of May 1, 1886, which led to the Haymarket Massacre a few days later in Chicago, was an epoch-making strike in the history of the American labor movement. On May 4, an open-air meeting was held in Chicago to protest the violent actions of the police during the strike. Just as a skirmish had broken out between the workers and the police, someone threw a bomb. Haymarket Square immediately became a battleground, and in the end there were scores of casualties. As a result of this incident, eight anarchists were arrested as suspects in the bomb throwing, and seven were sentenced to death; four of them were executed immediately. The evidence against the arrested men was insufficient, and afterwards the charges were found to be false. The incident was widely used by business as an excuse for an attack on labor unions, and the labor movement was in fact damaged.

Paralleling the organizing activities of farmers and workers, who either urged reforms as pressure groups or sought to obtain political power as third parties, demands for reform from writers and intellectuals also became vigorous. Strong attacks on the social contradictions in late nineteenth-century America became widespread. The journalist and politician Henry George, for example, in his best-selling *Progress and Poverty* (1879), attacked the system of private ownership of land as the fundamental cause of the extreme poverty which coexisted with America's wealth in the late nineteenth century (see the excerpt appended to this chapter). It criticized the enormous unearned incomes based on the increased value of land, and advocated the so-called Single Tax Movement, which called for a tax on land only. This was an extremely simplistic theory, but for that very reason it was widely accepted by the public; when George ran for the office of mayor of New York City, he was able to obtain a considerable number of votes, although he lost. His theory was widely accepted not only in America but also in Europe, and in particular in England, where it influenced the Labour Party.

Another bestseller of the time was Edward Bellamy's *Looking Backward 2000–1887* (1888), a socialist novel which hypothesized a utopian society under state socialism in the year 2000 and, through comparison with that society, pointed out the evils of monopoly at the end of the nineteenth century. It is said that over ten years nearly 400,000 copies were sold. Henry Demarest Lloyd's *Wealth Against Commonwealth* also attacked contemporary monopolization. These attacks, in novel or treatise, on the capitalist system were more readily accepted by the public because they were couched in terms of the reality of American society. They were followed in the early twentieth century by the works of the muckrakers, whom we shall meet again later.

Marxism, which was introduced to America by German immigrants and political exiles after 1848, had some influence at this time. The Socialist Labor Party was formed in 1876, but because its members were almost all Germans, it lacked the strength to permeate American society in general. The fear of alien influence, which was ubiquitous in American society at this time, was not helpful to the party's image. The party nominated presidential candidates from 1892 on, but never obtained more than 50,000 votes.

The organized and individual criticisms and attacks on the established system compelled the establishment to take countermeasures to protect the system. The dominant Republican Party effected several reform laws, which to some degree met the demands of the dissidents. For example, a drastic reform of the civil service system was initiated in response to criticism of corruption in government and to the assertion that the corruption originated in the spoils system, which had originally been part of democratic reform. Opposition to the spoils system had motivated a reformist group of Republicans to split off from the mainstream of the party in 1872 and form the Liberal Republican group, centering around the journalist and labor leader Horace Greeley. In the presidential election of that year, Greeley challenged Grant and lost. However, the demand for reform of the civil service system was deeply rooted among urban intellectuals and the middle class, and reform was finally effected in 1883 in the Pendleton Act. At first the system of civil service appointment by merit which was the essence of this law was only partially adopted. But gradually, as government service became increasingly complicated and specialized, it was applied to a broader range of government posts. By the end of the nineteenth century 50 percent, and by the 1930s 70 percent, of public servants were employed in accordance with this merit system.

The farmers' strong dissatisfaction with the railroad companies and their demand for the regulation of railroad freight charges also plagued the Republican administration. A Supreme Court decision in 1886 held that where railroad lines extended over several states, as almost all did, the regulatory authority did not rest in the individual state; the state laws establishing such regulations, even those which had previously been recognized in the Munn v. Illinois case, were declared unconstitutional. As a result, the farmers were pressing their demands for the regulation of railroad freight charges at the national level. Both major parties had to respond to this demand in some form; finally in 1887 the Interstate Commerce Act was passed, and the federal government began to supervise railroad companies. Because representatives of the railroad companies had influence in the Interstate Commerce Commission created by the act, it was impossible to effect a substantive revision of freight charges. Nevertheless, particular historical significance has been attached to this law as the first case in which the federal government intervened in the management of private enterprise on a national level.

In response to the strong dissatisfaction in various quarters with monopoly, a federal law which regulated industrial merger activities, the Sherman Anti-Trust Act, was passed in 1890. This law was significant in that it was the first time the federal government attempted to deal effectively with public antagonism toward the trend toward mergers and monopolization. However, the fact that this law was passed almost unanimously in Congress indicated that it had no significant impact in regulating trusts and that Congress enacted it with full knowledge that it would be a law with form but without effectiveness.

Indeed, the United States *v.* E. C. Knight Company decision of 1895 judged this anti-trust law not applicable to the American Sugar Manufacturing Company, which monopolized America's sugar refining industry, clearly demonstrating the nature of the law.

Crisis and Populism

At the convention of the American Historical Association held at the Chicago World's Fair in 1893, a young historian from the University of Wisconsin, Frederick Jackson Turner, claimed on the basis of the census of 1890 that the frontier had disappeared. He concluded his report on a somewhat exaggerated note: "And now, four centuries from the discovery of America, at the end of a hundred years of life under the Constitution, the frontier has gone, and with its going has closed the first period of American history" (see the excerpt appended to this chapter).

The word "frontier" was used rather vaguely even by Turner himself, and its disappearance did not necessarily mean the disappearance of free land. The disposal of public land continued on a large scale after 1890, but the disappearance of the frontier can certainly be considered to have symbolized a turning point in American history. Both Americans, beginning with Jefferson, and Europeans, including Hegel, recognized that the existence of a vast expanse of land had made American society different from that of Europe. As these expanses of land gradually narrowed, the various conflicts and contradictions fostered by the rapid development of American society inevitably came to be exposed.

American society was composed of various diverse races and nationalities. It was built under a federal system of government over a vast expanse of land. It integrated and unified because there existed among the people a certain conscious identity as Americans. Even if it was largely mythological, the social mobility symbolized by the expression "from a log cabin to the White House" was in principle guaranteed, and the dream of success based on equality of opportunity and free competition was an enduring one. By the end of the nineteenth century, however, monopolization was widespread and inequality in the distribution of wealth had become conspicuous. The flaunting of their wealth by the rich became an extremely important characteristic of the age. Thorstein Veblen called this phenomenon "conspicuous consumption" in his *The Theory of the Leisure Class* (1899). This display of wealth strongly stimulated the consciousness of those without wealth, and a sense of division between the top and the bottom in the structure of American society was awakened. Certainly, the last decade of the nineteenth century was a period in which the fissures in American society deepened markedly, taking such forms as conflict between business and labor, rural and urban dwellers, and old and new immigrants.[3]

Conflict between laborers and employers increased steadily through repeated strikes and the violent incidents accompanying them. Workers who had become radicalized at the time of the Haymarket Massacre of May 4, 1886, became even more militant in 1892 during a large-scale strike at the Carnegie Steel Company's Homestead factory, under the leadership of the AF of L. Because the strike was prolonged and the company mobilized against it a corporation which specialized in strikebreaking, Pinkerton's Detective Agency, the labor dispute escalated into a violent confrontation.

Farmers, who considered themselves the backbone of American society and who until then had in fact constituted the majority in that society, now were experiencing a relative decrease in numbers and in influence with the rapid development of industrialization and urbanization. The farmers feared that they and their way of life would gradually be left behind in the new society that seemed to be evolving. This strong sense of insecurity made more intense the farmers' expressions of discontent with the railroad campanies and the banks.

The rural-urban conflict overlapped with that between old and new immigrants. The old immigrants, mostly Protestants from northwestern and western Europe, were numerous in rural areas. In contrast, the immigrants from southern and eastern Europe,

[3] The political scientist Sebastian de Grazia perceived the end of the nineteenth century as almost the only period in American history characterized by "acute anomie," intense unrest and division. (*The Political Community: A Study of Anomie*, 1948, pp. 115–122). His book was published in 1948; the late 1960s and early 1970s probably constitute another such period.

many of whom were Catholic, were numerous among the urban masses. Consequently, the conflct between rural and urban was often perceived as a conflict between two different religions or cultures. To the old immigrants, the new immigrants were people to whom the American value system was unfamiliar and, in this sense, were "aliens"; moreover, they emerged as strong competitors for the old immigrants. The new immigrants, who had come to "the land of opportunity," often found it inhospitable; it was difficult for them to assimilate into American society, and they felt alienated from the people of native stock.

In this critical situation, a reform movement with a wide base of support began to gather strength, and in 1892, with the support of various local farmers' groups, the Knights of Labor, and local third parties, a national third political party called the People's Party of the United States, or the Populists, was organized.

The leader of the Populist movement was Ignatius Donnelly, a veteran of the Farmers' Alliance and a talented organizer. He emphasized that America was now in an absolutely critical condition morally—that due to the corruption of politics, two major classes, the millionaires and the poor, had been created.

In July 1892 the Populists held a national convention in Omaha, Nebraska; they nominated an independent presidential candidate, James B. Weaver, a Union general during the Civil War who was also the candidate of the Greenback Party in the 1880 election. The Populist platform echoed the traditional demand of the farmers for "free silver"—free and unlimited coinage of silver at a one-to-sixteen ratio with gold. It also called for the government ownership and operation of transportation and communication facilities such as railroads and the telephone and telegraph systems; the adoption of a graduated income tax; the establishment of postal savings banks which would give long-term, low-interest loans to farmers; the prohibition of alien land ownership; the direct election of U.S. senators, who in those days were elected by state legislatures; shorter working hours for industrial workers; and restrictions on immigration (see the excerpt from the platform appended to this chapter).

The Democrats ran former president Grover Cleveland as their candidate in the 1892 presidential election, and the Republicans ran the incumbent president Benjamin Harrison. The Populists received about one million votes in this election, which was not a bad showing for a party which had emerged suddenly as a third party; on the other hand, this constituted only about 8.5 percent of the total vote. The single-member electoral system—especially the presidential system, which is a sort of nationwide single-member electoral system—made the advance of a third party extremely difficult. The Socialist Labor Party, the first Marxist party to emerge in America, received only 21,000 votes in the 1892 election.

It is, however, significant to note that the nature of the Populist Party was reflected in the source of the votes it received. They came primarily from the west, while the party remained extremely weak in the east. This fact alone indicated that ultimately the Populist Party, while it advocated cooperation between workers and farmers, was a party of western farmers.

The Democratic administration under Cleveland, who took office as a result of this election, at first gave the impression that it differed from the Republicans. But in terms of basic policies, utimately there was little distinction between them. For example, although the Democrats had promised during the election campaign to lower the tariff, the Wilson-Gorman Tariff Act which they sponsored did not fundamentally revise the stringent protective tariff which had been instituted under the Republican administration. The Act did include an income tax provision which established a system of graduated taxation, thus responding to a certain degree to the demand of the reform movement for a progressive income tax system. However, the Supreme Court in the Pollock *v.* Farmers' Loan and Trust Co. case in 1895, by a five-to-four decision declared the relevant item of the Tariff Act unconstitutional.

In spite of widespread demands for the free coinage of silver, the Cleveland administration, confronted with the panic of 1893, advocated a sound financial policy based on the gold standard; in order to protect the gold reserves, the government forbade the purchase of silver. This measure resulted in deep discontent among the farmers. The march on Washington of Coxey's Army in 1894 was symbolic of the social unrest of the times. Jacob S. Coxey, an Ohio Populist, thought that the government ought to spend five hundred million dollars a year on public works for the relief of those unemployed due to the depression. Brandishing this demand, he rallied the unemployed and marched on Washington from all over the country. When they entered the Capitol grounds, however, they were all arrested, including Coxey.

Strikes by workers also occurred frequently. Of these, the strike against the Chicago Pullman Palace Car Company in May of 1894 was on a particularly large scale. The American Railway Union, under the leadership of Eugene V. Debs, struck in sympathy, and it developed into a major strike centering on Chicago and extending to twenty-four states. Faced with this workers' offensive, the Cleveland administration responded to the request of the companies being struck by dispatching federal troops and, under pretext of protecting the mail, intervened in the strike. The Supreme Court also issued an injunction against those union members who obstructed the mail and interstate commerce; because Debs did not observe the injunction, he was arrested for contempt of court. Finally the strike was suppressed.

The Cleveland administration naturally became unpopular among farmers and workers. In the mid-term elections of 1894, the Populist Party expanded its vote to 1,500,000, and by the time of the presidential election of 1896, it had become a political force which could not be ignored. Thus, within the Democratic Party a conflict emerged between the mainstream eastern faction which centered around Cleveland and the anti-mainstream faction of the western farmers, who were often called Silver Democrats. The two factions struggled violently for hegemony within the party. Finally, at the 1896 national convention in Chicago, the western faction won and nominated the thirty-six-year-old William Jennings Bryan as their presidential candidate. Bryan, a typical western "common man," gave his famous "Cross of Gold" speech at this national Democratic convention, attacking the gold standard and arguing that the party must pay serious attention to the problems of the farmers. One part of the eastern faction left the party and organized separately as the National Democratic Party.

The Republican Party, advocating its traditional high tariff policy, espousing the gold-standard system, and promising a vigorous foreign policy, nominated William McKinley, an advocate of the protective tariff, as its presidential candidate. One group within the Republican Party, however, opposed McKinley, withdrew from the party, and, under the name of National Silver Republicans, supported Bryan.

This course of events within the major parties posed a dilemma for the Populists. Many of the new policies of the Democratic Party dominated by the western faction were those previously advocated by the Populists, and consequently it was anticipated that many of the farmers' votes would go to the Democrats. For the third-party Populists, fusion with the Democratic Party meant extinction. The compromise adopted, therefore, was that the Populist Party would maintain its independent existence but would support the Democrat Bryan as its presidential candidate. For vice-president, they nominated the southern Populist Thomas Watson, rather than the Democratic vice-presidential candidate, and so tried to demonstrate the independence of their organization.

The election of 1896 was an extremely hard-fought battle. The Republicans poured enormous sums of money into their campaign. Bryan received funds primarily from the owners of silver mines; with his magnificent oratorical talent, he energetically campaigned throughout the country. In the end, the Republican McKinley won, receiving 51 against Bryan's 47 percent of the popular vote. McKinley got 271 electoral votes; Bryan, 176.

It is frequently said that this election was fought between two conflicting forces which cross-cut American society horizontally. However, that if had been completely true, Bryan, with the support of the lower classes who constituted the majority, would have won the election. It is also often said that money determined the outcome, and that the Republicans owed their victory to the skillful propaganda of Senator Marcus Alonzo Hanna, their campaign manager, as well as to the enormous amount of money they spent. It goes without saying that these factors contributed to McKinley's election. On the other hand, it must be pointed out that Bryan's views and personal style were rather anachronistic in an urbanized society in which the relative number of farmers was decreasing. Indeed, the vote distribution showed that Bryan had little appeal for voters in the eastern industrial cities.

Populism, as the term applied to both the Populist Party and Bryan's movement, sharply criticized the contradictions in American society at the end of the nineteenth century, and called for reform on the basis of the cooperation of workers and farmers. In the final analysis, however, in the sense that it hoped for a restoration of the old American society of the early nineteenth century, it was after all a backward-looking, rather than a forward-looking, reform. One can see in this movement both the uneasiness and the nostalgia of American agrarianism as it encountered a society which now was industrialized and urbanized. The religious fundamentalist Bryan personally symbolized the pathos of this movement: late in his life he again became prominent as an opponent of the teaching of evolutionary theory in public schools.

After the Republican Party regained political power in the election of 1896, the highest tariff rate in American history, the Dingley Tariff, was enacted, and in 1900 the gold standard was established. The Populist movement, which had in effect become identified with Bryan, collapsed with his defeat. Beginning around 1897, the demand in foreign markets for American agricultural products increased, and as business trends were also pointing towards recovery, to a certain extent the dissent and anxiety within the country abated, and the demands for reform grew less strident.

Documents

Resolutions of the Springfield, Illinois, Farmers' Convention, April 2, 1873

1. Resolved, by the farmers of Illinois, in mass meeting assembled, that all chartered monopolies, not regulated and controlled by law, have proved detrimental to the public prosperity, corrupting in their management, and dangerous to republican institutions.

2. Resolved, that the railways of the world, except in those countries where they have been held under the strict regulation and supervision of the government, have proved themselves arbitrary, extortionate and as opposed to free institutions and free commerce between states as were the feudal barons of the middle ages.

3. Resolved, that we hold, declare and resolve, that this despotism, which defies our laws, plunders our shippers, impoverishes our people, and corrupts our government, shall be subdued and made to subserve the public interest at whatever cost. . . .

5. Resolved, that in view of the present extortions, we look with alarm upon the future of an interest which can combine in the hands of a few men a capital

of nearly $250,000,000, and we believe it essential to the prosperity of all classes that this contest continue until these corporations acknowledge the supremacy of law.

6. Resolved, that we regard it as the undoubted power, and the imperative duty of the legislature, to pass laws fixing reasonable maximum rates for freight and passengers, without classification of roads, and that we urge upon our General Assembly the passage of such laws. . . .

Preamble of the Constitution of the Knights of Labor, January 1, 1878

The recent alarming development and aggression of aggregated wealth, which, unless checked, will invariably lead to the pauperization and hopeless degradation of the toiling masses, render it imperative, if we desire to enjoy the blessings of life, that a check should be placed upon its power and upon unjust accumulation, and a system adopted which will secure to the laborer the fruits of his toil; and as this much-desired object can only be accomplished by the thorough unification of labor, and the united efforts of those who obey the divine injunction that "In the sweat of thy brow shalt thou eat bread," we have formed the * * * * with a view of securing the organization and direction, by cooperative effort, of the power of the industrial classes; and we submit to the world the object sought to be accomplished by our organization, calling upon all who believe in securing "the greatest good to the greatest number" to aid and assist us:—

I. To bring within the folds of organization every department of productive industry, making knowledge a standpoint for action, and industrial and moral worth, not wealth, the true standard of individual and national greatness. . . .

Henry George, *Progress and Poverty,* 1879

. . . This association of poverty with progress is the great enigma of our times. It is the central fact from which spring industrial, social, and political difficulties that perplex the world, and with which statesmanship and philanthropy and education grapple in vain. From it come the clouds that overhang the future of the most progressive and self-reliant nations. It is the riddle which the Sphinx of Fate puts to our civilization, and which not to answer is to be destroyed. So long as all the increased wealth which modern progress brings goes but to build up great fortunes, to increase luxury and make sharper the contrast between the House of Have and the House of Want, progress is not real and cannot be permanent. The reaction must come. The tower leans from its foundations, and every new story but hastens the final catastrophe. To educate men who must be condemned to poverty, is but to make them restive; to base on a state of most glaring social inequality political institutions under which men are theoretically equal, is to stand a pyramid on its apex. . . .

Andrew Carnegie, *The Gospel of Wealth,* **1889**

. . . The price which society pays for the law of competition, like the price it pays for cheap comforts and luxuries, is also great; but the advantages of this law are also greater still, for it is to this law that we owe our wonderful material development, which brings improved conditions in its train. But, whether the law be benign or not, we must say of it, as we say of the change in the conditions of men to which we have referred: It is here; we cannot evade it; no substitutes for it have been found; and while the law may be sometimes hard for the individual, it is best for the race, because it insures the survival of the fittest in every department. We accept and welcome, therefore, as conditions to which we must accommodate ourselves, great inequality of environment, the concentration of business, industrial and commercial, in the hands of a few, and the law of competition between these, as being not only beneficial, but essential for the future progress of the race. Having accepted these, it follows that there must be great scope for the exercise of special ability in the merchant and in the manufacturer who has to conduct affairs upon a great scale. That this talent for organization and management is rare among men is proved by the fact that it invariably secures for its possessor enormous rewards, no matter where or under what laws or conditions. The experienced in affairs always rate the *man* whose services can be obtained as a partner as not only the first consideration, but such as to render the question of his capital scarcely worth considering, for such men soon create capital; while, without the special talent required, capital soon takes wings. Such men become interested in firms or corporations using millions; and estimating only simple interest to be made upon the capital invested, it is inevitable that their income must exceed their expenditures, and that they must accumulate wealth. Nor is there any middle ground which such men can occupy, because the great manufacturing or commercial concern which does not earn at least interest upon its capital soon becomes bankrupt. It must either go forward or fall behind: to stand still is impossible. It is a condition essential for its successful operation that it should be thus far profitable, and even that, in addition to interest on capital, it should make profit. It is a law, as certain as any of the others named, that men possessed of this peculiar talent for affairs, under the free play of economic forces, must, of necessity, soon be in receipt of more revenue than can be judiciously expended upon themselves; and this law is as beneficial for the race as the others. . . .

The Populist Party Platform, July 4, 1892

Assembled upon the 11th anniversary of the Declaration of Independence, the People's Party of America, in their first national convention, invoking upon their action the blessing of Almighty God, put forth in the name and on behalf of the people of this country, the following preamble and declaration of principles:

Preamble

The conditions which surround us best justify our co-operation; we meet in the midst of a nation brought to the verge of moral, political, and material ruin. Corruption dominates the ballot-box, the Legislatures, the Congress, and touches even the ermine of the bench. The people are demoralized; most of the States have been compelled to isolate the voters at the polling places to prevent universal intimidation and bribery. The newspapers are largely subsidized or muzzled, public opinion silenced, business prostrated, homes covered with mortgages, labor impoverished, and the land concentrating in the hands of capitalists. The urban workmen are denied the right to organize for self-protection, imported pauperized labor beats down their wages, a hireling standing army, unrecognized by our laws, is established to shoot them down, and they are rapidly degenerating into European conditions. The fruits of the toil of millions are boldly stolen to build up colossal fortunes for a few, unprecedented in the history of mankind; and the possessors of these, in turn, despise the Republic and endanger liberty. From the same prolific womb of governmental injustice we breed the two great classes—tramps and millionaires. . . .

Frederick Jackson Turner, *The Significance of the Frontier in American History,* **1893**

In a recent bulletin of the Superintendent of the Census for 1890 appear these significant words: "Up to and including 1880 the country had a frontier of settlement, but at present the unsettled area has been so broken into by isolated bodies of settlement that there can hardly be said to be a frontier line. In the discussion of its extent, its westward movement, etc., it can not, therefore, any longer have a place in the census reports." This brief official statement marks the closing of a great historic movement. Up to our own day American history has been in a large degree the history of the colonization of the Great West. The existence of an area of free land, its continuous recession, and the advance of American settlement westward, explain American development. . . .

But the most important effect of the frontier has been in the promotion of democracy here and in Europe. As has been indicated, the frontier is productive of individualism. Complex society is precipitated by the wilderness into a kind of primitive organization based on the family. The tendency is anti-social. It produces antipathy to control, and particularly to any direct control. The tax-gatherer is viewed as a representative of oppression. . . . Frontier conditions prevalent in the colonies are important factors in the explanation of the American Revolution, where individual liberty was sometimes confused with absence of all effective government. The same conditions aid in explaining the difficulty of instituting a strong government in the period of the confederacy. The frontier individualism has from the beginning promoted democracy.

The frontier States that came into the Union in the first quarter of a century of its existence came in with democratic suffrage provisions, and had reactive effects of the highest importance upon the older States whose peoples were being attracted there. An extension of the franchise became essential. It was *western* New York that forced an extension of suffrage in the constitutional convention of that State in 1821; and it was *western* Virginia that compelled the tide water region to put a more liberal suffrage provision in the constitution framed in 1830, and to give to the frontier region a more nearly proportionate representation with the tide water aristocracy. The rise of democracy as an effective force in the nation came in with western preponderance under Jackson and William Henry Harrison, and it meant the triumph of the frontier—with all of its good and with all of its evil elements . . . .

He would be a rash prophet who would assert that the expansive character of American life has now entirely ceased. Movement has been its dominant fact, and, unless this training has no effect upon a people, the American energy will continually demand a wider field for its exercise. But never again will such gifts of free land offer themselves. For a moment, at the frontier, the bonds of custom are broken and unrestraint is triumphant. There is no *tabula rasa*. The stubborn American environment is there with its imperious summons to accept its conditions; the inherited ways of doing things are also there; and yet, in spite of environment, and in spite of custom, each frontier did indeed furnish a new field of opportunity, a gate of escape from the bondage of the past; and freshness, and confidence, and scorn of older society, impatience of its restraints and its ideas, and indifference to its lessons, have accompanied the frontier. What the Mediterranean Sea was to the Greeks, breaking the bond of custom, offering new experiences, calling out new institutions and activities, that and more, the ever retreating frontier has been to the United States, directly, and to the nations of Europe more remotely. And now, four centuries from the discovery of America, at the end of a hundred years of life under the Constitution, the frontier has gone, and with its going has closed the first period of American history.

7

Maritime Empire and Progressivism

Concurrent with the reform movement within American society at the end of the nineteenth century was a movement to stabilize the system through extensive overseas expansion. In a sense, since the continental frontier disappeared, Americans had been seeking a new frontier at sea. The maritime empire envisioned by Hamilton at the end of the eighteenth century was realized one hundred years later as the result of the Spanish-American War of 1898.

At the same time, the American ruling class, fearing that the demands for social change from below had become so strong that they might fundamentally alter the system, sought to maintain and stabilize the system by reforming it from above. Both these movements, which spanned the end of the nineteenth and the beginning of the twentieth centuries, were conceived by an elite which belonged to the upper middle class—people who were afraid that the so-called *nouveaux riches* who had risen rapidly to power at the end of the nineteenth century would disregard the long-range perspective, because of their short-term interests, and who felt anxious about the power and organization of the new workers and the increasing numbers of new immigrants. Thus, they felt it was their responsibility to enter politics themselves in order to stabilize American society, to advance overseas and effect domestic reform. The period from the 1890s to the 1910s is therefore a period of overseas expansion, or "imperialism," and of domestic reform, or "progressivism."

The Spanish-American War and a Maritime Empire

By the 1850s, the continental territory of the United States of

America, except for Alaska, was almost fixed. At the same time, in 1853, the American squadron under Commodore Matthew Calbraith Perry arrived in Japan to break through its isolation. Some Americans at this time saw Asia as an extension of the American west. There was a theory which held that in world history, civilization had advanced westward: the civilization which had arisen in the Orient, Greece, and Rome had moved west from Europe to America, and within America from east to west, and finally was moving to Asia. One of those who, supported by this doctrine of the westward advance of civilization, had early believed in the idea of a maritime empire was William H. Seward, Secretary of State under President Lincoln. In 1852 Seward, then a senator, had pointed out that in due time the Pacific Ocean would probably become the main stage of international politics, and he emphasized that America had to become an "empire of the seas." In 1867, while Secretary of State, he purchased Alaska from Russia for $7,200,000, and he seriously viewed this land as a path to Asia, although in his day it was derisively called "Seward's icebox." Also in 1867, the Midway Islands, west of Hawaii, were occupied by the U.S. Navy and became American territory.

However, the development of American industry was still dependent on the growth of the domestic market; consequently, rather than giving serious consideration to overseas markets or to shipping which would extend to overseas markets, industry emphasized the domestic market and railroads as the means of expanding and unifying it. The lag in the development of the American shipping industry was evident in the almost total dependence of America's overseas trade on foreign ships. Naval expansion was also neglected after the Civil War.

However, as the United States assumed the position of one of the world's foremost industrial countries and with the saturation of the domestic market, the problem of overseas markets became more acute. The disappearance of the frontier, the symbol of opportunity, stimulated many Americans' consciousness of the need to seek opportunity overseas, and they began to advocate a vigorous advance overseas and the building of a maritime empire. Captain Alfred Thayer Mahan was perhaps the most influential of these people. Through his many writings, beginning with two seemingly very scholarly books, *The Influence of Seapower Upon History, 1660–1783* (1890) and *The Influence of Seapower Upon the French Revolution and Empire* (1892) and including his essay for the general public, "The United States Looking Outward" (1890), he advocated overseas expansion. (See the excerpt from his essay appended to this chapter.) In addition to being histories of naval battles and military affairs, his works were treatises written from a broader political and ideological perspective.[1] Politicians like Mahan's friend Theodore Roosevelt and his associates, Senators Henry Cabot Lodge and Albert J. Beveridge, saw the United States's overseas expansion as a natural course. This view was also supported by Social Darwinism, which was popular in those days, and also by a simple racism which held that the Anglo-Saxons, as a superior race, ought to bring Christian civilization to the backward races; there were many who preached the doctrine of the "white man's burden" which was later popularized by Rudyard Kipling.

The theory of "Manifest Destiny," once employed in the building of a continental empire, was expanded and adopted as a rationale which legitimized overseas expansion and the construction of a maritime empire, and beginning in the 1880s there was an augmentation of naval power. Steel warships were built for the first time, and the "New Navy" was established. The government also provided subsidies for the building of a merchant marine and encouraged its construction, but progress was slow since the American people in general, including the capitalists, still looked toward the country's interior and gave little consideration to overseas events.

Just as the century was about to end, however, the Spanish-American War of 1898 jolted the isolationists and speeded up

---

[1] Mahan's works were widely read and translated overseas as well, and their influence can be said to have been world-wide. Many of them were translated in Japan also. The above-mentioned two works were translated by the Japanese Navy under the titles *Kaijo Kenryoku Shiron* (Suikosha, 1894) and *Fukkoku Kakumei Jiddi Kai jo Kenryoku Shiron* (Suikosha, 1900), and were used as teaching material in the Naval War College. Among others which I know, there are translations of *Neruson den* [Biography of Nelson] (Kaigun Kyoiku Honbu, 1906) and *Kaigun Senryoku* [Naval Strategy] (Kaigun Gunreibu, 1932). Further, it is said that the Japanese Navy actually contemplated employing Mahan as an instructor at the Naval War College. See: Shimada Kinji, *Amerika ni okeru Akiyama Saneyuki* [Akiyama Saneyuki in America] (Asahi Shimbunsha, 1969). A portable edition of Mahan's works with an extensive introduction has recently been published in Japanese: Sadao Asada, *Alfred T. Mahan* (Kenkyusha, 1978).

America's overseas expansion. This war was touched off by the problem of Cuba, a Spanish possession in the Caribbean Sea. Cuba's emancipation from Spanish oppression was a popular goal of the American public, and in the presidential election of 1896 both the Democrats and the Republicans advocated Cuban independence. In February 1898, just when the so-called "yellow press" was demanding a strong policy with regard to Cuba, the American battleship *Maine* was blown up and sunk in Havana harbor. The Republican administration stiffened its posture toward Spain, and in April 1898 Congress formally authorized the use of the armed forces. The justification for the war was the liberation of Cuba from Spain's outmoded oppression, and both the Republicans and the Democrats, including Bryan, supported it. This so-called "Little War" ended after four months in overwhelming victory for the United States; however, it was strongly linked in both purpose and outcome to America's overseas expansion in the Pacific.

With the outbreak of the war, the American fleet, then at Hong Kong, proceeded to the port of Manila in the Philippine archipelago, which was Spanish territory; under Commodore George Dewey, it defeated the Spanish fleet and occupied Manila. Shortly thereafter, in July 1898, Hawaii, an independent Pacific nation which America had for some time intended to seize, was annexed by a joint resolution of both Houses of Congress on the grounds of protecting the ocean route to the Philippines. At the Paris Peace Conference following the war, the U.S. bought the Philippines from Spain for $20,000,000 and made it American territory. At the same conference Cuba's independence was recognized, but because of the island's political instability, it was placed under American military occupation for the time being. Possession of Puerto Rico and Guam was transferred from Spain to the United States at the same time.

The annexation of the Philippines by the United States aroused the strong opposition of the Filipinos under General Emilio Aguinaldo, who had cooperated with American forces during the war in expectation of independence from Spain. A rebellion occurred, and the American forces, paying a greater price in men and money than they expended in the war with Spain, endeavored to put down the Filipino insurrection. Only in 1902 was it suppressed and peace effected.

In observing the American acquisition of the Philippine Islands, one must note that it did not aim at the control of the territory of the islands themselves. The primary goal of the acquisition was not the possession of the islands nor the rule of a different race, but the possession of an important port of call, Manila. That is to say, seizing the opportunity of the Spanish-American War, the United States secured a base which connected Hawaii, Guam, and Manila in a sort of "bridge over the Pacific," thus successfully guaranteeing its trade routes.

Still, public opinion in the U.S. was critical of the colonization of the Philippines. On the principle that the territory of the United States should be limited to the American continent, the acquisition of the Philippines was criticized as an imitation of European "imperialism," and an "anti-imperialism movement" arose. At the same time, much of the criticism stemmed from the deeply-rooted opposition among American workers to possession of the Philippines, on the grounds that such possession would make the Filipinos Americans and a cheap Asian labor force would enter the American labor market. Many businessmen also feared that the Philippine sugar industry would begin to compete with the American sugar industry. However, the purpose for which these ocean routes and bases were secured was none other than the advance toward the Asian continent, a vast potential market for American goods; with the occupation of the Philippines, opposition to the war in business and economic circles changed to strong support.

The war had major significance for the United States's relationship with Cuba as well. The so-called Platt Amendment of 1901 inserted the following provisions into the Cuban constitution. First, Cuba would not conclude a treaty with any country other than the United States which would impair its independence or its territory. Second, Cuba would not issue a public loan without a guarantee for principal and interest. Third, there were provisions for the protection of Cuba's independence by the United States; for that purpose, the U.S. would have authority to intervene in Cuba's internal affairs at any time and would maintain military bases in Cuba. This amendment was incorporated into a treaty between the United States and Cuba in 1903. These changes made Cuba in essence an American protectorate, and this situation continued until the abrogation of those provisions in 1934.

Now, the completion of a "bridge over the Pacific" meant the completion of a road to the China market (or, broadly, the Asian market). But interest in China was by no means new. Even in the early years of independence, trade with China had yielded enormous profits, and this so-called "Canton trade" was very attractive to the shipping interests of eastern New England. After the 1840s and 1850s, however, a transfer from commercial to industrial capital occurred in the northeast, and trade with Asia declined rapidly. Economic interest in China was replaced by an image of China as the site of missionaries' evangelical work. At the same time, Chinese immigrants were welcomed in great numbers as cheap labor for the construction of the transcontinental railroad. As soon as this construction was completed, however, they were rejected as unassimilable, and in 1882 Chinese immigration was officially prohibited.

Thus trade with China actually represented only a small fraction of America's foreign trade; even in the 1890s exports to China did not exceed 5 percent of total American exports. However, although at the end of the nineteenth century the U.S. economic relationship with China was by no means close or indispensable, the China market was nonetheless implanted in the American consciousness as a potential "market of 300 million" (in the words of that time). Meanwhile, after the Sino-Japanese War (1895), China had begun to be divided into spheres of influence by the European imperialist powers. Imperial Russia's completion of the Trans-Siberian Railway and its scheme to advance into Manchuria, in particular, aroused the concern of the United States. This was because, within the China market, Manchuria was the region which had the greatest potential as a market for American cotton manufactured goods. The United States, despite its great productive power, was lagging behind other nations in opening foreign markets as a result of having concentrated on the development of the domestic market. It therefore strongly opposed the division of the China market by the other powers and insisted that this market should be kept open to any country—including, of course, the United States.

In 1899 Secretary of State John Milton Hay declared his so-called Open Door Policy. This policy, which was first presented in the form of a circular note to the powers (see the excerpt appended to this chapter), while recognizing the "spheres of interest" possessed by each country in China, stated that there should be equal opportunity for trade for every nation. The note had no binding force diplomatically, but because the powers recognized the principle, albeit with some conditions, Hay's policy was highly praised as a victory for American diplomacy. Shortly afterwards, however, the situation in China worsened; the Boxer Rebellion which broke out in June 1900 provided a pretext for further intervention in China by the European powers. In July of that year, the U.S. government issued another note to the powers advocating simultaneously the principle of equal opportunity in the entire territory of China and the territorial and administrative integrity of China. This Open Door Policy became the nucleus of America's China policy.

As a result of the acquisition of the Philippines and the Open Door Policy in China, America became involved in power politics in the Pacific region. From this time on, the United States was a Pacific power with a profound interest in the maintenance of the balance of power in Asia, and was always to oppose the monopolistic domination of the China market by any of the major powers.

New Nationalism and New Freedom

In September of 1901, McKinley, who had been reelected the previous year, was assassinated, and Vice-President Theodore Roosevelt took office at 42 to become the youngest president in American history. The three presidential administrations, from 1901 to 1920, of Roosevelt, William Howard Taft, and Woodrow Wilson are generally called the "Age of Progressivism." These three presidents all belonged to the old upper middle class of more or less distinguished families, were graduates of Ivy League colleges, and differed markedly from the previous "log-cabin to White House" type of president. Roosevelt was a graduate of Harvard, Taft of Yale, and Wilson of Princeton. Roosevelt wrote a number of books; Taft, after his retirement from the presidency, served as a professor at Yale and as chief justice of the Supreme Court; Wilson had been a professor and then president at Princeton before his election. Roosevelt and Wilson, in particular, had strong elite consciousness. Construing the presidency as a trust from the people, they consciously strove to demonstrate leadership. Behind this conscious leadership was a strong sense of crisis in America at the end of the nineteenth century. They felt that the politics of the *nouveaux riches,* or the machines which aimed only at obtaining votes, would be unable to heal the fissures in American society and prevent the internal disintegration of the system. In other words, Progressivism, at its foundation, aimed at the protection and stabilization of the established society through a series of reforms. Members of the old upper middle class, who had until then avoided politics, were entering the political world with a consciousness that might be called *"noblesse oblige"* and endeavoring to govern, not as "politicians" but as "statesmen."

In the election of 1900, the Republican bosses nominated Roosevelt as McKinley's vice-presidential candidate. Knowing that as governor of New York State Roosevelt had carried out reform policies and earned the reputation of a first-rate governor, they thought that the vice-presidency would keep him out of the way. Thus, Roosevelt's assumption of the presidency after McKinley's assassination was a major mishap for the bosses.

As president, however, Roosevelt was unable to carry out his reforms with a free hand; Congress, especially the Senate, was dominated by the conservative faction of the Republican Party, and such men as Nelson W. Aldrich, for example, held the real power. Thus, Roosevelt chose to attain what he could through his authority as chief executive rather than through legislative measures. At the same time, he attempted to put his own policies into effect by appealing to the general populace and mobilizing public opinion (in his own words, "over the heads of the Senate and House leaders"). His first goal was to show his determination to advocate "trust-busting" and to restrain giant combinations. In December 1902, the Roosevelt administration boldly proceeded to prosecute the Northern Securities Company on the grounds that it had violated the anti-trust law. This holding company had been organized to merge two large railroads, the Hill-Morgan and the

Harriman systems. Precisely because until now the collusion between the Republican Party and big businesses had been taken for granted, this action shocked the financial world and imparted a novel image of the Republicans to the general populace. In 1904, a Supreme Court decision ordered the holding company to dissolve on grounds of violation of the anti-trust law.

Yet although Roosevelt called for "trust busting" and actually did prosecute trusts, this did not mean that he rejected the merger of enterprises *per se*. Indeed, he recognized the amalgamation of enterprises as a sign of social progress. He took the position that in view of the fact that such mergers encouraged various abuses, the government must regulate them in the public interest. In reality, despite Roosevelt's advocation of "trust-busting" and his series of restraining measures against mergers, the amalgamation of enterprises advanced, and the actual prosecutions against mergers during his administration were few in number compared with those carried out by later administrations.

Roosevelt also advocated the so-called "Square Deal" toward both labor and business. In 1902, when a large-scale strike occurred in the Pennsylvania coal mines, he settled it by intervening in the name of protecting the public interest. In contrast with previous government intervention, which often under the pretext of mediation sided with the companies and suppressed the strikes, this intervention by Roosevelt actually attempted to mediate between the company and the workers. The settlement by no means completely satisfied the workers, but, because it created the image of a fair government that would also consider the position of the workers, this mediation had an extremely significant political effect.

The Roosevelt administration also embarked on a program of conservation of natural resources. By the end of the nineteenth century, it had become clear that the natural resources of the American continent, which until then had been thought to be inexhaustible, were limited, and it had therefore become necessary to make the most effective use of these limited resources. This conservation policy included the irrigation and reclamation of even the desolate desert zone.

Roosevelt's leadership within the Republican Party was firmly established by his record of performance as president. He was reelected in 1904 by an overwhelming margin. In his second term, Roosevelt was able to carry out his reforms not only by executive measures, but also in the form of Congressional legislation.

One such legislative reform was the Hepburn Act of 1906, which was adopted in order to strengthen the ineffective Interstate Commerce Act of 1887. Under the new act, the Interstate Commerce Commission was given the authority to prescribe fair railroad freight charges by decree. In addition, one must note the enactment of the Meat Inspection Act of 1906, which gave the federal government the authority to supervise the meat-packing trusts, and the Pure Food and Drug Act providing for the supervision of the manufacture of food and medicine. The federal government began to intervene in private enterprise as a guardian of the public interest.

Reform at the state level was also being advanced at this time. These state-level reforms were often motivated by public distrust of state legislatures, and one might say that they reflected a demand for direct, rather than indirect, democracy. Such men as Robert Marion LaFollette of Wisconsin and Hiram W. Johnson of California were representative leaders in the state reform movements. They demanded the adoption of a system of direct primaries which would select party candidates for office by the direct vote of all party members. Due to the efforts of LaFollette this system was adopted by Wisconsin in 1903, and by several other states. In 1910 this primary system was adopted at the national level as well for the nomination of presidential candidates. Many states also adopted a system of direct legislation, and the western states in particular often enacted legislation on the basis of initiative and referendum. The recall, a method of dismissing a public official by a vote of the people, was adopted. These reforms of the political system, in opposition to the traditional control by bosses, aimed at a broad, grass-roots extension of the opportunity for political participation. One could say that the expectation of a more democratic political system first took the form of a demand that the decision-making process itself be controlled by the citizenry at large. As a result of these changes in the political system, social reform legislation was adopted in some states.

In tandem with political reforms, there emerged a number of documentary writings which exposed the evils of contemporary political corruption and economic monopoly. Ida M. Tarbell's *History of the Standard Oil Company* (1904), originally serialized in *McClure's Magazine* beginning in 1903, was representative of these. One can also cite the works of Upton Sinclair and Lincoln Steffens. Because their works, which vividly described contemporary social and political conditions, exposed the dirt at the bottom of business and politics, these authors were called "muckrakers."

Before the 1908 election, Roosevelt, who believed that he had more or less achieved his goals, decided to retire from politics. In his nearly eight years as president he had firmly established presidential leadership and had succeeded in transforming the image of the Republican Party from that of a party of conservatism to one of progress and reform. He therefore concluded that he had succeeded in healing the rifts in American society and in stabilizing the system. As his successor, Roosevelt supported William Howard Taft, who had been Secretary of War under Roosevelt and was an able jurist and administrator. Against Taft, the Democratic Party ran Bryan for a third time, but Bryan had already lost his image as the brilliant popular politician, and the election ended in victory for Taft. Taft's popular image was that of a loyal successor to Roosevelt. Even during Roosevelt's term of office, however, a tenacious conservative Republican faction had continued to exist, and Taft's policies gradually began to reflect the viewpoint of this conservative faction.

As Roosevelt's successor, Taft to a certain extent continued "trust busting," extended the Interstate Commerce Act to apply to telegraphs and telephones as well as the railroads, and made possible the execution of a federal income tax through the Sixteenth Amendment to the Constitution. The Seventeenth Amendment, also passed during Taft's term of office, established the system for electing senators by direct popular vote. Thus, certainly, Taft was heir to the "reform" which had begun with Roosevelt, but at the same time, in the intense intraparty struggle between the conservative Republican faction, the "Old Guard," represented by such men as Aldrich, and the progressives, represented by such men as LaFollette, Taft gradually approached the position of the conservatives.

The progressives, who thus became the anti-mainstream faction within the Republican Party, tried to prepare for the election of 1912 by forming a separate organization within the party.

This was the National Progressive Republican League, organized around LaFollette, who, after serving as governor of Wisconsin, was elected to the Senate.

Roosevelt, who had returned from an extended trip to Africa and Europe, was greatly concerned about the split in the Republican ranks. He felt that the established, mainstream Republican Party should maintain a progressive image. The domination of the party by the conservative faction might bring to naught the foundation which he had built, and he began to make speeches in various places, advocating New Nationalism. This idea was in a way a popularization of the concept Herbert David Croly had expounded in his *The Promise of American Life* (1909). In sum, it advocated the need for a revision of *laissez-faire* and for the supervision of private enterprise in the interest of the public welfare. Roosevelt resolved to return to the political world and reunite the Republican Party under his own leadership. This decision, however, presented a dilemma for the progressive faction of the Republican Party: they had to decide whether to set aside LaFollette, whom they had upheld as their leader, in order to support Roosevelt. After many complications, at the party national convention the progressive faction supported Roosevelt while the conservative faction supported Taft. In the end Taft was nominated, and Roosevelt left the Republican Party to form a separate reformist party, called the Progressive Party. The platform of the Progressive Party, adopted at its convention in Chicago in August 1912, pledged to extend political participation to the broader masses. It advocated the direct primary and women's suffrage. In the economic sphere it called for strict supervision over the merger of enterprises, tariff reform, a graduated income tax system, reform of the banking system, and improvements in working conditions.

The Democratic Party, seeking a new face as a candidate, nominated Wilson, who after serving as president of Princeton University had won praise for his abilities as governor of New Jersey. In his two-year term as governor, Wilson had carried out many reforms and attacked the machine politics of the Democratic Party. He thus had established himself as a progressive.[2]

[2] Wilson, after graduating from Princeton University, transferred to The Johns Hopkins University, famous in those days for academic graduate education, and studied under Professor Herbert Baxter Adams, who was well known as a leader of the

In examining the election of 1912, in addition to the two major parties and the Progressive Party, one must also pay attention to the Socialist Party. Unlike the Socialist Labor Party, which was a Marxist party and had immigrants from Germany as its main constituents, the Socialist Party, though similarly advocating socialism, had American-born leaders and since 1900 had run its own candidate, Eugene Debs, in the presidential elections. Debs, whose leadership had been highly esteemed in the Pullman strike of 1894, ran as the Socialist Party's presidential candidate for the fourth time in 1912.

Thus, the election of 1912 was fought chiefly among the above four candidates; except for Taft they all professed to be progressives. The campaign came to focus on the fight between Roosevelt and Wilson. In contrast to Roosevelt's New Nationalism, Wilson advocated the New Freedom. He believed that American society, in its rapid transformation, had lost its traditional, special characteristics such as equality of opportunity and freedom of competition. His New Freedom (see the excerpt from one of his speeches appended to this chapter) was an attempt to reestablish those traditional characteristics in a new social environment. Roosevelt's New Nationalism recognized as an inevitable social trend the aggrandizement of organizations which had been taking place since the end of the Civil War, while Wilson's New Freedom assumed that this aggrandizement of organizations was itself an evil. (It is said that, just as Herbert Croly was behind Roosevelt's New Nationalism, Louis Dembitz Brandeis, the "people's attorney" who advocated public causes, was behind Wilson's New Freedom.) Wilson, although he failed to

positivist school of history. Inazo Nitobe, the well-known Japanese educator, was among his fellow students. Wilson, instead of becoming enchanted by the German school of history, was interested in the political theories of the British school, such as those of Edmund Burke and Walter Bagehot, and was strongly attracted to the English parliamentary cabinet system and the power it gave the prime minister. From this perspective, Wilson analyzed the American system of the separation of powers and particularly criticized Congress which was under the control of committees. The result was the excellent political science treatise *Congressional Government* (1885), for which he received his doctorate. When Wilson became president, he put this ideal into practice and, modeling himself after the British prime minister, revived the custom of the president himself reading his messages to Congress in person, which had been abolished since Jefferson's time. Thus, Wilson tried to, and actually did, exercise powerful leadership. In his later days as president, however, embittered by the failure of Congress to ratify the Versailles Peace Treaty which he had negotiated, he isolated himself from the people at large and even from his Cabinet.

obtain a majority of the popular vote, received 435 electoral votes, greatly outdistancing Roosevelt's 88 and Taft's 8 votes, and won the election. If one analyzes the votes received by Wilson, one can see that his main strength lay in the rural areas and the south; in the east he benefited from the split between Roosevelt and Taft. Further, one must note that in this election the Socialist Party's Debs received about 900,000 votes, or 6 percent of the total—a noteworthy achievement at a time when both the Democratic Party and the Progressive Party advocated reform.

Wilson's first major policy change was a reduction in the tariff on imported goods, which, despite long-standing demands, had not been realized because of vested interests in Congress. Wilson accomplished it with the Underwood Act of 1913. Under this law, a progressive income tax also became a reality. Next, Wilson effected reform of the currency and banking systems by the enactment of the Federal Reserve Act in 1913. This law, which divided the entire nation into twelve bank districts and decided to permit the issue of federal reserve notes, gave elasticity to the currency and became the basis of the American banking system. Third, in response to the ineffectuality of the existing anti-trust laws, Wison contrived a reform which would make trust supervision more effective, and in September 1914 the Federal Trade Commission Act was enacted. In the same year the Clayton Anti-Trust Act, which reinforced the existing anti-monopoly law, was also passed. While the old anti-monopoly law had been applied to worker and farmer organizations as well as to business, the Clayton Act prohibited such application and clearly protected the laborer. It also stipulated, for example, the prohibition of the system of interlocking corporate directorates and, compared with the earlier Sherman Anti-Trust Act, greatly advanced the effectiveness of trust regulation. The Clayton Act was often praised as "Labor's Magna Carta." In addition, in order to clear the way for long-term, low-interest loans to farmers, Wilson sponsored the Federal Farm Loan Act in 1916, and that same year also saw the passage of the Adamson Act, which specified an eight-hour work day for railroad workers. Thus during his first term Wilson was able to carry out a fair number of reforms through legislation.

I have mentioned that Roosevelt and Wilson were both conscious leaders—that is, they were presidents who exerted strong leadership. This fact, however, cannot be wholly attributed to their self-awareness and their elite consciousness. It must also be attributed to the social climate which encouraged this kind of strong presidency. By the end of the nineteenth century the so-called age of *laissez-faire* was gradually drawing to a close, and demands for the expansion of the central government were now heard from every corner of society. It would be most accurate to say that the primary cause of the emergence of strong presidents was the change from a legislative state to an executive state at the beginning of the twentieth century. This change was advanced by these progressive presidents with their strong individual personalities.

By 1916 Wilson was very popular. He was reelected, defeating the Republican Party's candidate, Charles E. Hughes, Supreme Court justice and former governor of New York. Wilson's victory reflected not only his past performance in domestic policies, but also the strong appeal of the campaign slogan "He kept us out of war"—referring to the First World War, which had been raging in Europe since 1914.

Here we must turn our attention to the foreign policy of the progressive era.

Progressivism and Foreign Policy

After the Spanish-American War, the United States had become a world power and had come to participate extensively in international politics. Progressivism primarily aimed at domestic reform, but it also developed a positive foreign policy.

In developing his foreign policy, Roosevelt emphasized his strong belief in power politics as symbolized by his "Big-Stick Diplomacy." Taft stressed the promotion of economic policies, widely referred to as "Dollar Diplomacy"; as Wilson's policy showed a strong ideological tinge, it was called "Missionary Diplomacy."[3] In this way the three progressive presidents together

[3] "I have always been fond of the West African proverb, 'Speak softly and carry a big stick, you will go far'" (T. Roosevelt, 1900). "The diplomacy of the present administration has sought to respond to modern ideas of commercial intercourse. This policy has been characterized as substituting dollars for bullets" (W. Taft, 1912). "Wilson and (Secretary of State) Bryan [were] . . . obsessed with the

symbolized the three fundamental elements of foreign policy—power, economic interests, and ideology; in addition, the three administrations had in common a strong interest in the international situation and in trying to improve America's international position. To be sure, behind their international activity was a desire, most conspicuous in Roosevelt, to alleviate domestic problems by deflecting the nation's attention to world affairs. Fundamentally, however, its international economic position as the leading industrial nation in the world made it difficult for the United States to maintain its traditional isolation from international affairs.

Towards Latin America, the Roosevelt administration's policies were based on a broadened interpretation of the Monroe Doctrine. The "Roosevelt Corollary" expanded the new interpretation of the Monroe Doctrine which the then Secretary of State, Richard Olney, had adopted in 1895 for his handling of a Venezuelan issue, and claimed for America an international police function in the western hemisphere. The concrete result of this was the so-called Caribbean Policy, which made the group of small countries in the Caribbean, including Cuba, the Dominican Republic, Nicaragua, and Haiti, virtual American protectorates. Roosevelt's plan for the construction of the Panama Canal demonstrated his "Big-Stick Diplomacy" most conspicuously. The United States had for some time been negotiating with England to build a canal which would link the Pacific and Atlantic Oceans, but negotiations remained unsuccessful, and in 1901 England withdrew, leaving the United States alone to build a canal in central America. Roosevelt chose the region of Panama, which was Colombian territory, as the canal site, following in the footsteps of the French engineer Ferdinand de Lesseps, the constructor of the Suez Canal, who had planned to build a canal through Panama but whose company failed financially. Roosevelt tried to conclude with the Colombian government a treaty stipulating the payment of a lump sum of $10,000,000 and a yearly payment of $25,000 for the lease of a six-mile-wide canal zone for ninety-nine years. The Colombian Senate rejected Roosevelt's offer, but in November 1903 the residents of the

concept of America's mission in the world. Finally, they were both fundamentally missionaries, evangelists, confident that they comprehended the peace and well-being of other countries better than the leaders of those countries themselves" (Arthur S. Link, *Woodrow Wilson and the Progressive Era; 1910–1917* [1954], p. 81).

Panama Canal Zone declared independence from Colombia and proclaimed the establishment of the independent Republic of Panama. The United States sent Marines to the Zone and immediately recognized its independence. Thereupon, by treaty with the Republic of Panama, America acquired the right to lease the Panama Canal Zone in perpetuity. This almost coercive method of building the canal met with intense criticism from within and without the United States. However, the linkage of the Atlantic and Pacific oceans now became possible; construction of the canal began in 1904 and was completed in 1914.

The Taft administration basically continued the "Caribbean Policy," although it favored the use of dollars rather than bayonets to achieve policy objectives. The main concern of Taft and his Secretary of State, Philander C. Knox, was expansion and protection of foreign investments. Wilson seemed at first to oppose military intervention in small countries, but when a revolution occurred in Mexico, he asserted that he could not recognize the new regime because it was a military dictatorship; taking advantage of the murders of American citizens, he went so far as to dispatch troops. The Wilson administration also intervened militarily and financially in Haiti and Nicaragua. Thus, the progressive administrations established the precedent of interference by the "Northern Giant" in the domestic affairs of Latin American countries. The overt presence of the Marines in particular aroused a strong resentment and distrust of the United States among the peoples of Latin America.

Wilson's refusal to recognize Victoriano Huerta's military regime can be said to be a forerunner of the United States's unique recognition policy. The usual practice of international law was to recognize any *de facto* government. U.S. policy, however, determined whether or not to recognize a regime on the basis of ideological considerations.

The United States at this time had an interest in the maintenance of the balance of power in Asia. Roosevelt, at the time of the Spanish-American War, advocated annexation of Hawaii and the acquisition of the Philippines, but he realized that the Philippines, while serving as an American outpost in Asia, would at the same time be a strategic vulnerability, an "Achilles heel" for the U.S. Consequently, he recognized that some arrangement with Japan was unavoidable in order to secure the possession of the Philippines. From the balance-of-power viewpoint which opposed monopolistic control in Asia by any one nation, he had supported Japan financially and morally in the Russo-Japanese War (1904–05) for the sake of countering Russian influence in the region. At the same time, however, he watched carefully lest the war result in Japan's overwhelming victory and a monopolistic advance toward China. He sent Secretary of War Taft to Japan to issue the Taft-Katsura Memorandum in July 1905; in this memorandum the U.S. recognized Japan's suzerainty over Korea and Japan confirmed U.S. possession of the Philippines. At the same time, Roosevelt mediated the Portsmouth Treaty and succeeded in bringing the war to an end and maintaining a balance of power between Japan and Russia. In November 1908, Secretary of State Elihu Root concluded the Root-Takahira agreement, which bound Japan to the existing *status quo* in the Pacific and the Open Door policy in China (see the text appended to this chapter). Japan, however, interpreted the *status quo* as U.S. recognition of Japan's paramount interests in Korea and southern Manchuria.

After the Russo-Japanese War, relations between Japan and the U.S. rapidly deteriorated. Since Matthew Perry's ship had been the symbolic first wedge in the opening of Japan to the outside world in 1853, America thought of itself as the main outside agent of "modernization" in Japan, and Japan also had a sense of affinity with America as a model of a modern society. Because the two countries had had no particular point of dispute which might have caused conflict, Japanese-American relations were basically friendly during the half-century from 1850 to 1900. When the division of China by the powers took place, the U.S. expected that Japan would function to maintain the balance of power. However, Japan's victory in the war with Russia inevitably greatly changed the relations between the two countries. The United States became alert to the possibility that Japan, rather than the European powers, might take an aggressive stance toward China.

Having achieved victory over Russia, Japan, with greatly invigorated nationalism, endeavored to establish a powerful military force; the so-called "8.4 (eventually 8.8) fleet" was constructed, aiming at the U.S. as the hypothetical enemy. To make matters worse, at this time segregated education for the children of Japanese immigrants in the city of San Francisco and a movement for the exclusion of Japanese immigrants further provoked nationalistic feeling in Japan. Relations between Japan and the U.S. rapidly worsened, to the point where rumors of a Japanese-American war were heard frequently in both countries. The immigration issue was, for the U.S., essentially a local problem and not a matter over which the federal government had immediate jurisdiction, but Roosevelt attempted to appease Japanese public opinion by such tactics as summoning prominent Californians to the White House. In the so-called Gentlemen's Agreement of 1907, Japan agreed to voluntarily regulate emigration, and the problem seemed to be solved for the time being. Roosevelt had planned an around-the-world cruise of seventeen battleships in order to sell the idea of a big navy to the American public; the cruise took place between December 1907 and February 1909, and, with the implicit purpose of displaying America's military strength to Japan, the fleet included Japan on its itinerary. Japanese leaders, however, had no intention of fighting the United States immediately after the Russo-Japanese War, and the visit of the fleet to Japan took place in a friendly atmosphere. This visit, however, along with Japan's construction of a new fleet, symbolically indicated that the two countries were facing off, while continuing to increase their respective military strengths in the Pacific.

Taft basically carried on the Roosevelt administration's Asian policy. His administration, with Philander C. Knox as Secretary of State, advocated the neutralization and internationalization of the South Manchurian Railway. This attempt at "internationalization" was frustrated by the opposition of Japan and Russia, but the Taft administration continued to promote America's interests in China through an international consortium.

Wilson welcomed the 1911 revolution in China. Believing that China had changed from a corrupted monarchy to a new republic, he entertained the image of a "sister republic." The revolution, along with the activities of the many missionaries who had been sent to China, led to an illusory, emotional sense of unity between America and China. Wilson, at least in the early days of his tenure, was opposed to American participation in an international consortium for China, because he believed that it would violate China's sovereignty and that the United States would be thought of in Asia as a partner of the imperialistic European powers, though he later had to revise his attitude toward the issue of loans. The maintenance of China's sovereignty and the Open Door had become a major problem for the Wilson administration. When, soon after the outbreak of the First World War, Japan thrust the so-called Twenty-one Demands on China, America was confronted with a dilemma. Given the outbreak of war in Europe, the United States could not afford to be engrossed in Asia. At the same time, Japan's Twenty-one Demands clearly violated the Open Door policy in China. In May 1915, Secretary of State Bryan protested to Japan that the Twenty-one Demands impaired the territorial and political integrity of China, and declared that the United States would not recognize any settlement arrived at between Japan and China. On the other hand, however, the United States was finally obliged to intervene in the war in Europe; as a nation associated with the Allied Powers, it found itself fighting on the same side as Japan, and so a temporary, provisional compromise was reached. This was the Lansing-Ishii Agreement, between Secretary of State Robert Lansing and Ambassador Extraordinary Kikujiro Ishii, concluded in November 1917 (see the extract appended to this chapter). This agreement reaffirmed the principle of the "open door" or equal opportunity for commerce and industry in China on the one hand, and recognized Japan's special interests in Manchuria, based on its territorial propinquity, on the other. In addition to indicating the dilemma which America faced, it can be said to demonstrate the realism of Wilsonian foreign policy.

Documents

Alfred T. Mahan, *The United States Looking Outward,* **1890**

. . . Indications are not wanting of an approaching change in the thoughts and policy of Americans as to their relations with the world outside their own borders. For the past quarter of a century, the predominant idea, which has asserted itself successfully at the polls and shaped the course of the Government, has been to preserve the home market for the home industries. The employer and the workman alike have been taught to look at the various economical measures proposed from this point of view, to regard with hostility any step favoring the intrusion of the foreign producer upon their own domain, and rather to demand increasingly rigorous measures of exclusion than to acquiesce in any loosening of the chain that binds the consumer to them. The inevitable consequence has followed, as in all cases when the mind or the eye is exclusively fixed in one direction, that the danger of loss or the prospect of advantage in another quarter has been overlooked; and although the abounding resources of the country have maintained the exports at a high figure, this flattering result has been due more to the superabundant bounty of Nature than to the demand of other nations for our protected manufactures.

For nearly the lifetime of a generation, therefore, American industries have been thus protected, until the practice has assumed the force of a tradition, and is clothed in the mail of conservatism. In their mutual relations, these industries resemble the activities of a modern ironclad that has heavy armor, but inferior engines and guns; mighty for defense, weak for offense. Within, the home market is secured; but outside, beyond the broad seas, there are the markets of the world, that can be entered and controlled only by a vigorous contest, to which the habit of trusting to protection by statute does not conduce.

At bottom, however, the temperament of the American people is essentially alien to such a sluggish attitude. Independently of all bias for or against protection, it is safe to predict that, when the opportunities for gain abroad are understood, the course of American enterprise will cleave a channel by which to reach them. . . .

The interesting and significant feature of this changing attitude is the turning of the eyes outward, instead of inward only, to seek the welfare of the country. To affirm the importance of distant markets, and the relation to them of our own immense powers of production, implies logically the recognition of the link that joins the products and the markets—that is, the carrying trade; the three together constituting that chain of maritime power to which Great Britain owes her wealth and greatness. Further, is it too much to say that, as two of these links, the shipping and the markets, are exterior to our own borders, the acknowledgment of them carries with it a view of the relations of the United States to the world radically distinct from the simple idea of self-sufficingness? We shall not follow far this line of thought before there will dawn the realization of America's unique position, facing the older worlds of the East and West, her shores washed by the oceans which touch the one or the other, but which are common to her alone. . . .

Hay's Circular Letter, September 6, 1899

Sir: At the time when the Government of the United States was informed by that of Germany that it had leased from His Majesty the Emperor of China the port of Kiao-chao and the adjacent territory in the province of Shantung, assurances were given to the ambassador of the United States at Berlin by the Imperial German minister for foreign affairs that the rights and privileges insured by treaties with China to citizens of the United States would not thereby suffer or be in anywise impaired within the area over which Germany had thus obtained control.

More recently, however, the British Government recognized by a formal agreement with Germany the exclusive right of the latter country to enjoy in said leased area and the contiguous "sphere of influence or interest" certain privileges, more especially those relating to railroads and mining enterprises; but, as the exact nature and extent of the rights thus recognized have not been clearly defined, it is possible that serious conflicts of interest may at any time arise, not only between British and German subjects within said area, but that the interests of our citizens may also be jeopardized thereby.

Earnestly desirous to remove any cause of irritation and to insure at the same time to the commerce of all nations in China the undoubted benefits which should accrue from a formal recognition by the various powers claiming "spheres of interest" that they shall enjoy perfect equality of treatment for their commerce and navigation within such "spheres," the Government of the United States would be pleased to see His German Majesty's Government give formal assurances and lend its cooperation in securing like assurances from the other interested powers that each within its respective sphere of whatever influence—

First. Will in no way interfere with any treaty port or any vested interest within any so-called "sphere of interest" or leased territory it may have in China.

Second. That the Chinese treaty tariff of the time being shall apply to all merchandise landed or shipped to all such ports as are within said "sphere of interest" (unless they be "free ports"), no matter to what nationality it may belong, and that duties so leviable shall be collected by the Chinese Government.

Third. That it will levy no higher harbor dues on vessels of another nationality frequenting any port in such "sphere" than shall be levied on vessels of its own nationality, and no higher railroad charges over lines built, controlled, or operated within its "sphere" on merchandise belonging to citizens or subjects of other nationalities transported through such "sphere" than shall be levied on similar merchandise belonging to its own nationals transported over equal distances. . . .

Theodore Roosevelt, *The New Nationalism,* **1910**

. . . Combinations in industry are the result of an imperative economic law which cannot be repealed by political legislation. The effort at prohibiting all combination has substantially failed. The way out lies, not in attempting to prevent such combinations, but in completely controlling them in the interest of the public welfare. . . .

National efficiency has many factors. It is a necessary result of the principle of conservation widely applied. In the end it will determine our failure or success as a Nation. National efficiency has to do, not only with natural resources and with men, but it is equally concerned with institutions. The State must be made efficient for the work which concerns only the people of the State; and the Nation for that which concerns all the people. There must remain no neutral ground to serve as a refuge for lawbreakers, and especially for lawbreakers of great wealth, who can hire the vulpine legal cunning which will teach them how to avoid both jurisdictions. It is a misfortune when the national legislature fails to do its duty in providing a national remedy, so that the only national activity is the purely negative activity of the judiciary in forbidding the state to exercise power in the premises.

I do not ask for overcentralization; but I do ask that we work in a spirit of broad and far-reaching nationalism when we work for what concerns our people as a whole. We are all Americans. Our common interests are as broad as the continent. . . . The national Government belongs to the whole American people, and where the whole American people are interested, that interest can be guarded effectively only by the national Government. The betterment which we seek must be accomplished, I believe, mainly through the national Government.

The American people are right in demanding that New Nationalism, without which we cannot hope to deal with new problems. The New Nationalism puts the national need before sectional or personal advantage. It is impatient of the utter confusion that results from local legislatures attempting to treat national issues as local issues. It is still more impatient of the impotence which springs from overdivision of governmental powers, the impotence which makes it possible for local selfishness or for legal cunning, hired by wealthy special interests, to bring national activities to a deadlock. This New Nationalism regards the executive power as the steward of the public welfare. It demands of the judiciary that it shall be interested primarily in human welfare rather than in property, just as it demands that the representative body shall represent all the people rather than any one class or section of the people. . . .

Woodrow Wilson, *The New Freedom,* 1912

. . . There is one great basic fact which underlies all the questions that are discussed on the political platform at the present moment. That singular fact is that nothing is done in this country as it was done twenty years ago.

We are in the presence of a new organization of society. Our life has broken away from the past. The life of America is not the life that it was twenty years ago; it is not the life that it was ten years ago. We have changed our economic conditions, absolutely, from top to bottom; and, with our economic society, the organization of our life. The old political formulas do not fit the present problems; they read now like documents taken out of a forgotten age. The older cries sound as if they belonged to a past age which men have almost forgotten. . . .

We have come upon a very different age from any that preceded us. We have come upon an age when we do not do business in the way in which we used to do business—when we do not carry on any of the operations of manufacture, sale, transportation, or communication as men used to carry them on. There is a sense in which in our day the individual has been submerged. In most parts of our country men work, not for themselves, not as partners in the old way in which they used to work, but generally as employees—in a higher or lower grade—of great corporations. There was a time when corporations played a very minor part in our business affairs, but now they play the chief part, and most men are the servants of corporations.

You know what happens when you are the servant of a corporation. You have in no instance access to the men who are really determining the policy of the corporation. If the corporation is doing the things that it ought not to do, you really have no voice in the matter and must obey the orders, and you have oftentimes with deep moritfication to cooperate in the doing of things which you know are against the public interest. Your individuality is swallowed up in the individuality and purpose of a great organization.

It is true that, while most men are thus submerged in the corporation, a few, a very few, are exalted to a power which as individuals they could never have wielded. Through the great organizations of which they are the heads, a few are enabled to play a part unprecedented by anything in history in the control of the business operations of the country and in the determination of the happiness of great numbers of people.

Yesterday, and ever since history began, men were related to one another as individuals. To be sure there were the family, the Church, and the State, institutions which associated men in certain wide circles of relationship. But in the ordinary concerns of life, in the ordinary work, in the daily round, men dealt freely and directly with one another. Today, the everyday relationships of men are largely with great impersonal concerns, with organizations, not with other individual men. . . .

Root-Takahira Agreement, November 30, 1908

Excellency: I have the honor to acknowledge the receipt of your note of to-day setting forth the result of the exchange of views between us in our recent interviews defining the understanding of the two Governments in regard to their policy in the region of the Pacific Ocean.

It is a pleasure to inform you that this expression of mutual understanding is welcome to the Government of the United States as appropriate to the happy relations of the two countries and as the occasion for a concise mutual affirmation of that accordant policy respecting the Far East which the two Governments have so frequently declared in the past.

I am happy to be able to confirm to Your Excellency, on behalf of the United States, the declaration of the two Governments embodied in the following words:

1. It is the wish of the two Governments to encourage the free and peaceful development of their commerce on the Pacific Ocean.

2. The policy of both Governments, uninfluenced by any aggressive tendencies, is directed to the maintenance of the existing status quo in the region above mentioned, and to the defense of the principle of equal opportunity for commerce and industry in China.

3. They are accordingly firmly resolved reciprocally to respect the territorial possessions belonging to each other in said region.

4. They are also determined to preserve the common interest of all powers in China by supporting by all pacific means at their disposal the independence and integrity of China and the principle of equal opportunity for commerce and industry of all nations in that Empire.

5. Should any event occur threatening the status quo as above described or the principle of equal opportunity as above defined, it remains for the two Governments to communicate with each other in order to arrive at an understanding as to what measures they may consider it useful to take.

Accept, Excellency, the renewed assurance of my highest consideration.

Elihu Root

His Excellency
Baron Kogoro Takahira,
Japanese Ambassador

Lansing-Ishii Agreement, November 2, 1917

. . . The Governments of the United States and Japan recognize that territorial propinquity creates special relations between countries, and, consequently, the Government of the United States recognizes that Japan has special interests in China, particularly in the part to which her possessions are contiguous.

The territorial sovereignty of China, nevertheless, remains unimpaired and the Government of the United States has every confidence in the repeated assurances of the Imperial Japanese Government that while geographical position gives Japan such special interests they have no desire to discriminate against the trade of other nations or to disregard the commercial rights heretofore granted by China in treaties with other powers.

The Governments of the United States and Japan deny that they have any purpose to infringe in any way the independence or territorial integrity of China, and they declare, furthermore, that they always adhere to the principle of the so-called "open door" or equal opportunity for commerce and industry in China. . . .

8

The First World War
and the Twenties

The First World War has not until now occupied a very important position in the discussion of American history. Compared to its decisive importance in European history, in American history the First World War has often been treated as a mere episode. Indeed, the postwar settlement and the U.S. failure to ratify the Versailles Treaty have drawn more attention than the war itself or its impact on American society. However, the nation was totally mobilized for the war, thus making its domestic impact on American society extremely significant, and the war itself decisively altered America's international position.

The 1920s, which followed the First World War and can be seen in retrospect as a sort of valley between Progressivism and the New Deal, have also not been given very serious consideration. Certainly this was an era of "mediocrity"; politically, aside from a series of scandals, there were neither truly spectacular events nor the development of new policies. Beneath this superficial calm and "normalcy," however, American society, building on the expansion of productivity during the First World War, began to move decisively toward an era of mass production and mass consumption, toward so-called "mass society" and mass democracy. In this respect, the 1920s can be said to have been the era in which "modern" American society was established. Naturally, this development had an impact on America's party politics as well, and caused a wide-scale reorganization of the parties. During the 1920s, the Democratic Party transformed itself from a rural party to an urban one and created the basis upon which it became the new majority party in American politics.

The First World War and the U.S.

While the Wilson administration was carrying out domestic reform under the banner of New Freedom, the First World War broke out in Europe in the summer of 1914. Wilson immediately declared America's neutrality, and the American people, regarding this as Europe's war, as a whole supported him.

When the war broke out, the American economy was suffering from a slight depression, but the war soon created a demand from Europe for war matériel, with a corresponding stimulation of the American economy. The demand by the English and the French, in particular, increased astronomically, but as the war continued, England and France came to lack the dollars with which to pay for them, and the sale of war supplies on credit became an issue. Ultimately, American banks lent to England and France so that they could purchase military goods. As a result, by the time of its entry into the war in 1917, America held $2,300,000,000 in bonds from the Allied powers, while in German and Austrian bonds it held less than one hundredth that amount. One might say that America had come to hold a large mortgage on the Allied powers.

However, as a more fundamental reason for the entry of America into the war, one must cite its traditional basic foreign policy toward Europe—the policy of attempting to maintain the balance of power among the European countries in order to avoid the rise to dominance of one specific country which might eventually interfere in the American continents. After 1871 the German Empire had gradually become dominant on the European continent; under the "world policy" of Wilhelm II, it had shown an inclination to interfere as far away as Mexico, and this raised American suspicions toward Germany. The defeat of the Allied nations and the resulting overwhelming dominance of Germany on the European continent would have been by no means desirable for the United States.

The United States had fought its mother country, England, in the War for Independence, and Americans had often harbored antagonism toward England. At the same time, many Americans had English ancestors, and there was a certain sense of cultural and ethnic unity. Because the U.S. had become the world's leading industrial nation and there was no longer a need for an inferiority complex toward England, and because, partly due to the influence of Social Darwinism, the theory of Anglo-Saxon racial superiority had been widely circulated, this sense of unity was on the rise. Indeed, some Americans even advocated an Anglo-American alliance. Moreover, President Wilson had deep respect for the English political system and practice of politics, and personally he was emotionally pro-England.

For these reasons, America began to show growing sympathy toward the Allies. There were many German and Austrian immigrants in America, and their sympathy for the German-Austrian side imposed considerable restrictions on the government in reaching its final decision. Despite the influence of these German and Austrian immigrants, however, American anti-German sentiment was strongly incited by the German Army's violation of Belgian neutrality and English and French propaganda concerning this violation, by Germany's surprise submarine attack in the "war zone," and, above all, by the sinking of the British steamer *Lusitania* in May 1915, which took the lives of many Americans.

Wilson's reelection in 1916, under the slogan "He kept us out of war," caused Germany to mistakenly assume that America would not enter the war, at least for some time. Counting on American neutrality and aiming for a quick and decisive victory, Germany resumed unrestricted submarine warfare in February 1917. This finally led the U.S. Congress to declare a state of war against Germany in April 1917. The vote was not unanimous: six Senators and fifty Representatives cast votes against the war resolution in Congress. Many of them represented midwestern states where German immigrants were numerous. But many of these negative votes were motivated, not only by considerations of ethnic background, but also by the isolationist-progressive idea which urged America to ignore the quarrels among the corrupt European powers and instead to give undivided attention to domestic reform.

After entering the war, the government quickly established a system of total mobilization in the military, economic, social, and intellectual spheres. At the beginning of the century, the army had undergone some limited reform under Secretary of War Elihu Root, but even so, it had only 80,000 regular troops. With entry into the war, a selective service system was enacted, mobilizing over four million soldiers. Of these, 2,080,000 were sent to the French front as the American Expeditionary Force (A.E.F.) commanded by Gen. John J. Pershing. The navy also had gradually been modernized since the turn of the century. In 1916, a large-scale naval construction plan had been developed in order to establish a "Navy Second to None." After war was declared, the "bridge of ships" strategy was adopted in order to safeguard the supply of military and other materials and the transport of troops. Escorting convoys were employed against German submarines by the gifted Admiral William S. Sims. The War Industries Board was established in order to expand the production of war matériel. After its reorganization and expansion under the directorship of Bernard M. Baruch in March 1918, the board had the power to place the economy under government control. The encouragement of production and the regulation of consumption applied not only to war materials, but also to food and fuel. In order to transport such products effectively, the railroads were placed under government management. Such action was unprecedented in the history of the American economy, which had made *laissez-faire* its basic principle. In the wartime boom, production expanded remarkably, and the government even mediated actively between labor and management. An extremely high graduated income tax and a corporation tax were imposed, and public bonds were issued in order to procure the vast sums needed for war expenditures.

Along with economic controls, a vigorous propaganda campaign was carried out in order to "sell" the policy of intervention in a European war to the people. For the execution of the war, it was necessary to unify the ethnically divisive populace and to obtain and secure their loyalty. A propaganda agency called the Committee on Public Information was established in 1917, with George Creel as chairman, and a vast psychological mobilization for war was carried out. Repressive thought control measures were taken in order to eliminate the influence of those who would obstruct the prosecution of the war. These were embodied in the Espionage Act of 1917 and the Sedition Act of 1918. Under these acts, many of those who actively opposed the war, such as Eugene Debs, were imprisoned. The external war for democracy thus ironically gave rise to internal thought control.

Even before the war ended, President Wilson made public his conception of the postwar peace. In January 1917, before the American entry into the war, he urged "Peace Without Victory," suggesting that the war should end with neither side standing in the position of victory. The Bolshevik government in Russia made public the secret treaties concluded by the Allied powers and criticized the Allies for their imperialist intentions. The U.S. urgently needed to make clear its war aims. In January 1918, with the help of Colonel Edward House, his adviser on foreign affairs, Wilson presented his famous "Fourteen Points" as the conditions for peace, and urged to the American people and the belligerent nations the restoration of peace on that basis (see the excerpts from his address appended to this chapter). The first of Wilson's four-teen points was the advocacy of open—rather than the old secret —diplomacy. Second was the principle of freedom of the high seas which America had advocated for many years. Third was the removal of barriers to commerce—in other words, free trade. This had been a long-standing goal of Wilson's, but it was not necessarily shared by the majority of Americans. Fourth was reduction of armaments, and fifth was the impartial adjustment of the demands of colonial peoples. There were also several con-crete proposals based on the so-called principle of national self-determination. Last was the creation of an international associa-tion of nations by convenant.

These fourteen points are often claimed to represent Wilson's *idealistic* foreign policy. When one considers America's interna-tional political and economic position, and the changes in that position which the great war had brought about, however, his conception must be considered extremely realistic in terms of the long-term interests of the United States.

In October 1918, Germany proposed peace negotiations on the basis of the Fourteen Points. With an armistice on November 11, the First World War tentatively came to an end. Wilson himself went to Paris and undertook the negotiation of the peace treaty. Ironically, however, the negotiations were conducted not according to Wilson's "open diplomacy" but in Machiavellian secrecy. More-over, back in the U.S., the mid-term election of 1918 had already given the Republicans, although by a small margin, the majority position in the Senate and weakened Wilson's domestic leadership.

Once the government had decided on war, the American people participated vigorously, even enthusiastically, in the European conflict. With the Armistice, however, their overwhelming desire was to separate themselves rapidly from Europe's problems. The Versailles Peace Treaty was signed, and Wilson returned with it to seek its ratification by the Senate. However, domestic unity was breaking down into a power struggle between the political parties. Despite Wilson's pleas to the people at large, the treaty failed in the end to obtain the Senate's consent. Thus, the United States did not join the League of Nations which had been created under the leadership of its own president.

In its refusal to ratify the Versailles treaty, it seemed as if the U.S. had again returned to its traditional isolation. The First World War had been billed as a war to defend democracy, but it ended in disillusionment, and soon many intellectuals of the "lost generation" began to criticize America's participation in the war. The army was rapidly demobilized. The various economic controls also were quickly rescinded with the end of the war, and the principle of *laissez-faire* again began to be glorified. In this sense, the First World War seemed to have been nothing more than a passing episode.

Whether or not the American people were keenly conscious of it, however, this world war had an enormous impact on American society. Domestically, the mobilization actually put into effect the government intervention in and regulation of the activities of private enterprise which Progressivism had advocated but been unable to carry out. The mutual cooperation and unity of the government, business, and labor, although a temporary and exceptional wartime occurrence, was an extremely significant phenomenon in American history. It foreshadowed the pattern of the American economic system under the New Deal, during the Second World War, and in the postwar world. On the international level, the U.S., which had had only a small-scale standing army, eventually sent overseas more than 2,000,000 troops and played a decisive role in the outcome of the war. Despite the postwar demobilization, the U.S. had shown itself to be a great military power and to be strong enough to determine the European balance of power.[1] Economically, the war transformed the United States from a debtor to a creditor nation; for this reason, and because its vast economic strength had supported the wartime economies of the Allies, after the war the U.S. began to exert great economic influence in Europe. Thus, despite the return of isolationist sentiment after the war, the First World War marked a turning point in American involvement in international politics.

As a result of the nation's increasing involvement in international politics, events and movements in Europe and elsewhere came to have a greater effect on American society than ever before. The emergence of a socialist state as the result of the Russian Revolution of 1917, in particular, had a strong impact in the United States. Not only did it intensify the ideological conflict between capitalism and socialism; the creation of the Third International (Comintern) of 1919 and the birth of an American Communist Party were seen as the advent of international communism which threatened, from without and within, America's internal political unity. For American society, which had neither racial nor cultural unity, an artificial unity of belief was essentially indispensable, and for that reason Americans were extremely suspicious of the influence of alien or international beliefs or organizations. The appearance of a socialist state and the advent of an international communist organization with a (supposed) branch in the United States were perceived as a threat and a danger to the unity of American society, and gave rise to excessive antagonism and suspicion. The "Red Hunt" under Attorney General Alexander Mitchell Palmer; the arrest and expulsion from his seat in Congress of Socialist Party Congressman Victor Louis Berger; the expulsion of five Socialist Party members from the New York state legislature; and the arrest and execution of the anarchists Nicola Sacco and Bartolomeo Vanzetti for murder (1927)—in these and

[1] While the army effected a rapid demobilization, the navy, although decreasing the number of sailors, did not scrap vessels but rather continued its previous naval construction program. Consequently, even after the war, the navy expanded. Essentially, the large naval construction program of 1916 aimed at achieving the control of sea power as advocated by the Mahan school, taking advantage of the opportunity afforded by the war. In 1914 the Panama Canal was opened, and in 1919, when the American navy transferred some of its battleships from the Atlantic to the Pacific Ocean and organized a Pacific Fleet, it became a two-ocean navy in both name and reality. In fact, with the end of the world war, the naval expansion race among Japan, England, and America accelerated, and came in due time to stimulate an acute awareness of the need for an armaments limitation treaty.

other cases, the specter of threats from the outside were raised in the desperate efforts to maintain ideological unity. The Ku Klux Klan, which had nothing in common with the post-Civil War KKK, was reorganized in 1915 and during the 1920s extended its power not only in the south but in the midwest and the northeast as well. The KKK advocated not only discrimination against blacks, but also nativism and anti-foreignism, and it attacked the new immigrants, socialism, communism, Catholics, and the League of Nations. The influence of this organization demonstrated the potential for paranoia in American society toward what seemed to be foreign, international, or un-American, whether race, idea, or organization.

"Return to Normalcy" and the Development of Mass Society

Because of the unpopularity of the incumbent Democratic president, the Republican Party's victory in the presidential election of 1920 was almost assured. There was a flood of Republican contenders for the nomination that promised almost certain victory, and after intense competition and a series of deals, Warren Gamaliel Harding, a senator from Ohio, was nominated. Harding, although he possessed only mediocre ability, had an imposing presidential appearance. Under the slogan "Return to Normalcy," he advocated a transition from wartime to peacetime and, broadly speaking, from progressivism and reform to conservatism. James Middleton Cox, governor of Ohio, ran on the Democratic ticket pledging to continue Wilson's policies. Assistant Secretary of the Navy Franklin Delano Roosevelt, from New York State, was nominated as his running mate. The Socialist Party's Debs was in prison, but he ran again anyway.   .

One of the central campaign issues was whether the United States should join the League of Nations. The Democratic Party, in response to Wilson's call to make the election "a solemn referendum," advocated joining the League, which was already a lost cause. The Republican slogan "Return to Normalcy" appealed more widely to the people, who were weary of war and reform. The result, as predicted, was an overwhelming Republican victory; the Democratic Party barely managed to carry its power base in the south. It should be noted that the voter turnout in this election was only 51 percent. In part, this was the result of the doubling of the electorate when the Nineteenth Amendment to the Constitution extended suffrage to women. However, the virtual lack of difference between the Republican and Democratic candidates and their policies also contributed to the public apathy.

Harding was the first of three successive Republican presidents: he was succeeded by Calvin Coolidge, his vice-president, and Herbert Hoover. Harding is notorious because of the scandals which came to light after his death in 1923. He has often been criticized as the worst president in American history. However, he did appoint capable Cabinet members such as Secretary of State Charles E. Hughes, Secretary of Commerce Herbert C. Hoover, and Secretary of the Treasury Andrew W. Mellon.

The 1920s were generally considered a time of prosperity. This period saw the emergence of a number of so-called "new industries" based on such technological innovations as the electric light, the automobile, the motion picture, and new chemicals. With their spectacular growth these enterprises influenced other related industries. Along with the development of these newly rising industries, rationalization and mechanization of production advanced. As symbolized by the automobile industry's adoption of mass production based on the assembly-line system, large-scale production was made possible. However, mass production raised the problem of guaranteeing a market for the increasing volume of goods being produced. In order to expand the foreign market, American businesses tried to restore the purchasing power of the European economy, which had been impoverished by the world war, by making loans to European countries for the purchase of American manufactured goods. At the same time, in order to preserve high prices and keep the domestic market safe, the tariff on imported goods, which had been temporarily lowered during the Wilson administration, was raised in 1921 and again in 1922. A protective tariff policy was also adopted for those agricultural products which were in competition with foreign commodities. While *laissez-faire* and individualism were strongly advocated as ideologies, Secretary of Commerce Hoover, claiming the need to prevent excessive competition, effectively promoted the formation of combinations. Manufactured goods became standardized and uniform. In the 1920s cooperation between government and business advanced. The federal government, cooperating with "big business," gradually and inconspicuously developed into "big government."

The victims of the Republican administration's pro-industry policy were the farmers. During the First World War, agricultural production had expanded remarkably due to the increase in military procurements and exports. But with the end of the war, demand stagnated and overproduction resulted. The combination of increased productivity and mechanization widened the price differential between agricultural products and industrial manufactured goods. The decline in the prices of agricultural goods deprived a growing number of farmers of their mortgaged land. By 1930, 42 percent of all farm land had become tenant-farmed land. In response, the farmers organized themselves into a pressure group to voice their discontent. The farm bloc in Congress was organized and the American Farm Bureau Federation was founded to promote their interests. Their discontent surfaced politically with the formation of such organizations as the Farmer-Labor Party in 1920 and the Conference for Progressive Political Action (CPPA) in 1922.

The American Federation of Labor, which in the nineteenth century had been a craft union of skilled workers, was still the focus of the American labor movement. Because the AF of L was rigidly exclusive, however, its membership, which numbered approximately 4,000,000 in 1921, decreased to about 3,000,000 by 1929, even though the numbers of industrial workers were increasing. Meanwhile, the courts often issued injunctions prohibiting strikes, and many company unions were created. As a result, the entire labor movement stagnated during the 1920s.

At the time of the 1924 presidential election, the main base of the Republican Party was the industrial cities of the east. But the party's anti-mainstream progressive faction members, such as La-Follette, focused their attention on the farmers of the midwest. In response to the agricultural depression of the 1920s, LaFollette, with the support of the western farming class, organized the Conference for Progressive Political Action and split off from the

Republican Party in 1924. As its policy platform, the CPPA advocated public ownership of the means of transportation and communication, such as railroads and telegraphs, opposition to court injunctions against strikes, the organization of farmers and workers, and the reduction of taxes. The Socialist Party cooperated with the CPPA. Thus LaFollette became the central figure of a number of groups of political and economic dissidents.

The election of 1924 exposed the Democratic Party's internal contradictions. In essence, the party had traditionally been the party of the farmers, making the farming class of the south and west its basis of support. However, it was also a party of the urban masses, with the support of the new immigrants of the large cities. Before the 1920s, the southern wing of the party had succeeded in having things mostly its own way. However, the rapid increase in the number of immigrants around the turn of the century had strengthened the influence of the northeastern machines and their bosses. In 1924, the farmers' faction of the Democratic Party supported William Gibbs McAdoo, Woodrow Wilson's son-in-law, for the party's presidential nomination. The northeastern urban group supported Alfred Emmanuel Smith. Born in a New York slum as a son of Irish immigrants, Al Smith rose step by step in the political world and became governor of New York State. He was a symbol of the urban masses. The two candidates fought to a dead-lock at the party's national convention. Finally, on the 103rd ballot, a Chicago banker, John W. Davis, was nominated as a compromise candidate. Thus, in the end the Democrats' nominee was not much different from the Republicans', Calvin Coolidge, who had served as president since Harding's death the previous year. The election ended in Coolidge's overwhelming victory. It must be noted, however, that LaFollette, with the support of the Socialist Party and the AF of L, put up a good fight, receiving 4,820,000 votes and the 13 electoral votes of the state of Wisconsin. After this election the farmers began to attempt to promote their interests, not by means of national political organi-zations, but through the activities of special pressure groups. The election indicated that it was the urban masses who would possess the decisive influence in the American political parties; the farmers would henceforward be a minority. This trend was clearly shown by the fact that in 1920 for the first time more Americans lived in urban than in rural areas. The 1920 census showed that the urban population had reached 51.2 percent of the total.

The increase in the urban population meant the growth of a potential labor force. Previously, the United States had made the encouragement of immigration a national policy in order to mitigate its labor shortage and guarantee reasonable labor costs. But as the number of immigrants increased and as the labor shortage eased, pressure on the government to limit them intensified. The immigrants' difficulty in assimilating into American society became the first argument for exclusion. The first to be excluded were the Chinese immigrants: a Chinese exclusion law had been passed as early as 1882. The Japanese became the next target. In accordance with the 1907 and 1908 Gentlemen's Agreements with the United States, Japan began a voluntary restriction of emigration. Then the voices against the immigrants from Europe—Latins, Eastern Europeans, and Jews—became more clamorous. Racism was one motivating force behind the exclusion movement. In view of a labor surplus, however, labor unions were also demanding the exclusion of the cheap immigrant labor in order to protect the relatively high level of wages. Despite prosperity, during the 1920s a labor surplus became a serious issue.

In 1921, as emergency legislation, an immigration restriction law was passed limiting the number of immigrants to 357,000 per year. In 1924 the National Origins Act, setting a limit of 150,000, was enacted as permanent legislation. This restrictive act took as a basis the number of a given nationality in the American population in 1890 and set an immigration quota of 2 percent of that number each year. The choice of 1890 gave an advantage to northern and western Europeans and was extremely disadvantageous to people from eastern and southern Europe—the so-called "new immigrants." (Later the government would make 1920 the base year.) Japanese immigrants, who could not be naturalized, were permanently excluded by this law. Just as the disappearance of the frontier in 1890 had symbolized an end to the image of America as unlimited space, this immigration act can be said to have symbolized an end to the image of America as the land of opportunity. In fact, after the passage of this act, immigration decreased to 294,314 in 1925; in 1934, affected by the depression, it declined to 29,490. The immigration act was not revised in substance until 1965, when the national quota system was abolished.

Urbanization in the 1920s meant not only an increase in the population of the cities, but also the urbanization of American society at large. Methods of mass production were adopted by many industries, and uniform, standardized manufactured goods were sold and consumed all over the country with the help of extensive advertising. During this era the mass media of communications were developed, and from New York in the east to California in the west, through the consumption of the same kinds of goods and information, life styles and opinions became standardized to a great extent. The 1920s stressed consumption more than production, and a so-called "consumer culture" gradually emerged. This trend was also reflected in the ideal image of a successful life during this period: consumer-type heroes, such as movie stars or athletes, grew in popularity.

These widespread social changes markedly altered the voting trends of the electorate. The political parties, which had traditionally advocated the expansion of opportunity, now responded to the demands of the urban masses and stressed security rather than opportunity in their central policies: they all came to advocate, as a means of obtaining votes, some sort of social welfare legislation. In the 1920s, however, such social welfare legislation was more often enacted at the state than at the national level, especially in states with many large cities. For example, New York State under Governor Al Smith passed a great deal of social legislation. During this same period many occupations became highly professionalized, and pressure groups within each profession vigorously worked to protect and promote their respective special interests. For example, the AF of L and the American Farm Bureau Federation came to pursue, rather than the general welfare of workers and farmers, the "job interests" of skilled workers and the particular interests of farmers of some affluence. Such groups as the American Medical Association, the American Bar Association, and the American Legion promoted their own special interests.

During this decade, despite the principle of *laissez-faire*, in reality the role of the state expanded and government began to reach into the daily lives of the people. However, the relationship between specific government policies and the interests of ordinary people was extremely complicated. It was not necessarily clear to the individual citizen what his own interest was and what policy would attain it. Consequently, political apathy gradually grew among the voters, and the rate of abstention from voting increased. Under such conditions, election campaigns focused not on discussing specific policies but on creating an emotional affinity between the voters and the candidate on the basis of his personality or image. On this score the election of 1928 was no exception. The Republicans ran Herbert Hoover, who, since becoming Secretary of Commerce in 1921, had built a solid reputation as an able administrator. Born in Iowa, Hoover graduated from Stanford University, working to pay for his own education. Upon graduation, he became an engineer, and at the time of the First World War he gained fame by ably administering food relief for Europe and the management of food production at home. In a sense, Hoover, who had succeeded as engineer, businessman, and federal administrator, symbolized the older type of success story. In contrast, the Democratic Party on the first ballot nominated Al Smith, a second-generation American from New York, as its candidate. Smith symbolized a new type of success based on the changing composition of the American population.

The result of the election, as expected from the beginning, was Hoover's overwhelming victory. It was a time of prosperity, and no one doubted the victory of the Republican Party, as the party of prosperity. More interesting than Smith's predictable defeat *per se* are the early signs of transfiguration which the Democratic Party showed in the midst of that defeat. The party's defeat in the southern states indicated the eventual collapse of the Democratic one-party system in the south. On the other hand, the Democrats won in the highly industrialized states of Massachusetts and Rhode Island. Moreover, even though they lost in other northern states, they carried many of the large cities. This suggested that in the future the Democratic Party would build a powerful base in the large northern cities. Al Smith, the child of immigrants and of the cities, symbolized a qualitative change in the Democratic Party.

In the election of 1928, policy itself was hardly a point of dispute. The Democratic Party advocated abolishing the prohibition clause, while the Republican Party favored its preservation.

This gives the impression that prohibition itself sharply divided the two major parties.[2] Prohibition was a specific and divisive issue. More broadly, however, it illustrated a conflict between two cultures in the United States, the traditional agrarian culture and the new city culture. It was, in other words, a conflict between the old rural Protestant ethic and the growing urban Catholic or non-religious way of life. In 1928 the Republican Party, which supported the old morality, won. But the time was approaching when the Democratic Party, which adopted as its base the growing urban majority, would dominate.

It is often said that in the 1920s America returned to isolationism. Certainly, in view of its rejection of Wilsonianism and the League of Nations, one could say that the U.S. withdrew from the arena of international politics. However, America's predominant position in world politics had been too firmly established by the nation's wartime military and (especially) economic activities to disappear with the end of the war. In fact,

[2] The 1920s are often called the era of prohibition. In January 1919, the Eighteenth Amendment came into effect, and with the enactment of the Volstead Act, a strict national prohibition (the prohibition of the manufacture and sale of beverages with an alcoholic content of more than 0.5 percent) was put into practice. The prohibition movement began in the 1840s as a part of the humanistic reform movement, and from early on prohibition laws were put into effect in several northern states. After the Civil War, however, the prohibition movement weakened; the brewery business and bars became very prosperous and were often involved in political corruption. A prohibition movement centering around the Protestant churches once again became widespread. In 1895 the Anti-Saloon League of America was formed, developed into a powerful movement as a pressure group, and was active as one wing of the reformist movement to clean up politics. As a result, prohibition was effected in many states and counties, with varying degrees of success; at the end of 1917, nineteen states had enacted prohibition laws. The Anti-Saloon League hoped for a unified prohibition on a national scale, and initiated a movement to amend the Constitution, but there was also strong opposition, from the proponents of states' rights, to regulation of individual preferences by the federal government. However, the outbreak of World War I and the entry into war stimulated the rise of nationalism; parallel to the national regulation of the economy, national intervention in moral issues was made possible. The Eighteenth Amendment was ratified by all but two states. However, the prohibition laws, enacted as an expression of conformity, became throughout the 1920s a point of dispute between two groups in American society. This conflict was symbolized by the presence within the same Democratic Party of the ardent prohibitionist, Bryan, and the antiprohibitionist Al Smith. In the industrial states, the large cities, and areas with many new immigrants, not only was this "noble experiment" difficult to put into effect, but it also promoted the growth of criminal organizations which obtained their income from bootlegging of alcohol. In 1932 the Democratic Party advocated the repeal of the Eighteenth Amendment; in December 1933, prohibition was abolished by the Twenty-First Amendment, and the "noble experiment" was over. However, there are several areas in which prohibition has been maintained on a state or local level.

despite the isolationist sentiment which hung over American society, the 1920s saw the U.S. involved more deeply than ever before in both Europe and Asia. In Europe, there were the intricate problems of war debts and reparations. The war had made the U.S. a creditor of several European countries, having advanced loans totaling nearly $12 billion, including post-armistice loans and credits. The American people, with their strong postwar nationalism, would not consider cancellation of the debts and persistently urged the European nations to pay. However, a thoroughly impoverished Europe had no ability to comply with the American demand, and the Allies tried to pay their war debts with the reparations from Germany. As a result, the U.S. government was working to reduce the amount of reparations and at the same time providing Germany with funds for its economic recovery, hoping to facilitate Germany's payment of reparations to the Allies. This policy was formulated by the (Charles G.) Dawes Plan of 1924 and the (Owen D.) Young Plan of 1929.

Although it had rejected the League of Nations itself, the U.S. thus played a positive role in maintaining the Versailles system which it had helped to create by participating in League affairs. Another fruit of American diplomacy in the 1920s was the treaty for the renunciation of war. This multinational treaty was concluded in 1928 through the efforts of American Secretary of State Frank B. Kellogg and French Foreign Minister Aristide Briand. Although this antiwar treaty had virtually no substantive effect, it was noteworthy because it demonstrated American interest in international politics and its willingness to cooperate with other countries. On the other hand, the reservations that the U.S. maintained on the issue of participation in the World Court showed the traditional American fear of curtailing the full pursuit of its independent national interest.

In Asia and the Pacific region, the basic U.S. policy was, needless to say, based on maintenance of the Open Door in China. When the European war broke out, Japan took advantage of it to advance on the Chinese continent, issuing the Twenty-one Demands to China. The U.S., as we have noted, on the one hand maintained a policy of non-recognition toward the Twenty-one Demands while, on the other hand, it arrived at a provisional compromise through the Lansing-Ishii Agreement. In this agreement, the U.S. recognized the special postion of Japan in China based on geographic propinquity. After the war, however, American policy began to reassert its principle of the Open Door. At the same time, it sought to avoid conflict with Japan. The U.S. was particularly anxious to prevent the naval armaments race from escalating. Japan's unwillingness to withdraw its troops from Siberia after the joint American-Japanese intervention there at the end of the war did nothing to allay U.S. suspicions of Japan, and the government began looking for a way to compromise and adjust the conflicting American and Japanese interests on the Asian continent and in the Pacific. As a result, at American urging, the Washington Conference was convened in November 1921. The conference sought a naval arms reduction and solutions to the various pending problems in Asia. First, a naval armaments limitation treaty was concluded, whose five signatory powers pledged to limit their respective naval holdings such as capital ships and aircraft carriers. Second, they agreed to keep military fortifications in the Pacific at the existing level. A Four-Power Treaty to guarantee peace in the Pacific was concluded among Japan, England, America, and France; this resulted in the termination of the Anglo-Japanese Alliance. Third, a Nine-Power Treaty concerning China was concluded, which for the first time upheld the Open Door principle at the level of a multilateral treaty. Each signatory nation promised to preserve the sovereignty of China and to uphold the principle of equal opportunity for trade and industry in that country. These treaties irritated some people in Japan; having achieved considerable economic progress during the First World War, the nation was assertive of its first-class power status, and some in Japanese military circles came to view the treaties as barriers to Japan's further development. Nonetheless, it must be noted that the Washington treaty system to some extent alleviated the tension between Japan and America at that time. In the Nine-Power Treaty, America had gained recognition from the signatory nations for the Open Door principle in China. Indeed, the United States would continuously invoke the treaty to protest the Japanese advance into China.

Turning to Latin America, it could be said that at this point the U.S. still considered the western hemisphere a region in which its own special interest predominated. In practice, America's Latin American policy worked to control the region's small and medium-sized countries through investment and other financial and economic means rather than by the "big stick." This new policy orientation was particularly noticeable in relations with Cuba, Panama, the Dominican Republic, Haiti, and Nicaragua; Marines were withdrawn from several of these countries. It is true that at times the U.S. resorted to direct military intervention, but at least in principle, American policy toward Latin America shifted gradually towards the "good neighbor" orientation and promotion of Pan-Americanism.

The Great Depression and the 1932 Election

In his speech accepting the nomination as Republican presidential candidate in 1928, Herbert Hoover stated that the day was not far off when poverty would be erased from America. With the unprecedented prosperity of the 1920s the American people in general accepted this idea. However, behind the prosperity of the 1920s was the shadow of the agricultural depression, which persisted for many years. Twice, in 1927 and 1928, President Coolidge vetoed the McNary-Haugen Bill, which aimed at stabilizing agricultural prices by means of government purchase of agricultural commodities. Immediately upon assuming office, Hoover took up the issue of agricultural relief. In June 1929 he successfully enacted the Agricultural Marketing Act and attempted to stabilize prices. This lukewarm measure, however, failed to achieve his objective, and American agriculture entered a period of major depression. To make matters worse, Congress passed the Hawley-Smoot Tariff Act in June 1930, once again raising the tariff rates to protect the prices of domestic products. This policy resulted in reducing the foreign export market for American industry, and many economists expressed their opposition to the bill in joint statements and urged the president to veto it. Many commodities which had been manufactured in great quantities could no longer be consumed solely in the limited domestic market, and the manufacturers had to seek overseas markets. High U.S. tariffs, however, induced other countries to adopt similarly high tariffs, and as a result the export market for American products was narrowed.

The stock market panic which struck Wall Street on October 24, 1929, immediately spread to the entire country and in a single stroke destroyed the dream of prosperity. The U.S. depression touched off a world-wide depression which lasted several years. America's export trade stagnated, prices declined sharply, the national income was reduced by half, and many businesses went bankrupt. In 1932 the number of unemployed was as high as 13 million, one-fourth of the potential labor force. In addition, the wage level of those who remained employed was approximately 60 percent of the pre-depression level, and the American national economy was severely shaken.

Many factors can be cited as causes of this depression. First, as indicated above, even during the prosperity of the 1920s, agriculture had been in a state of chronic depression, and the purchasing power of the farmers in the domestic market was extremely limited. Second, while the 1920s was a period of mechanization and rationalization, and saw a rapid rise in productivity, this meant that in the latter half of the decade the American economy harbored inherent structural unemployment. Third, although prosperity was real, differences in income were marked, and the wage level of workers was relatively low. Consequently, despite prosperity, the imbalance between productivity and consumption gradually intensified. Finally, though American manufacturers needed to expand into foreign markets, the indebted European nations had little purchasing power. Moreover, their high tariffs restricted the amount of imports from America. In general, Europe was economically incapable of purchasing large quantities of goods, and thus America's foreign market could not keep up with its productive power. Behind the prosperity of the 1920s lay these latent causes of depression; they were revealed with devastating effect after the stock market panic of October 1929.

Hoover and the Republican administration asserted that the depression was temporary. Claiming that prosperity was around the corner, the government first put its hopes in the self-regulating ability of the American economy. However, the depression became increasingly severe, and the public denounced the Hoover administration for its failure to take vigorous measures. The shanties built at the fringe of the cities were often called "Hoovervilles," and they became symbols of the resentment toward the government. The Hoover administration was not, however, completely inactive and resourceless. It applied the Agricultural Marketing Act to prevent the further decline of agriculture prices, and persuaded business leaders to maintain existing wages. Stressing that relief of the unemployment was primarily the responsibility of local and state governments, the Hoover administration promised federal aid to the state governments for relief programs. The Reconstruction Finance Corporation (RFC) was established to provide financial aid for banks and other large corporations.

The Hoover administration's basic depression policy was revealed in the creation of the RFC: it believed that once big business had recovered, the effect would seep down directly to small businesses, leading in due course to the total economic recovery of the nation. But the self-regulating power of the American economy proved ineffective in dealing with this Great Depression, and the impatience and resentment of the American people gradually intensified. Those who had lost their land began to seek its recovery by means of forced auction. In the early summer of 1932 veterans of the First World War began the so-called Bonus March on Washington, demanding the settlement and early payment of their pensions in lump sums. The deepening discontent naturally damaged the incumbent Republican Party, and conversely benefited the Democratic Party in the election of 1932.

In 1932 the Republicans again nominated Hoover. The Democrats nominated Franklin Delano Roosevelt, who had succeeded Al Smith as governor of New York. Roosevelt was from a well-known New York family and in a sense a typical member of the elite; in this respect he was the antithesis of Smith, the child of immigrants, though the personal friendship between the two men was strong. Roosevelt had carried out some noticeable anti-depression policies, and was therefore regarded as a progressive new politican. After becoming a presidential candidate, Roosevelt assembled a "Brain Trust" of university professors and other intellectuals to undertake policy planning, including such men as Columbia University's Raymond Moley, Adolf Berle, Jr., and Rexford Tugwell and Harvard University's Felix Frankfurter. At the same time, he used veteran machine politicians like James A.

Farley to get votes. As soon as he received the nomination, Roosevelt flew to the Democratic Party convention in Chicago, and there announced his famous New Deal policy. His advisors agreed on several fundamental principles: the priority of domestic affairs; the positive intervention of the government in the economy; the rejection of the so-called Wilson–Brandeis idea—the positive use of concentration of enterprises as a tool of economic recovery. The Democratic Party platform itself differed little from that of the Republican Party. Yet, regardless of the content of the New Deal, the American people expected from it something new and different from Hoover's Republican policies. (See the excerpt from Roosevelt's Commonwealth Club speech appended to this chapter.)

As expected, the election resulted in a major victory for the Democratic Party. Roosevelt received 57 percent of the popular vote and 472 electoral votes, compared to Hoover's 59 electoral votes. The Democratic Party, through its gradual transformation in the 1920s, replaced the Republican Party as the new national majority party.

It has often been the case in American history that a third party emerged at a time of crisis. At the time of the Great Depression, however, the role played by third parties was insignificant. The Socialist and Communist parties both increased their share of the vote somewhat; however, they made no epoch-making gains. This relatively poor showing was attributable partially to the weakness and internal dissension of the third parties themselves. But more important was the fact that under Al Smith the Democratic Party had established its image as the party of the property-less masses. Roosevelt inherited this image, and his New Deal, although vague, gave people some hope. In this sense one could say that with its nomination of Al Smith in 1928, the Democratic Party had been preparing itself for its big opportunity.[3]

[3] In the election of 1932, the candidates receiving the most votes after the Democrats and the Republicans were the Socialist Party's Norman Thomas, with over 880,000 votes, and the Communist Party's William Z. Forster, with approximately 103,000. Even including the votes received by other small third parties, the vote of third parties constituted a mere 4 percent of the total popular vote. Since its emergence in the election of 1900, the Socialist Party had expanded its influence under Debs's leadership and in 1912 had received nearly 6 percent of the total vote. Essentially, however, in both ideology and organization, the Socialist Party was a fusion of a variety of constituents. The First World War greatly affected the American socialist movement. On the one hand, party members who opposed the war, beginning with Debs, were arrested and imprisoned, and the party's activities were hindered. On the other hand,

Roosevelt won in November 1932, but in accordance with the provisions of the Constitution he, and the nation, had to stand by until his inauguration in March 1933 to mark the beginning of a new Democratic era.

Documents

"The Fourteen Points": Wilson's Address to Congress, January 8, 1918

. . . I. Open covenants of peace, openly arrived at, after which there shall be no private international understandings of any kind but diplomacy shall proceed always frankly and in the public view.

II. Absolute freedom of navigation upon the seas, outside territorial waters, alike in peace and in war, except as the seas may be closed in whole or in part by international action for the enforcement of international covenants.

III. The removal, so far as possible, of all economic barriers and the establishment of an equality of trade conditions among all the nations consenting to the peace and associating themselves for its maintenance.

IV. Adequate guarantees given and taken that national armaments will be reduced to the lowest point consistent with domestic safety.

V. A free, open-minded, and absolutely impartial adjustment of all colonial claims, based upon a strict observance of the principle that in determining all such questions of sovereignty the interests of the populations concerned must

people who positively advocated entry into the war emerged from within the party. In both ways, the wartime system of total morale mobilization and the postwar conformity created conditions which were disadvantageous to the socialist movement. Moreover, the Russian revolution and the establishment of the Bolshevik regime had a serious influence on the Socialist Party. The Left and Right factions within the party were violently opposed, and the party finally split at its Chicago convention in August 1919. The Leftist faction withdrew from the party and organized the Communist Party. The radical elements within the Socialist Party turned to the Communists or were banished by the leadership of the Socialist Party, which became an organization of the rightist faction. The composition of the party members also changed from worker-centered to intellectual-centered. During the "prosperity" of the 1920s, the influence of the Socialist Party again declined, and in 1926 Debs, the father of the party, died. The depression of 1929 revived the party, but despite its activity under party president Norman Thomas, it had already lost the power to appeal widely to the masses. Thomas was an intellectual who had graduated from Princeton and Union Theological Seminary and worked as a minister in New York City's Harlem district. In 1912 he supported the Progressive Party. Such people as the philosopher John Dewey and the theologian Reinhold Niebuhr supported the Socialists. From 1933 on, the development of Roosevelt's New Deal policies impeded the expansion of the Socialist Party's strength; with 187,000 in 1936 and 100,000 in 1940, the number of votes it received kept decreasing.

have equal weight with the equitable claims of the government whose title is to be determined. . . .

XIV. A general association of nations must be formed under specific covenants for the purpose of affording mutual guarantees of political independence and territorial integrity to great and small states alike.

Japanese Ambassador M. Hanihara to Secretary of State Charles Evans Hughes, April 10, 1924

. . . It is needless to add that it is not the intention of the Japanese Government to question the sovereign right of any country to regulate immigration to its territories. Nor is it their desire to send their nationals to the countries where they are not wanted. On the contrary the Japanese Government showed from the very beginning of this problem their perfect willingness to cooperate with the United States Government to effectively prevent by all honorable means the entrance into the United States of such Japanese nationals as are not desired by the United States, and have given ample evidences thereof, the facts of which are well-known to your Government. To Japan the question is not one of expediency, but of principle. To her the mere fact that a few hundreds or thousands of her nationals will or will not be admitted into the domains of other countries is immaterial, so long as no question of national susceptibilities is involved. The important question is whether Japan as a nation is or is not entitled to the proper respect and consideration of other nations. . . .

Relying upon the confidence you have been good enough to show me at all times, I have stated or rather repeated all this to you very candidly and in a most friendly spirit, for I realize, as I believe you do, the grave consequences which the enactment of the measure retaining that particular provision would inevitably bring upon the otherwise happy and mutually advantageous relations between our two countries.

Speech of Henry Cabot Lodge, April 4, 1924

. . . Mr. President, I regret to say that the letter addressed to our State Department by the ambassador from Japan seems to me a letter improper to be addressed by the representative of one great country to another friendly country. It contains, I regret much to say, a veiled threat. Now, Mr. President, the United States can not legislate by the exercise by any other country of veiled threats. Owing to this, what we are now doing assumes the character of an international precedent; and I think it should be understood, and understood by the whole world, that the United States alone is to say who shall come into the United States to form part of its citizenship. What our country determines as to its immigration is neither a just cause of offense nor a subject for war or threats of war. It is an undoubted sovereign right and nothing else.

Herbert Hoover, "Rugged Individualism," October 22, 1928

. . . And what have been the results of our American system? Our country has become the land of opportunity to those born without inheritance, not merely because of the wealth of its resources and industry, but because of this freedom of initiative and enterprise. Russia has natural resources equal to ours. Her people are equally industrious, but she has not had the blessings of 150 years of our form of government and of our social system.

By adherence to the principles of decentralized self-government, ordered liberty, equal opportunity and freedom to the individual, our American experiment in human welfare has yielded a degree of well-being unparalleled in all the world. It has come nearer to the abolition of poverty, to the abolition of fear of want, than humanity has ever reached before. Progress of the past seven years is the proof of it. This alone furnishes the answer to our opponents who ask us to introduce destructive elements into the system by which this has been accomplished. . . .

I have endeavored to present to you that the greatness of America has grown out of a political and social system and a method of control of economic forces distinctly its own—our American system—which has carried this great experiment in human welfare further than ever before in all history. We are nearer today to the ideal of the abolition of poverty and fear from the lives of men and women than ever before in any land. And I again repeat that the departure from our American system by injecting principles destructive to it which our opponents propose will jeopardize the very liberty and freedom of our people, will destroy equality of opportunity, not alone to ourselves but to our children. . . .

Franklin D. Roosevelt, Commonwealth Club Speech, September 23, 1932

. . . A glance at the situation today only too clearly indicates that equality of opportunity as we have known it no longer exists. Our industrial plant is built. The problem just now is whether, under existing conditions, it is not over-built.

Our last frontier has long since been reached, and there is practically no more free land. More than half of our people do not live on the farms or on lands and cannot derive a living by cultivating their own property.

There is no safety valve in the form of a Western prairie to which those thrown out of work by the Eastern economic machines can go for a new start. We are not able to invite the immigration from Europe to share our endless plenty. We are now providing a drab living for our own people.

Our system of constantly rising tariffs has at last reacted against us to the point of closing our Canadian frontier on the north, our European markets on the east, many of our Latin-American markets on the south and a goodly proportion of our Pacific markets on the west through the retaliatory tariffs of those countries.

It has forced many of our great industrial institutions, who exported their surplus production to such countries, to establish plants in such countries, within the tariff walls.

This has resulted in the reduction of the operation of their American plants and opportunity for employment.

Just as freedom to farm has ceased, so also the opportunity in business has narrowed. It still is true that men can start small enterprises, trusting to native shrewdness and ability to keep abreast of competitors; but area after area has been pre-empted altogether by the great corporations, and even in the fields which still have no great concerns the small man starts under a handicap. . . .

Put plainly, we are steering a steady course toward economic oligarchy, if we are not there already.

Clearly, all this calls for a re-appraisal of values.

A mere builder of more industrial plants, a creator of more railroad systems, an organizer of more corporations, is as likely to be a danger as a help.

The day of the great promoter or the financial titan, to whom we granted anything if only he would build or develop, is over. Our task now is not discovery or exploitation of natural resources or necessarily producing more goods.

It is the soberer, less dramatic business of administering resources and plants already in hand, of seeking to re-establish foreign markets for our surplus production, of meeting the problem of under-consumption, of adjusting production to consumption, of distributing wealth and products more equitably, of adapting existing economic organizations to the service of the people.

The day of enlightened administration has come. . . .

9

The New Deal
and the Second World War

Roosevelt took office in March 1933. He was elected to an unprecedented four terms and for more than twelve years, until his death in April 1945, executed his duties as Chief Executive. Domestically, his New Deal greatly altered the American economy; although it has been highly praised for stimulating the recovery of the economy, at the same time it has also been criticized as "creeping socialism." The Roosevelt administration's foreign policy has also been the object of both praise and criticism. It has received high praise for its performance in the Second World War, but its conciliatory policy toward the Soviets was later attacked by its political opposition. More recently, Roosevelt's New Deal and his foreign policy have been criticized in the New Left revisionist interpretations of American history. In this sense, the policies of the Roosevelt administration, whether domestic or foreign, continue to be defended or criticized from the perspective of contemporary politics. Keeping in mind that the policies of the Roosevelt administration continue even now to possess a contemporary character, my object here is to examine their meaning within the broad context of American history.

The New Deal Policies

The New Deal had no consistent philosophy. It was no more than a collection of policies which were invented as they were needed. Fundamentally, however, the three elements of economic recovery, relief for the "forgotten man," and reform constituted the basis of Roosevelt's New Deal policies. While so characterizing the New Deal, however, one must note that there are important differences between the so-called First New Deal, which lasted until around the summer of 1935, and Roosevelt's later policies. Even the composition of the Brain Trust changed: while Raymond Moley dominated during the first term, a younger generation of advisers emerged to play major roles in the second term.[1]

When Roosevelt was inaugurated as president on March 4, 1933, the financial panic was at its worst. In various places depositors made runs on the banks, bank closings occurred, and the American economy was in a state of hopeless paralysis. In his inaugural address, Roosevelt asserted his belief that the only thing Americans had to fear was fear itself, and he immediately made a series of policy moves. During a period of one hundred days, displaying powerful leadership, he proposed a series of successive emergency programs, and Congress, gravely frightened in the face of the hopeless situation, approved—or, rather, "rubber-stamped"—the novel policies. Relief and recovery became the first urgent task. The Brain Trust, led by Moley, thought that the economic depression had essentially domestic causes; centering their depression policy on domestic measures, they attempted to restore the economy by means of government intervention (see the excerpt from Moley's writings appended to this chapter). The administration first enacted the Emergency Banking Relief Act, which closed the nation's banks for a fixed period and then permitted only those which were sound to reopen at the discretion of the government. This was a rather drastic measure, but it was not intended to put the banks under public ownership, and it greatly restored confidence in financial agencies. Next, to come to the

---

[1] The members of Roosevelt's Brain Trust did not always agree among themselves, but Roosevelt utilized these men skillfully and fully, putting the right men in the right place at the right time. This was one of the special characteristics of Roosevelt's leadership. The appellation Brain Trust started with and has been remembered in relation to the Roosevelt administration, but more basically it must be regarded as a structural phenomenon which accompanied the expansion of the role of the state and of executive authority. As the pressure of the work of the presidency increased with the expansion of the state's function, the president needed alter egos who could identify themselves completely with him and act as his "brains" and at his beck and call. Roosevelt, confronting the great economic depression at home and the Second World War abroad, freely created and replaced his alter egos, but the necessity for such people did not end with him. The White House staff system had been established by 1939, but in the Eisenhower era in particular it was more comprehensively institutionalized. It is well known that President Kennedy made extensive use of advisers. The Watergate Incident could be described as a tragedy in which an individual president used for his personal power the alter ego system which had become indispensable to the presidency.

aid of the unemployed, the Federal Emergency Relief Act was passed and Harry L. Hopkins, a social worker, was appointed federal Relief Administrator. Heeding the fact that the immediate cause of the Great Depression had been the panic which originated in the speculative stock exchange, the administration gained passage of the Federal Securities Act in May 1933 and the Securities Exchange Act the next year to tighten government control of the securities business and establish the Securities and Exchange Commission.

More even than these emergency measures, however, it was the National Industrial Recovery Act (NIRA), a long-term economic recovery policy, which became the focus of the New Deal. The NIRA can be divided into three main parts. The first, Title I, through production restrictions and price regulation, aimed at the recovery of business itself. For the purpose of aiding recovery, the government encouraged the merger of businesses and exempted these officially approved mergers from the application of the anti-trust laws. The New Deal employed the trend toward merger positively rather than regarding it as an unmitigated evil. Hugh S. Johnson, a retired general and expert in army logistics, became the head of the National Recovery Administration (NRA), with jurisdiction over NIRA policies, and began to enforce high price levels, which aided business. The second project of the NIRA (Section 7a) was relief for workers. While recognizing the workers' right to organize and prevent the decline of wages, the NIRA established the National Labor Board. The board guaranteed workers' right to bargain collectively and tried to improve labor-management relations. The third NIRA project (Title II) was the promotion of public works to relieve the unemployed and aid in the recovery of the economy. After the spring of 1935, the Works Progress Administration (WPA) was to manage this program, but until then, the Public Works Administration (PWA) under the NIRA took charge of the project. Secretary of the Interior Harold L. Ickes was appointed chief of the PWA, and under him the policy of so-called "pump-priming" through public works was put into practice. The National Industrial Recovery Act, encompassing all these measures, was designed to achieve the simultaneous relief of capital, labor, and the unemployed, and in this sense it formed the nucleus of the New Deal.

What policies did the Roosevelt administration adopt for agriculture, which had been afflicted by chronic depression since the 1920s? First, in 1933 the Agricultural Adjustment Act was passed. Secretary of Agriculture Henry A. Wallace was appointed to head the Agricultural Adjustment Administration (AAA) created by this act. Recognizing the need to restrict production in order to eliminate surpluses, stabilize prices, and restore the purchasing power of farmers, the Agricultural Adjustment Act curtailed agricultural production, and in return, the government paid compensation. A policy of agricultural recovery through low-interest, long-term financing for farmers was also put into effect.

The Tennessee Valley Authority (TVA) Act, which is often regarded as a symbol of the New Deal, is noteworthy because it sought to achieve several goals at the same time: developing electric power under the auspices of the national government at a price cheaper than that of private enterprise; easing unemployment; and coordinating regional development. This national enterprise plan was originally intended for many other regions as well as the Tennessee Valley, but it met with intense opposition from private enterprise, and in the end TVA remained an isolated experiment.

What were the actual results of this series of high price policies implemented through the economic intervention of the government? The American economy, which was at its nadir when Roosevelt first took office in 1933, gradually improved thereafter. If one creates an index with 1929 as 100, the economy, which in 1932 was 63, had recovered by 1935 to 75. The gap between agricultural and industrial prices also shrank, and on the whole a trend toward economic recovery, although slight, could be seen. Consequently, workers, businessmen, and farmers at first gave their support to the New Deal which had to various degrees helped them. Although the American economy thus seemed to emerge at least from the crisis situation, it did not achieve full recovery in this period, and the prospects for a return to the pre-depression level remained dim. One might say, paradoxically, that the limited recovery from the crisis served only to perpetuate a latent crisis situation. This condition led to a flow of criticism and dissatisfaction with the New Deal from groups which until then had wholly supported it. Criticism first came from business circles.

Business leaders had realized that the self-regulating mechanism of the American economy could not overcome the depression, and therefore sought government intervention and hoped for a recovery through political measures. However, government assistance meant government control of the economy. As soon as some expected recovery was achieved, business began to regard the government control as a fetter and to criticize the New Deal. For example, in August 1934, the Du Ponts, a leading business family, and others organized the American Liberty League as an anti-New Deal force.

The judiciary also emerged as a force strongly critical of the New Deal. At the height of the crisis the Supreme Court had acquiesced in the many drastic New Deal measures. As soon as the crisis situation had been somewhat eased, however, it took the position that much of the New Deal legislation was unconstitutional. The bases of the judicial attack on the New Deal were several. First, the legislative branch had delegated too broad an authority to the executive branch, violating the principle of separation of powers. Second, the federal government, exceeding the powers granted by the Constitution, had encroached on the powers of state governments. On these grounds, the National Industrial Recovery Act, which was the foundation of the New Deal, was judged unconstitutional in May 1935, as was another New Deal mainstay, the Agricultural Adjustment Act, in January 1936. The Supreme Court declaration of unconstitutionality of the two crucial elements of the New Deal was a serious blow to the Roosevelt administration, or at least to its image.

The attack on the New Deal was not confined to business and the courts; it came also from the workers. The New Deal aimed originally at a balance between business and labor, as symbolized by the Industrial Recovery Act. The continuing existence of a large gap between commodity prices and wages, however, caused discontent among workers, and strikes broke out in various places. In San Francisco a general strike took place in July 1934. The National Recovery Administration was criticized for being more interested in business than in labor.

Worker discontent was not directed solely at the government or at business. The center of the American labor movement had been the skilled worker craft union, with the AF of L as its central organization. However, with the arrival of the era of mass production, opposition to the craft union system emerged among industrial workers. Soon a movement to organize industrial labor unions appeared within the AF of L, culminating in the formation of the Congress of Industrial Organizations under the leadership of John L. Lewis, president of the United Mine Workers. It was originally organized in November 1935 as the Committee of Industrial Organizations, an opposition group within the AF of L. In 1938 the CIO finally separated from the AF of L, and its membership expanded rapidly to three million. New labor leaders like Sidney Hillman of the Amalgamated Clothing Workers emerged, and labor unions began to play a major role in American politics. Although the unions criticized some aspects of the labor policies advanced under the Roosevelt administration, they were basically strong supporters of the New Deal.

The New Deal effected some degree of economic recovery and partially achieved the relief of the "forgotten man." However, before either recovery or relief was complete, a new crisis emerged. Exploiting the deep-rooted mass anxiety of the depression years, political demagogues began to appeal to the masses by advocating radical utopian policies. Particularly notable among these was Huey P. "Kingfish" Long, governor and senator from Louisiana. With his traditional populist background, he appealed strongly not only to farmers but also to the urban masses. Long proposed a "Share-Our-Wealth" movement, which demanded that the government restore prosperity and reduce the gap between rich and poor by imposing a high property tax and distributing the tax revenue to each household. The movement had a wide appeal, and it was predicted that Long would play a major role in the 1936 presidential election. However, he was assassinated in 1935 in the Louisiana state capitol. Besides Long, one must note the National Union for Social Justice movement, led by Father Charles E. Coughlin of Michigan. While centered in the midwest, this movement reached the whole nation over the radio. Coughlin's utopian, abstract criticism of the New Deal appealed strongly to people who were dissatisfied with their daily lives. The old age pension scheme of Dr. Francis Townsend of California also had considerable influence. To stimulate spending for economic recovery, Townsend proposed to give a monthly pension of $200 to

every citizen over the age of sixty. As the election of 1936 approached, these radical yet popular movements could not be ignored.

Having achieved some success, the First New Deal faced criticism
from the courts, business, labor, and grass-roots reform movements.
In response, Roosevelt began to consider a new set of policies.

The Second New Deal and the Roosevelt Coalition

Vehemently criticizing big business, and at the same time pro-
posing alternatives to the panaceas offered by the demagogues,
Roosevelt attempted to rejuvenate the New Deal and regain the
support of the masses. He said, "I am fighting Communism, Huey
Longism, Coughlinism, Townsendism." To replace the Industrial
Recovery Act, which had been declared unconstitutional, he
obtained passage of the National Labor Relations Act, popularly
known as the Wagner Act. This law strengthened the workers'
right to organize, and thus mobilized their support for Roosevelt's
New Deal programs. The Fair Labor Standards Act of 1938 further advanced the regulation of labor-management relations. It
stipulated minimum wages and maximum working hours for the
unorganized majority of workers. The Emergency Relief Appropriation Act established the Works Progress Administration
(later called the Works Projects Administration, administered by
Harry L. Hopkins), which undertook immense public works
projects in order to provide work for vast numbers of unemployed,
including not only manual laborers but also white-collar workers
and intellectuals such as teachers, musicians, writers, and the like.
It is said that within one year after WPA's formation, 3,400,-
000 people were employed by its programs. The First New Deal
had established the Civilian Conservation Corps (CCC), which
combined unemployment relief and training of youth in work
camps for the conservation of natural resources. In 1935, as part
of the Works Progress Administration, the National Youth Administration (NYA) was established; this agency provided part-
time work for young people unable to afford to attend school,
thus allowing them to continue their education.

However, it was the Social Security Act of August 1935 which
more than anything became the focus of the Second New Deal.

Based on careful planning by Secretary of Labor Frances Perkins, (the first woman to hold a Cabinet post in the U.S. government), the act established a broad program including old-age pensions, unemployment insurance, and welfare aid for the physically handicapped. To put these measures into practice, a Social Security Board was established. The federal government's creation of a national-level social security system, regardless of its scale, was an epoch-making event from the perspective of the traditional theory of states' rights and the philosophy of Social Darwinism. The fact that the national government directly undertook to guarantee the livelihood of its citizens constituted a major change in the idea of the function of the central government.

In order to raise the revenue for this social security program, and at the same time as an answer to the "Share Our Wealth" concept of Long and his followers, Roosevelt instituted a progressive income tax and a corporate tax. and raised gift taxes and inheritance taxes to higher levels. This measure provoked intense argument even within the Brain Trust; Raymond Moley, calling the tax a "soak-the-rich" tax scheme, and several others left the administration in disagreement over this issue, afterwards joining those who were intensely critical of Roosevelt.

The 1936 election took place within the context of the Second New Deal, the Roosevelt administration's turn to the left. This election is famous in American history for the intensity of its campaign. The Republican Party and groups like the American Liberty League, whose members included many anti-Roosevelt Democrats like Al Smith, raised their anti-New Deal banners and began a vigorous campaign. The Republicans nominated the governor of Kansas, Alfred L. M. Landon, as their presidential candidate. Landon had been elected in the mid-term election of 1934 in spite of the overwhelming defeat of the Republican Party elsewhere; moreover, during his term he had achieved. a reputation as a governor who had conquered the depression in his state. The election campaign clearly focused on the issue of the New Deal, and many newspapers, supported by big business, published articles attacking Roosevelt's policies (see the excerpt from the Republican Party platform appended to this chapter). Louisiana's Huey Long and others had been planning to form a third party under an anti-New Deal banner. After Long's assassination, his successor, Representative William Lemke of North Dakota, continued the midwestern populist tradition and became a candidate on a Union Party ticket, which gathered together the various radical groups advocating drastic reforms. However, because it had lost the charismatic Huey Long, and because the Roosevelt administration, by its leftward turn, had co-opted many of its proposals, the Union Party was not much of a factor in the 1936 election. Meanwhile the Socialist Party ran Norman Thomas for the third time, and the Communist Party ran Earl Browder. Many progressive parties appeared at the state level in this election, running their own candidates locally but supporting Roosevelt in the presidential election. Examples were the American Labor Party in New York and the Farmer-Labor Party and the Progressive Party in the midwest. Labor unions such as the AF of L and the CIO also supported Roosevelt; the CIO, under Lewis and Hillman, created the Labor's Non-Partisan League, which involved itself actively in the election campaign.

The election resulted in overwhelming victory for Roosevelt: he received about 61 percent of the popular vote and 323 electoral votes, while Landon received only 8 electoral vote. The Union Party received 890,000 votes, the Socialist Party 187,000, and the Communist Party 80,000. The fact that their total did not exceed 3 percent of the popular vote indicated that the Democratic Party under Roosevelt almost completely absorbed the discontent vote. Workers, small farmers, the unemployed, immigrants, and blacks voted almost solidly for Roosevelt, creating the so-called "Roosevelt coalition." Blacks, who had formerly supported the Republican Party because of Abraham Lincoln, voted Democratic as beneficiaries of the New Deal, though Roosevelt himself did not propose desegregation.

In his second inaugural address, Roosevelt, pointing to "one-third of a nation ill-housed, ill-clad, ill-nourished," promised to continue his New Deal policies. He proposed the Wagner-Steagall National Housing Act, enacted in September 1937, which included a plan to eliminate slums and provide public housing for low-income families. In February 1938, the administration obtained passage of a new Agricultural Adjustment Act. Supported by his overwhelming victory, Roosevelt went out to do battle for his policies; however, he encountered serious obstacles.

During his first term, the Industrial Recovery Act and the Agricultural Adjustment Act had been declared unconstitutional by the Supreme Court, and the nation waited eagerly to see what kind of judgments other New Deal legislation would receive. In order to protect his policies, Roosevelt planned to revamp the Supreme Court and to appoint justices friendly to the New Deal. The reform of the courts had been an issue in Congress as well, and there had been talk of measures to restrain the Supreme Court's right of judicial review. But Roosevelt perceived this not as an institutional problem but as a personnel problem, one which could be solved by the substitution of new judges for old ones. His "Court-packing" bill, as it came to be called, under the pretext of a decline in the justices' capabilities due to their increasing age, aimed at retiring justices over the age of seventy, and stipulated that when justices over the age of seventy would not retire, the president would be permitted to appoint an equal number of justices up to a maximum number of fifteen. Roosevelt's plan, however, clearly injured the pride of the elderly judges. Further, he had not conferred sufficiently with Congressional leaders and had proceeded secretly with the drafting of the bill, so it met with violent opposition from Congress and the press. Roosevelt immediately appealed to the general public by his usual method, a "fireside chat" radio broadcast, but his frontal attack on the Supreme Court, which is sometimes called the "dignified part" of the American political system, aroused hostility among the public. The plan to reform the Court was ultimately opposed in Congress even by the Democrats, and was defeated. In the event, however, due to the timely retirement of some elderly judges, Roosevelt was able to appoint justices known to be friendly to the New Deal, and gradually the Supreme Court changed into a liberal court, known as the "Roosevelt Court." Among the liberal justices appointed by Roosevelt were Hugo L. Black, Felix Frankfurter, and William O. Douglas. Beginning with the Wagner Act, several New Deal laws were declared constitutional. In essence the opposition between the executive and the judicial branches was dissolved, and the Court, observing the "judicial restraint" principle, thereafter made it a practice to desist whenever possible from handing down decisions on politically sensitive cases.

The controversy over reform of the Supreme Court unexpectedly revealed conflict between the executive and the legislative branches as well. On this issue, Roosevelt was unable to control the Congressional members of his own Democratic Party, and a split between the presidential Democratic Party and the congressional Democratic Party resulted. Roosevelt attempted to tighten his control over the party and planned to purge the anti-New Deal Democrats from Congress in the midterm election of 1938. However, his attempt failed; a number of Democrats opposed to him were nominated at the state party conventions and subsequently elected. American political parties are at base confederations of local parties, and Roosevelt failed in his bold attempt to challenge this basic nature of party structure through asserting national control.[2]

The economic recession beginning around 1937 was also a serious blow to the Roosevelt administration. As soon as some economic recovery had been achieved the government tried to cut back public spending; the economy was immediately set back and the number of unemployed again increased. At this point some people began to think that public spending, which had originally been conceived as mere temporary "pump-priming," should be institutionalized in order to guarantee the smooth flow of the American economy.

The Second New Deal gradually came to emphasize structural reform more than recovery, and, at least in theory, the welfare of

[2] The conflict between Roosevelt and the Democratic Party members in Congress revealed the complicated nature of the American political party system. Corresponding to the basic structure of the federal system and the separation of the three powers, the political parties also maintain a decentralization of power. The party is a mechanism for obtaining votes in elections; it is not a policy-making organization. With regard to voting behavior in Congress, the party often does not act as a solid unit; voting which transcends party lines—"cross-over voting"—is common. In this sense the American political party can be said to be both non-partisan and bi-partisan: the legislators often vote in accordance with regional or special interests. From another perspective, the cross-voting could also be said to stem from the ideological similarity between the two major parties. In any case, due to this lack of discipline within the Congressional parties, even when the president's party enjoys the majority in Congress, there is no guarantee that he will be able to obtain the consent of the majority to his own policies. Therefore special efforts are required of the American president in handling Congress, which differ from those of the English or Japanese prime minister under the parliamentary cabinet system. In the more than forty years from the 1932 election to the present, except for a mere four years, the Democratic Party has always had a majority in Congress, but Democratic presidents have always been troubled by conflicts with some faction of their own Democratic Party in Congress.

the people came to take precedence over the interest of capital. This trend was demonstrated by the creation in June 1938 of the Temporary National Economic Committee (TNEC), a large-scale joint committee of the legislative and executive branches to investigate the tendency toward monopoly and to suppress the concentration of economic power. However, with the deterioration of the international political situation in Europe, emphasis was gradually shifted from social security to national security as the area of public spending. In May 1938, a plan for naval expansion was drawn up, and expenses of over one billion dollars were approved. One could say that the economy was gradually moving toward wartime status.

If one takes the period up to 1939 (when the Second World War broke out) as the era of the New Deal, one could question, at least in strictly economic terms, whether or not it really achieved economic recovery. The production index during this period failed to return to the pre-1929 level, and a high rate of unemployment persisted until the shift to a wartime economy brought full employment. In this sense, it is debatable whether, without the wartime stimulus, the New Deal could have achieved economic recovery. Further, it is doubtful that the American economic philosophy, which traditionally gave precedence to private enterprise, would have actually allowed long-term public spending in a form other than military expenditures. However, although we often tend to give negative or mixed reviews to the New Deal in strictly economic terms, there is no doubt that in its political aspect it contributed greatly to the preservation of the American social system in a crisis, when people's insecurity had reached a critical point both materially and psychologically. By broadening and elaborating the role of the federal government, the New Deal made the masses the beneficiaries of a "welfare state," and thus offered the people at least psychological security. Aided by the personal identification with Roosevelt which emerged among the people, the New Deal to a certain extent eliminated mistrust toward the American social system itself and contributed to its preservation. In this sense the New Deal, despite its progressive policies, succeeded in playing a conservative role in preserving the American system. This might be said to have been the ultimate goal of the Roosevelt administration and its New Deal policy.

The Roosevelt Administration's Foreign Policy

The Roosevelt administration was preoccupied with domestic economic problems during the early years, and at first adopted a rather uncooperative attitude internationally. Its foreign policy was sometimes called one of "economic nationalism." Despite the deterioration of the international situation with the advance of Japan in Asia and the rise of the Nazis in Europe, the Roosevelt administration did not adopt a positive foreign policy. It did emphasize the exploration of foreign markets, in the interests of upholding the Open Door policy and as one step on the road to economic recovery.

This emphasis was illustrated by U.S. policy toward Latin America. Roosevelt advocated the Good Neighbor policy, and made it clear that he would adopt a position of non-interference toward the Latin American countries. In 1934 the Platt Amendment was rescinded; the U.S. relinquished the right to interfere in Cuba and withdrew its troops from Haiti and Nicaragua. Beginning at the end of 1933, the U.S. government convened several Pan-American conferences and stressed strengthening solidarity among the nations of the American continents. However, the fundamental premise of American policy remained the unity of the North and South American continents, and the new policy did not deviate from the underlying basis of the Monroe Doctrine. During this period, the value of American exports and capital investment in Latin America increased rapidly. Traditional protective tariff policies were liberalized under the Roosevelt administration. In order to expand foreign markets, Secretary of State Cordell Hull, a southern advocate of free trade, urged the conclusion of mutual trade agreements with a number of nations, which aimed at the reciprocal reduction of tariffs. In June 1934, Congress approved Hull's idea and gave the president the authority to lower the tariff by as much as 50 percent. This constituted a shift from the traditional high protective tariff policy, but because the tariff problem always involved domestic special interests which had to be pacified, completely free trade was impossible.

Also at this time, the U.S. government officially recognized the Soviet Union, for a number of reasons, foremost among them the desire to develop a new foreign market. Adhering to the peculiar American doctrine of ideological non-recognition, the preceding Republican administrations had never recognized the Soviet Union. However, the Soviet Union appeared to the Roosevelt administration to be a market which had escaped the depression, and also as an Asian power with the potential might to restrain Japan, which was continuing its advance on the Chinese mainland after the Manchurian Incident.

Basically, the tendency of public opinion in the early 1930s was to advocate undivided attention to the American domestic crisis without entanglement in the struggles of other nations. This tendency can be seen in the creation in 1934 of a Senate special committee to investigate the munitions industry, headed by Senator Gerald P. Nye of North Dakota, a progressive Republican. This committee sought to show that America's entry into the First World War had been due to the schemes of the "merchants of death"—munitions makers. Once again the principle of neutrality was advocated. In August 1935, immediately after Italy began its invasion of Ethiopia, Congress passed the Neutrality Act, which prohibited the shipment of arms to belligerent countries. Thereafter, the Neutrality Act was stiffened and was also applied to the Spanish Civil War.

However, the establishment of the Nazi regime in Germany and the expansion of its power, together with Japan's invasion of Chinese territory, made many Americans apprehensive about the future. Japan's military actions on the Chinese mainland—the "China Incident"—excited American public opinion. In response, in October 1937 Roosevelt gave his famous "Quarantine Speech" in Chicago, in which he took a firm position, declaring that in order to prevent the threat of international anarchy, the aggressor nations should be "quarantined" (see extract appended to this chapter). This speech was extremely unpopular in America, and no specific policy resulted. Nonetheless, pursuing the naval armaments race which had begun with Japan's announcement of the abrogation of the Washington Naval Treaty at the end of 1934, Congress approved in 1938 a large appropriation for naval armaments (the Vinson Plan).

Nazi Germany's push into neighboring countries finally led to the invasion of Poland, and in September 1939 the Second World War broke out. The advance of of Japan in Asia and of Germany in Europe greatly undermined the balance of power in their respective regions. In the United States, two opposing factions simultaneously emerged, one demanding neutrality and non-intervention, the other urging the restraint of Germany and Japan in order to restore the balance of power in both regions. The Roosevelt administration, while balancing these two opposing opinions, groped for a foreign policy stance with regard to the war.

America's traditional foreign policy, as we have seen, consciously or unconsciously aimed chiefly at the prevention of the emergence of any dominant power in Europe or Asia. A dominant power in Europe was considered a direct threat to the western hemisphere, while the appearance of a dominant power in Asia would threaten the Open Door in China and result in the monopolistic control of the China market. Consequently, as Germany grew stronger, not only American sympathy with England and France in terms of political system, culture, and sentiment, but also, and more fundamentally, the fear of German domination of Europe made aid to England and France and the overthrow of Germany the central object of U.S. European policy. Thus the Roosevelt administration, although declaring itself committed to neutrality, in actuality endeavored to create a situation beneficial to England. First, in November 1939, the Neutrality Act was revised to repeal the arms embargo clause and approve the export of munitions on a "cash and carry" basis—that is, provided that buyers would pay in cash and transport on their own ships. With this revision, the U.S. in practice began to assist the Allies. In the spring of 1940, the Nazi blitzkrieg by Panzers and Luftwaffe began. Denmark, Norway, Holland, Belgium, and France were forced to surrender. Shocked and alarmed, the American public at last felt the reality of the war. In September 1940, Roosevelt concluded an executive agreement with England, offering fifty destroyers in exchange for bases in the West Indies. Meanwhile the creation of a joint defense system among the American nations was planned: at the 1938 Pan-American Conference in Lima, the Panama Conference in 1939, and the Havana Conference in 1940, the participants agreed to a common defense treaty.

Chanting the slogan "Don't change horses in midstream," the Democratic Party nominated Roosevelt for a third term as president in 1940. The Republican Party nominated the able and charming corporation lawyer Wendell L. Willkie. In the face of the international crisis brought about by the fall of France, the people trusted and supported Roosevelt, who had had a successful record over eight years, more than Willkie, who was an unknown quantity, and Roosevelt won an unprecedented third term.

In his campaign Roosevelt pledged that the U.S. would not enter the war and that he would not send America's sons to a European battle front. However, soon after his election, he announced that America would be the "great arsenal of democracy"; he gradually converted the economic system to a wartime posture, and a selective military service system was approved and put into effect. In January 1941 he advocated the "Four Freedoms," picturing the war as an ideological and moral confrontation between freedom and tyranny. In March 1941 the Roosevelt administration obtained passage of the Lend-Lease Act and began to give military aid to England, the Soviet Union, and other allies. Thus, the United States gradually strengthened its commitment to the European war, and in fact economically participated in the war as one of the Allies; the only remaining question was when the nation would enter the war militarily.

In Asia as well as in Europe, the U.S. confronted a dilemma. While the necessity of containing Japan's advance in China was felt strongly by Americans, the need to oppose German aggrandizement had a more direct importance. Since Germany was the primary enemy, the administration felt that a head-on collision with Japan should be avoided, and it did not prohibit the exportation of such militarily important commodities as scrap iron and petroleum. However, when Japan concluded a military alliance with Germany in September 1940, and the Axis alliance among Japan, Germany, and Italy was established, the U.S. inevitably took a firmer stance toward Japan. After Japan's occupation of French Indo-China, the government froze Japanese assets in the United States and imposed an embargo on the shipment of oil to Japan, and Japanese-American relations further deteriorated. Negotiations between the two governments, which began in the spring of 1941, became deadlocked on such American demands as the Japanese Army's total withdrawal from China and the suspension of the Tripartite Pact, and failed to settle the issues. On December 7/8, 1941,* with the Japanese surprise attack on Pearl Harbor, hostilities began, and the United States formally entered the Second World War.[3] Public opinion, which had been split between neutrality and entry into the war, was unified at a single stroke, and the energy of the American people was concentrated on the execution of the war. Since entry into the war was sparked by Japan's "sneak" attack on Pearl Harbor, national sentiment regarded Japan as the number one enemy, but stragegically, from first to last the U.S. regarded Germany as the primary enemy, and its basic strategy was to work for the defeat of Germany first. Europe and the Atlantic became the principal war theater; Asia and the Pacific were secondary as far as the land war in particular was concerned.[4]

Well before December 7, 1941, the United States had begun preparations for war. In October 1940, under the first peacetime selective service system, 16,400,000 young men were registered for military service, and in August 1941 the active-duty terms of 900,000 enlisted soldiers had been extended. In June 1941 the Alien Registration Act (Smith Act) had been passed. This law, in addition to regulating the registration and control of foreigners, aimed broadly at controlling the subversive activity of the American citizenry in general. In December, the Office of Production Management was created to promote the work of the "arsenal of democracy."

With entry into the war, mobilization became total. In January

---

*In Japan the time was early morning, December 8, when the attack took place.

[3] After the Japanese attack on Pearl Harbor, on the basis of Roosevelt's presidential message on December 8, Congress declared the existence of a state of war between Japan and the U.S. by a vote of 83–0 in the Senate and 388–1 in the House. The lone dissenter was Jeannette Rankin of Montana, who, as a Quaker conscientious objector, cast the historic one dissenting vote literally in tears. Representative Rankin had also cast a negative vote at the time of entry into the First World War in 1917, and later would oppose the Vietnam War.

[4] For Japan, the Second World War meant principally a war with the United States, and the Japanese people have tended to forget that for the U.S. this was primarily a war with Germany and only secondarily a war with Japan. Similarly, Japanese often have the illusion that the importance of America in Japan's foreign policy is reciprocal. This is an illusion which the Japanese people have tended to have with regard to Japanese-American relations ever since the arrival of Perry in Japan.

1942 the War Production Board was created; absorbing and expanding the role of the Office of Production Management, it controlled the production of munitions and industrial production in general. In April, the War Manpower Commission was created, and it carried out a comprehensive mobilization and management of human resources. An executive order of February 1942 "relocated" 110,000 Japanese-Americans, whose loyalty had become suspect, from their Pacific coast residences to the interior of the continent. Afterwards the second-generation Japanese-Americans formed Nisei regiments, and had to prove their loyalty to America literally with their blood on the European front. Other wartime measures included the control of prices and wages; the restriction of labor union activities, especially of strikes in munitions industries; the procurement of scarce military resources; the abolition of racial discrimination in order to guarantee efficiency in munitions production; the national management of the railroads; and the control of domestic and foreign intelligence-gathering. Beginning in August 1942, the "Manhattan Project" to produce an atomic bomb was organized and conducted in extreme secrecy. In order to establish bipartisan national unity, Roosevelt had appointed leading Republicans to important posts with responsibility for the execution of the war: former Secretary of State Henry Lewis Stimson was Secretary of the Army, and Frank Knox was Secretary of the Navy. The atomic bomb project was placed under Stimson's jurisdiction.

Traditionally, when engaged in fighting a war the United States distinguished between the peacetime system and the wartime system; during war everything was decided on the basis of military considerations. European nations did not make such a clear distinction between wartime and peacetime; in a sense they viewed wartime as an extension of peacetime and so tended to give greater consideration to postwar power politics. In wartime America, however, the military perspective was affirmed in every aspect. This peculiar American view of war was responsible for Roosevelt's insistence on the unconditional surrender of the Axis nations.

The strategic considerations in the execution of the war inevitably affected ideas about the postwar world. The Allies often held important summit conferences at which they discussed both their plans for joint operations and their plans for the postwar world.

At the meeting of American and British leaders at Casablanca in January 1945, the Cairo Conference in November of the same year, the Teheran Conference, the Yalta Conference of February 1945, and, last, the Potsdam Conference, the Allies' postwar plans steadily advanced. Roosevelt's basic desire was to create a United Nations, which would replace the League of Nations and would be led by the major Allied countries. At this time Roosevelt assumed that after the war it would be possible to continue to cooperate with the Soviets, and this premise was the basis for his attitude toward the Soviet Union at the Yalta Conference, which was later criticized as too great a concession to that country. After the Yalta Conference, Roosevelt died suddenly without seeing the end of the war, and Vice-President Harry S Truman succeeded him as president. One month later Germany surrendered; in August, having faced the American use of the atomic weapon and the Soviet Union's entry into the war, Japan accepted the terms of the Potsdam Declaration (see the excerpt appended to this chapter), and the Second World War came to an end.

The Second World War confirmed the "Pax Americana" which had been established to a certain extent after the First World War, and in the postwar world the United States came to exercise its influence literally as a superpower economically and militarily. As a result of the total mobilization which lasted such a long time, the Second World War established a strong sense of nationalism among the American people. Moreover, the wartime economy had reached nearly full employment. Consequently, the New Deal system lost its ideological novelty, and the vast mechanism of government, which had expanded through the New Deal and the Second World War, remained in operation.

Documents

Raymond Moley, "The Birth of the New Deal," from *After Seven Years* (**Harper Brothers, 1939**)

. . . What was taking shape was distinctive in three respects.

First was what we might have called the "Look Homeward, Angel" interpretation of the depression: we proceeded on the assumption that the causes of our ills were domestic, internal, and that the remedies would have to be internal too. How unorthodox this was at the time may be judged by the amount of bitterness with which we were called "nationalists" by older economists.

Second was the belief that there was need not only for an extension of the government's regulatory power to prevent abuses (stock-market regulation and the abolition of child labor, for instance) but for the development of controls to stimulate and stabilize economic activity ("planning" for agriculture and the concentration of greater powers in the Federal Reserve Board, for instance). The former, designed to curb economic power and special privilege, did not depart in principle from the lines of policy laid down in the administrations of Theodore Roosevelt and Woodrow Wilson. But the latter carried us pretty far from ancient moorings.

Third was the rejection of the traditional Wilson-Brandeis philosophy that if America could once more become a nation of small proprietors, of corner grocers and smithies under spreading chestnut trees, we should have solved the problems of American life. We agreed that the heart of our difficulty was the anarchy of concentrated economic power which, like a cannon loose on a frigate's deck, tore from one side to another, crushing those in its path. But we felt that the remedy for this was not to substitute muskets for cannon or to throw the cannon overboard. We believed that any attempt to atomize big business must destroy America's greatest contribution to a higher standard of living for the body of its citizenry—the development of mass production. We agreed that equality of opportunity must be preserved. But we recognized that competition, as such, was not inherently virtuous; that competition (when it was embodied in an employer who survived only by sweating his labor, for example) created as many abuses as it prevented. So we turned from the nostalgic philosophy of the "trust busters" toward the solution first broached in modern times by Charles Richard Van Hise's *Concentration and Control*. . . .

The Republican Party Platform, 1936

America is in peril. The welfare of American men and women and the future of our youth are at stake. We dedicate ourselves to the preservation of their political liberty, their individual opportunity and their character as free citizens, which today for the first time are threatened by Government itself.

For three long years the New Deal Administration has dishonored American traditions and flagrantly betrayed the pledges upon which the Democratic Party sought and received public support.

The powers of Congress have been usurped by the President.

The integrity and authority of the Supreme Court have been flouted.

The rights and liberties of American citizens have been violated.

Regulated monopoly has displaced free enterprise.

The New Deal Administration constantly seeks to usurp the rights reserved to the States and to the people. . . .

Franklin D. Roosevelt, "Quarantine Speech" at Chicago, October 5, 1937

. . . It seems to be unfortunately true that the epidemic of world lawlessness is spreading.

When an epidemic of physical disease starts to spread, the community approves and joins in a quarantine of the patients in order to protect the health of the community against the spread of the disease.

It is my determination to pursue a policy of peace and to adopt every practicable measure to avoid involvement in war. It ought to be inconceivable that in this modern era, and in the face of experience, any nation could be so foolish and ruthless as to run the risk of plunging the whole world into war by invading and violating in contravention of solemn treaties the territory of other nations that have done them no real harm and are too weak to protect themselves adequately. Yet the peace of the world and the welfare and security of every nation is today being threatened by that very thing. . . .

War is a contagion, whether it be declared or undeclared. It can engulf states and peoples remote from the original scene of hostilities. We are determined to keep out of war, yet we cannot insure ourselves against the disastrous effects of war and the dangers of involvement. We are adopting such measures as will minimize our risk of involvement, but we cannot have complete protection in a world of disorder in which confidence and security have broken down.

If civilization is to survive the principles of the Prince of Peace must be restored. Shattered trust between nations must be revived.

Most important of all, the will for peace on the part of peace-loving nations must express itself to the end that nations that may be tempted to violate their agreements and the rights of others will desist from such a course. There must be positive endeavors to preserve peace.

America hates war. America hopes for peace. Therefore, America actively engages in the search for peace.

Joseph C. Grew to Cordell Hull, November 3, 1941

. . . (d) The Embassy in Japan has never been convinced by the theory that Japan's collapse as a militaristic power would shortly result from the depletion and the eventual exhaustion of Japan's financial and economic resources, as propounded by many leading American economists. Such forecasts were unconsciously based upon the assumption that a dominant consideration would be Japan's retention of the capitalistic system. The outcome they predicted has not transpired, although it is true that the greater part of Japan's commerce has been lost, Japanese industrial production has been drastically curtailed, and Japan's national resources have been depleted. Instead, there has been a drastic prosecution of the process to integrate Japan's national economy, lacking which there might well have occurred the predicted collapse of Japan. What has happened to date therefore does not support the view that continuation of trade embargoes and imposition of a blockade (proposed by some) can best avert war in the Far East.

(3) The Ambassador mentions his telegram No. 827, September 12, 1940 (which reported the "golden opportunity" seen by Japanese army circles for expansion as a consequence of German triumphs in Europe). He sent this telegram under circumstances and at a time when it appeared unwise and futile for the United States to adopt conciliatory measures. The strong policy recommended in the telegram was subsequently adopted by the United States. This policy, together with the impact of world political events upon Japan, brought the Japanese Government to the point of seeking conciliation with the United States. If these efforts fail, the Ambassador foresees a probable swing of the pendulum in Japan once more back to the former Japanese position or even farther. This would lead to what he has described as an all-out, do-or-die attempt, actually risking national hara-kiri, to make Japan impervious to economic embargoes abroad rather than to yield to foreign pressure. It is realized by observers who feel Japanese national temper and psychology from day to day that, beyond peradventure, this contingency not only is possible but is probable.

(4) If the fiber and temper of the Japanese people are kept in mind, the view that war probably would be averted, though there might be some risk of war, by progressively imposing drastic economic measures is an uncertain and dangerous hypothesis upon which to base considered United States policy and measures. War would not be averted by such a course, if it is taken, in the opinion of the Embassy. However, each view is only opinion, and, accordingly, to postulate the correctness of either one and to erect a definitive policy thereon would, in the belief of the Embassy, be contrary to American national interests. It would mean putting the cart before the horse. The primary point to be decided apparently involves the question whether war with Japan is justified by American national objectives, policies, and needs in the case of failure of the first line of national defense, namely, diplomacy, since it would be possible only on the basis of such a decision for the Roosevelt administration to follow a course which would be divested as much as possible of elements of uncertainty, speculation, and opinion. The Ambassador does not doubt that such a decision, irrevocable as it might well prove to be, already has been debated fully and adopted, because the sands are running fast.

(5) The Ambassador emphasizes that, in the above discussion of this grave momentous subject, he is out of touch with the intention and thoughts of the Administration thereon, and he does not at all mean to imply that Washington is pursuing an undeliberated policy. Nor does he intend to advocate for a single moment any "appeasement" of Japan by the United States or recession in the slightest degree by the United States Government from the fundamental principles laid down as a basis for the conduct and adjustment of international relations, American relations with Japan included. There should be no compromise with principles, though methods may be flexible. The Ambassador's purpose is only to ensure against the United States becoming involved in war with Japan

because of any possible misconception of Japan's capacity to rush headlong into a suicidal struggle with the United States. While national sanity dictates against such action, Japanese sanity cannot be measured by American standards of logic. The Ambassador sees no need for much anxiety respecting the bellicose tone and substance at present of the Japanese press (which in the past several years has attacked the United States intensely in recurrent waves), but he points out the shortsightedness of underestimating Japan's obvious preparations to implement an alternative program in the event the peace program fails. He adds that similarly it would be shortsighted for American policy to be based upon the belief that Japanese preparations are no more than saber rattling, merely intended to give moral support to the high pressure diplomacy of Japan. Action by Japan which might render unavoidable an armed conflict with the United States may come with dangerous and dramatic suddenness.

The Yalta Conference, February, 1945

Agreement Regarding Japan.

The leaders of the three great powers—the Soviet Union, the United States of America and Great Britain—have agreed that in two or three months after Germany has surrendered and the war in Europe has terminated, the Soviet Union shall enter into the war against Japan on the side of the Allies on condition that:

1. The status quo in Outer Mongolia (the Mongolian People's Republic) shall be preserved;

2. The former rights of Russia violated by the treacherous attack of Japan in 1904 shall be restored, viz.:

(a) The southern part of Sakhalin as well as the islands adjacent to it shall be returned to the Soviet Union;

(b) The commercial port of Dairen shall be internationalized, the preeminent interests of the Soviet Union in this port being safeguarded, and the lease of Port Arthur as a naval base of the U.S.S.R. restored;

(c) The Chinese-Eastern Railroad and the South Manchurian Railroad, which provide an outlet to Dairen, shall be jointly operated by the establishment of a joint Soviet-Chinese company, it being understood that the preeminent interests of the Soviet Union shall be safeguarded and that China shall retain full sovereignty in Manchuria;

3. The Kurile Islands shall be handed over to the Soviet Union. It is understood that the agreement concerning Outer Mongolia and the ports and railroads referred to above will require the concurrence of Generalissimo Chiang Kai-shek. The President will take measures in order to obtain this concurrence on advice from Marshal Stalin.

The heads of the three great powers have agreed that these claims of the Soviet Union shall be unquestionably fulfilled after Japan has been defeated.

For its part, the Soviet Union expresses its readiness to conclude with the National Government of China a pact of friendship and alliance between the U.S.S.R. and China in order to render assistance to China with its armed forces for the purpose of liberating China from the Japanese yoke.

The Potsdam Conference, Proclamation Defining Terms for Japanese Surrender, July 26, 1945

(1) We—The President of the United States, the President of the National Government of the Republic of China, and the Prime Minister of Great Britain, representing the hundreds of millions of our countrymen, have conferred and agree that Japan shall be given an opportunity to end this war.

(2) The prodigious land, sea and air forces of the United States, the British Empire and of China, many times reinforced fly their armies and air fleets from the west, are poised to strike the final blows upon Japan. This military power is sustained and inspired by the determination of all the Allied Nations to prosecute the war against Japan until she ceases to resist.

(3) The result of the futile and senseless German resistance to the might of the aroused free peoples of the world stands forth in awful clarity as an example to the people of Japan. The might that now converges on Japan is immeasurably greater than that which, when applied to the resisting Nazis, necessarily laid waste to the lands, the industry and the method of life of the whole German people. The full application of our military power, backed by our resolve, will mean the inevitable and complete destruction of the Japanese armed forces and just as inevitably the utter devastation of the Japanese homeland.

(4) The time has come for Japan to decide whether she will continue to be controlled by those self-willed militaristic advisers whose unintelligent calculations have brought the Empire of Japan to the threshold of annihilation, or whether she will follow the path of reason.

(5) Following are our terms. We will not deviate from them. There are no alternatives. We shall brook no delay.

(6) There must be eliminated for all time the authority and influence of those who have deceived and misled the people of Japan into embarking on world conquest, for we insist that a new order of peace, security and justice will be impossible until irresponsible militarism is driven from the world.

(7) Until such a new order is established *and* until there is convincing proof that Japan's war-making power is destroyed, points in Japanese territory to be designated by the Allies shall be occupied to secure the achievement of the basic objectives we are here setting forth.

(8) The terms of the Cairo Declaration shall be carried out and Japanese sovereignty shall be limited to the islands of Honshu, Hokkaido, Kyushu, Shikoku and such minor islands as we determine.

(9) The Japanese military forces, after being completely disarmed, shall be permitted to return to their homes with the opportunity to lead peaceful and productive lives.

(10) We do not intend that the Japanese shall be enslaved as a race or de-

stroyed as a nation, but stern justice shall be meted out to all war criminals, including those who have visited cruelties upon our prisoners. The Japanese Government shall remove all obstacles to the revival and strengthening of democratic tendencies among the Japanese people. Freedom of speech, of religion, and of thought, as well as respect for the fundamental human rights shall be established.

(11) Japan shall be permitted to maintain such industries as will sustain her economy and permit the exaction of just reparations in kind, but not those which would enable her to re-arm for war. To this end, access to, as distinguished from control of, raw materials shall be permitted. Eventual Japanese participation in world trade relations shall be permitted.

(12) The occupying forces of the Allies shall be withdrawn from Japan as soon as these objectives have been accomplished and there has been established in accordance with the freely expressed will of the Japanese people a peacefully inclined and responsible government.

(13) We call upon the government of Japan to proclaim now the unconditional surrender of all Japanese armed forces, and to provide proper and adequate assurances of their good faith in such action. The alternative for Japan is prompt and utter destruction.

10

Postwar America

I have said that American historical thought generally has a contemporaneous character. In the case of postwar history this contemporaneous character is particularly strong. Partly because much of the data is not yet available, interpretations of postwar history are extremely diverse. Furthermore, interpretation is frequently affected by the historian's political standpoint. The "revisionist" interpretation of postwar American foreign policy is a well-known example. Approaches to postwar history differ considerably in nuance depending on how historians evaluate the "Liberal Establishment" represented by the Kennedy administration. While fully aware that it is rather risky to include the period up to the 1970s in a discussion of American history, I shall dare to attempt to sketch roughly the "facts" of the thirty years following the war.

During these thirty years, America exercised great influence in the world, not only militarily, but economically and culturally as well. When it manifested the "arrogance of power," it ran into limits both externally and internally. With lost prestige and self-confidence, American society was thrown into confusion. In racial strife and the war in Vietnam, America, two hundred years afer independence, has confronted, both physically and spiritually, profound ordeals, and is overcoming them.

The Cold War and the Fair Deal

With the dropping of the atomic bombs, the United States was able to bring an end to the Second World War. Setting aside the question of whether the dropping of the atomic bombs was solely intended to bring an early end to the war or whether it was meant at the same time to be the first strategic blow in postwar international policy, the development of a nuclear weapon with devastating destructive power caused the U.S. to feel unsure of its own security. Because the secret of atomic weapons could not remain an American monopoly forever, the loss of the natural, or "free," security which it had enjoyed until now was only a matter of time. Thus the conclusion of the Second World War was accompanied by tacit fears of another world war, which must be a cataclysmic one, on the part of policy-makers.

The common people, however, welcomed the end of the war as a "return to normalcy." They looked forward to the end of the long-term total mobilization system, and the soldiers on the battlefronts and their families in particular sought a rapid demobilization. Some soldiers overseas even rioted. The government, under public pressure, had little choice but to effect a rapid and wide-scale demobilization. The army, which at the end of the war numbered 8,260,000 troops, was reduced by the summer of 1946 to 1,500,000 and in 1947 to as few as 550,000. Wartime economic controls were relaxed; in October 1945 the War Production Board was disbanded, and the system of commodity rationing (except that for sugar) was abolished.

With the end of the war, however, the internal unity which had been maintained in the face of external enemies and under Roosevelt's powerful leadership slackened. Truman, who became "president by accident" after Roosevelt's death, had to tread a fine line in confronting the strong demands of diversified interests. The people were anxious that the full employment which had been achieved by the wartime economy be maintained despite the disappearance of wartime demands, and they feared the return of depression and unemployment. Business demanded the complete abolition of price controls; labor unions sought wage increases, and strikes occurred frequently. The Truman administration desired the continuation of price controls, but under popular pressure for a "return to normalcy," the regulations collapsed, prices rose, and the administration had to try desperately to devise an anti-inflation policy. In order to prevent the return of the depression, a full-employment bill was introduced and enacted as the Employment Act of 1946. This act was a compromise, but under it, the federal government came to bear full responsibility for maximum employment. This act also created the President's Council of Economic Advisers to conduct long-term economic analysis and planning.

Roosevelt's sudden death and the end of the war provided a good opportunity for the Republican Party, which had been out of power for a long time, to regain the majority. In fact, in the midterm elections of 1946, the Republicans became a majority in both houses of Congress for the first time in sixteen years. Taking advantage of their victory, the Republicans embarked on a campaign to revise the New Deal policies; in June 1947, overriding President Truman's veto, they succeeded in enacting the Taft-Hartley Labor-Management Relations Act and revised the Wagner (National Labor Relations) Act.

Meanwhile, the postwar international political situation was deteriorating, and tension between America and the Soviet Union gradually mounted. Remembering the military intervention against it which had followed the First World War, the Soviet Union attempted to make Eastern Europe its own sphere of influence; the Allies, centering around England, feared the advance of the Soviet Union in Europe and endeavored to secure the Balkan region. Already during the war, the conflict between the Soviet Union (Stalin) and England (Churchill) had been covertly growing and had required continuous mediation by America (Roosevelt). In other words, England's traditional balance-of-power concept and America's concept of collective security—the United Nations system based on cooperation among the three superpowers—were in conflict.

After the war, however, the U.S. began to move closer to the English view. In March 1946, Churchill propounded his vision of the "Iron Curtain" and warned the United States to watch Soviet behavior closely. Truman also adopted an uncompromising position towards the Soviets; he opposed Secretary of Commerce Henry Wallace, who advocated reconciliation with the Soviets, and finally, in September 1946, removed him from office. England, severely impoverished after the war, had to abandon its aid to Greece and Turkey, and the United States was asked to shoulder the responsibility. This meant that the U.S. was forced to commit itself to the European balance of power both economically and militarily.

The Truman Doctrine of March 1947 represented an appeal to the American people for their support of this commitment. The Truman administration framed its appeal for aid to Greece and Turkey in terms of the broad issue of a confrontation between two political systems, or two ways of life—a free system and a totalitarian (*i.e.*, communist) system. In order to remobilize a people who were absorbed in a mood of demobilization, it had to appeal not merely politically, in terms of a conflict between the two superpowers, America and the Soviet Union, but also ideologically, in terms of a conflict between the "free world" and communism. This grandiose ideological formula cast American foreign policy in an inflexible mold, that of the so-called "Cold War diplomacy." In May 1947 the U.S. formally committed itself to aiding Greece and Turkey—and, in the process, to involvement in postwar European politics.

The following month, Secretary of State George C. Marshall, in a speech at Harvard University, proposed what became known as the Marshall Plan; if the European countries together proposed a reconstruction plan, he said, America was prepared to respond to it with large-scale, long-term assistance. In response, a number of Western European countries created the Organization of European Economic Cooperation (OEEC). Partly in response to the shock of the establishment of a communist regime in Czechoslovakia in February 1948, the U.S. Congress two months later passed the Foreign Assistance Act and created the Economic Cooperation Administration; in the following three years the U.S. gave aid totaling approximately $12 billion for Europe's economic rehabilitation. The Marshall Plan, while accomplishing its major purpose of countering the Soviets by aiding Europe's economic recovery, also expanded the market for American exports.

The 1948 presidential election came in the midst of strong dissension over the course of both domestic and foreign policy. The Democratic Party nominated Truman, but it faced the election severely weakened by internal dissension. The southern conservative delegation, which opposed the Truman administration's policy of guaranteeing the civil rights of blacks, walked out of the convention and nominated J. Strom Thurmond of South Carolina as their presidential candidate on a States' Rights ticket. At the same time a group from the Democratic left wing, who opposed the administration's hard-line policy toward the Soviet Union, organized the Progressive Party around Henry Wallace, and ran him as their presidential candidate. With both the left and right wings splitting from the party, the prospects for a Democratic victory seemed slim. The Republican Party, seeing its chance to regain power, again nominated Thomas Dewey, who was well known as the able governor of New York. Public opinion polls predicted a Republican victory. The result of the election, however, was a victory for Truman. This seeming "miracle" showed that the structure of the Democratic majority which had been created under Al Smith and Franklin Roosevelt had not been destroyed. The image of the Democratic Party as the party of the "have-nots," and the fact that enormous numbers of people had benefited directly from the policies of the Democratic administration under the New Deal and the Second World War, caused the voters to seek a "continuation" under the Democrats, rather than a "change" with the Republicans.

In his inaugural address, the victorious Truman promised to carry out a Fair Deal policy. In other words, he intended to take over and expand the New Deal in his domestic policies. The raising of the minimum wage, the expansion of public housing, the stabilization of agricultural prices, and the expansion of social security were undertaken. However, Truman was unable to achieve the guarantee of civil rights for blacks or the abolition of the Taft-Hartley Act, both of which he had publicly pledged. The Democratic Party had a majority in both Houses, but the alliance of southern conservative Democrats and Republicans exercised a powerful veto in Congress.

In due course, however, international political tensions overshadowed the Fair Deal in domestic politics, and with the outbreak of the Korean War in 1950, America again changed from a welfare state into a warfare state. In actuality, the domestic political milieu had already been transformed by the Cold War. Almost simultaneously with the pronouncement of the Truman Doctrine, in March 1947, an executive order to investigate the loyalty of federal government employees was issued. In 1950 the McCarran Act, or the Internal Security Act, was passed over presidential veto, and the government began to suppress so-called "subversive movements," which in practice meant supposedly communist-related groups. In this context, Senator Joseph R. McCarthy began his anticommunist demagogy. In the name of protecting freedom, these anticommunist activities resulted more often than not in the suppression of freedom.[1]

In July 1947, shortly after the announcement of the Truman Doctrine, the National Security Act was passed, and the National Security Council was created as a unified organ coordinating all aspects of diplomatic, military, and domestic affairs in order to prepare for total war. A Department of Defense was created to unify the three services, and the Central Intelligence Agency was created as the headquarters for intelligence-gathering activities. The Selective Service System was established in June 1948, and preparations were made for remobilization. Parallel with these preparations of the domestic system, the North Atlantic Treaty was signed in April 1949; twelve countries, including the United States, formed a regional collective defense organization for the North Atlantic. With this treaty the U.S. committed itself for the first time to a military alliance in peacetime, and it began to give military and economic aid on a large scale to the West European countries. Meanwhile, in Asia, a revolutionary war was under way in China, with the Nationalist government and the Chinese Communist Party continuing their fierce struggle. The United States attempted intermediation but failed, and the Nationalist Party government disintegrated. The main body of the Nationalists, from Generalissimo Chiang Kaishek on down, moved to Taiwan, and in October 1949 the Chinese People's Republic was established. This was a severe shock to the U.S., which since the end of the nineteenth century had regarded China as a latent market for American goods, civilization, and Christianity, and since the establishment of the Nationalist Party government had cherished a sentimental identification with this "sister republic." Partly in response to the propaganda of the so-

[1] There are various interpretations of McCarthyism, ranging from one which regards it as temporary hysteria based on the acrobatics of McCarthy the individual, to one which regards it as a structural phenomenon. Even when one regards it as a product of the Cold War system, it is insufficient to dismiss it merely as an anticommunist movement within the context of capitalism versus communism. From a broader perspective, it was, after all, deeply connected with the American nation's inevitable need for artificial unity, composed as it is of various races and nationalities. From a narrower perspective, it was closely linked to the Republican Party's desire to seize the reins of government, having been out of power since 1933.

called "China Lobby," many Americans regarded the communist takeover as the "loss" of China. The responsibility for this "loss" was ascribed to the Truman administration, especially to Secretary of State Dean Acheson and those in charge of Asian policies in the State Department, and they were made the objects of violent attack by the right wing of the Republican Party. Just at this juncture, in the summer of 1950, North Korean forces crossed the 38th parallel into South Korea, and war broke out. The U.S. immediately decided to aid South Korea and sent troops on the basis of a resolution by the United Nations, and General Douglas MacArthur, the commander of the Allied forces occupying Japan, was appointed Supreme Commander of the United Nations forces. The UN forces, which had been pushed back to Pusan in the south, mounted a counterattack by means of a landing at Inchon; having crossed the 38th parallel, they advanced to the Manchurian border, finally provoking the participation of the Chinese "Volunteer Corps." MacArthur was willing to risk all-out war with China, but Truman, who feared a total war in Asia, relieved the General of his duties in April 1951, and America divided violently over the Korean War. Public opinion supported MacArthur, and he was welcomed upon his return as a victorious general, but eventually this enthusiasm abated, and sentiment which favored an end to the war grew strong. The truce negotiations which opened in July 1951 were extremely complicated and prolonged; in the cold war situation, the distinction between war and peace was ambiguous. The American people, confronting a limited war new to their experience, were tormented by frustration and impatience.

America's policy toward Japan also changed its direction as the Cold War developed. After Japan's surrender in accordance with the Potsdam Declaration, Allied forces led by Americans had occupied Japan, and General MacArthur had been conducting the administration of the occupation as Supreme Commander for the Allied Powers (SCAP). On September 22, 1945, barely a month after the end of the war, the U.S. government had announced its policy aiming at the demilitarization and democratization of Japan. This policy included such measures as the destruction of Japan's military power, the punishment of war criminals, the purge of public officials, and the dissolution of the *zaibatsu*. Indeed, the initial stage of the occupation was managed in accordance with this policy line. However, with the shift in the international situation the U.S. government gradually came to see Japan part of the United States's anti-Soviet, anti-Chinese security system, and the possibility of Japan's rearmament began to be contemplated. The establishment of the Chinese Peoples' Republic in the fall of 1949, the conclusion of a Sino-Soviet alliance in the spring of 1950, and the outbreak of the Korean War in the summer of that year significantly altered the outlook of the occupation forces in Japan, and at the same time changed the role of Japan as an occupied country. In September 1951 the Japanese Peace Treaty and the Japan-United States Security Treaty were signed in San Francisco. Japan, in return for its independence, would become one part of America's Cold War system. In fact, during the Korean War Japan functioned as a supply base for American troops, and the Japanese economy benefited from the "special procurements" orders from the American forces.

The Eisenhower and Kennedy Administrations

As the Korean War was being fought abroad, and McCarthyism and inflation were raging at home, the 1952 election was held. The Republican presidential candidate was widely expected to be Senator Robert A. Taft, who was known as "Mr. Republican." However, many Republicans questioned how much the orthodox Taft, with his strongly anti-New Deal, isolationist position, could actually appeal to the voters. Accordingly, the "national hero" General Dwight D. Eisenhower, with his sincere personality and wide popularity, was nominated instead, and was promoted with the slogan "I like Ike." Senator Richard M. Nixon from California, a well-known champion of anticommunism, was nominated for vice-president. On the Democratic side, Truman showed no interest in renomination, and eventually the governor of Illinois, Adlai E. Stevenson, was nominated. The urbane Stevenson obtained the support of intellectuals, but he lacked mass appeal, and the election ended in sweeping victory for Eisenhower. The Republican Party thus retook the reins of government for the first time in twenty years, but it is doubtful whether one can consider this the victory of the party itself. In Congress, the Republican Party barely managed to win a majority, and in the mid-term election of 1954 it again fell to the postion of a minority party. In 1956, though Eisenhower was reelected, the Republicans remained the minority party. The election of 1952 must be regarded as the personal victory of Ike rather than of the Republican Party.

At his inauguration, Eisenhower emphasized a change from the preceding Democratic administration; and certainly an anti-New Deal, anti-internationalist mood was dominant. However, this did not necessarily imply that wide-scale policy changes were carried out under the Republican administration. Despite the Republican Party's emphasis on financial retrenchment, vast public expenditures were by now regarded as necessary in order to guarantee the smooth functioning of the American economy. The continuation and expansion of social security measures were considered necessary in order to maintain the support of the masses. Thus, the New Deal as a symbol was rejected, but the New Deal as a policy could not be rejected, for it had already been built into the modern American system. Neither could America, in the postwar world, return to its traditional position of isolationism. The only question was whether its world-wide involvement would be unilateral or multilateral, in cooperation with other Western countries such as England. The Republican Party, which had criticized the foreign policy of the Democratic administration as an "appeasement policy" and as Anglophilia, could not avoid presenting, at least in its rhetoric, an increasingly firm stance against communism.

In the Eisenhower administration, many financiers were appointed to cabinet posts, beginning with the selection of the president of General Motors, Charles E. Wilson, as Secretary of Defense. The well-known Wall Street lawyer John Foster Dulles was appointed Secretary of State. Eisenhower was not a leader with an egocentric personality but rather a coordinator of various interests. He had used this ability during his military career, and he capitalized on it as president by appointing advisers. Former New Hampshire governor Sherman Adams, as Eisenhower's special assistant, played the role of chief of staff.

One decisive factor in Ike's election victory was the pledge he made at the close of the campaign that he would go to Korea if elected president. The people, tired of the seemingly endless war without definite victory, sought its early conclusion, and they expected that Ike's trip to Korea would somehow bring this about. Thus, in December, only one month after his election, Eisenhower inspected the Korean battle lines. The truce negotiations somehow progressed, and a cease-fire agreement was concluded at Panmunjom in July 1953. This did not, however, mean the arrival of peace in Asia. During the Korean War, not only did American and Chinese troops fight directly on the Korean battlefield; the American Seventh Fleet, cruising the Taiwan Straits, also prevented the "liberation" of Taiwan by China. In December 1954 America concluded a Mutual Defense Pact with Taiwan's Chiang Kai-shek regime and became committed to the defense of the island.

Shortly after Eisenhower's election, but before he took office, President Truman announced the successful testing of the hydrogen bomb. In January 1954 Secretary of State Dulles proposed his New Look policy, a massive retaliation strategy. As a result of the spectacular development of nuclear weapons, the United States and the Soviet Union came to possess the means of massive slaughter, and the "balance of terror" came into being. As the tension between East and West mounted, it became clear that some method must be devised to prevent the outbreak of a third world war which would destroy mankind. In March 1953, Stalin had died; this caused a change in the internal power situation in the Soviet Union, and signs of an East-West thaw began to appear. In July 1955, a summit conference attended by British Prime Minister Anthony Eden, Soviet Prime Minister Nikolai Bulganin, French Prime Minister Edgar Fauré, and President Eisenhower was held in Geneva. The leaders discussed problems such as disarmament and the unification of Germany, but no agreement was reached. On the other hand, while East-West talks continued, the nuclear weapons race intensified, and in the summer of 1957 the Soviet Union succeeded in developing an intercontinental ballistic missile (ICBM). That October, the Soviets launched the man-made satellite Sputnik I, making the competition to develop new military and space technology all the more intense. The repeated testing of nuclear weapons and the threat of a nuclear war aroused public opinion and gradually gave rise to strong opposition within the United States. Soviet Premier Nikita Khrushchev visited the United States and met with Eisenhower at Camp David to seek a solution to the Berlin crisis. The trend toward a thaw became stronger, but in 1960 an ultra-high-flying reconnaissance plane, a U-2, crashed in Soviet territory, revealing the fact that the U.S. was conducting reconnaissance flights. A summit conference scheduled in Paris was cancelled, and East-West tension continued.

1960 was also a presidential election year. The Republican Party had grasped the reins of government by capitalizing on the personal appeal of Ike, and now its major task was building on this foundation in order to make the Republican Party itself a majority party. In the final analysis, Ike's administration had basically continued the policies of the Democratic administration in both domestic and foreign affairs. In this respect it could not but incur the criticism of its own right wing for "me-tooism"— imitating the Democratic Party. The Democrats had their own problems. Although a great number of people had benefited from the vast public spending since the New Deal, these people had now become middle class and were inclined to desert the Democratic Party, the party of the "have-nots." The children of the party's supporters, who were once from urban slums, had now moved to suburban residential areas of the large cities, and tended to support the Republican Party. The Republican Party nominated as Ike's successor Richard Nixon, who had served as vice-president under Eisenhower. The Democratic Party nominated the young (forty-three-year-old) John F. Kennedy. The second son of the millionaire ambassador to England and a descendant of Irish immigrants, Kennedy was expected to infuse a new style into the political world. One notable feature of this election campaign between the two young political opponents was a series of public television debates, spread over four days. As was fitting in an age of mass media, people in every part of America saw these men debate before their very eyes. In the end, Kennedy won by the narrow margin of 110,000 votes, and the Democratic Party regained the White House.

Seen in the context of American political history, Kennedy's victory was significant in that for the first time a Catholic descendant of Irish immigrants came to occupy the White House. The long political monopoly of the White Anglo-Saxon Protestant (WASP) majority was gradually being broken, and Catholicism or Irish descent was no longer an insuperable barrier in presidential politics.[2] This suggested that other minorities would also come to demand a share of power.

In his inaugural address Kennedy, with a rather stirring rhetorical flourish, stated his aspirations to the people. The major problem which confronted the Kennedy administration was basically the Cold War problem, *i.e.*, the establishment of peaceful coexistence with the Soviet Union. Kennedy appointed a number of faculty members from Harvard and the Massachusetts Institute of Technology (MIT) as presidential assistants, undersecretaries, and ambassadors: MacGeorge Bundy, Arthur Schlesinger, Jr., W. W. Rostow, Edwin O. Reischauer, and John K. Galbraith are well-known examples. The president of the Ford Motor Company, Robert S. McNamara, was appointed Secretary of Defense, and developed foreign and military policies based on cool calculation. In such international crises as the one in Berlin in 1961 and the installation of Soviet missiles in Cuba in 1962, Kennedy confronted Soviet Prime Minister Khrushchev, and succeeded in avoiding war. One could say that both the United States and the Soviet Union recognized the futility of nuclear war. The trend toward conciliation and coexistence between America and the Soviet Union was confirmed by the Cuban missile crisis and its resolution, and the Cold War, which was based on the rivalry between the two major powers, America and the Soviet Union, was in this sense being resolved. In fact, in June 1963, in a speech at American University, Kennedy advocated reconciliation between America and the Soviet Union, and in August of that year a Partial Nuclear Test Ban Treaty among the U.S., the Soviet Union, and England was signed in Moscow.

[2] The image of the Kennedy family as a born elite is strong, especially in Japan. Certainly, the Kennedy children were born to wealth and able to receive the best educations; their father was ambassador to England, and the sons were Harvard graduates. On the other hand, the Kennedys had crossed the Atlantic as poor immigrants at the time of the famine in Ireland in 1848, and were a typical Irish immigrant family which made its way to the slums of Boston. Over a period of nearly one hundred years, they climbed the ladder of success step by step, finally struggling to the White House itself. In this respect the Kennedy family's history could be said to be a typical success story, rather than typical of the traditional elite in America, such as the Adams family.

This U.S.-Soviet reconciliation, however, did not directly mean the arrival of world peace. Although it gave rise to a policy of East-West coexistence, it did not bridge the gulf between South and North. In other words, although it aimed at the solution of European problems, it did not resolve the problems of Asia. As China grew increasingly powerful, the conflict between China and the Soviet Union intensified. China also criticized American imperialism. The Kennedy administration endeavored to avoid all-out war between America and the Soviet Union, but continued to prepare for possible local wars with conventional weapons. This included the preparation of military force which could deal with guerrilla warfare in politically unstable Southeast Asia. Under the Kennedy administration, military aid to the South Vietnamese government increased. It would not be an overstatement to say that the later tragic intervention in Vietnam began during the Kennedy administration, whatever the president's personal intentions may have been.

Another element in the Kennedy administration's foreign policy which must be noted is the intervention, soon after Kennedy took office, in the internal affairs of Cuba, and the failure of that intervention. This incident revealed the limits of the traditional Monroe Doctrine. When outlining the foreign-policy events of these years, one must also remember the promotion of a liberalization of trade by the Kennedy Trade Act of 1962.

Essentially, the Kennedy administration was foreign affairs-oriented. The opposition of the conservative Democrats in Congress made it difficult to develop effective domestic policies through legislation. Of all the domestic issues, one which the Kennedy administration did confront seriously was the problem of racial discrimination.

Racial Tensions and the Vietnam War

After reconstruction ended in 1877, a system of racial segregation of blacks had been established in the southern states through the revision of the state constitutions and the enactment of so-called "Jim Crow laws" discriminating against blacks, and blacks had become politically, economically, and socially alienated. The 1896 "separate but equal" decision by the Supreme Court (Plessy *v.*

Ferguson) made this system legal despite the provisions of the Fourteenth Amendment to the Constitution. In spite of the founding of the National Association for the Advancement of Colored People (NAACP) in 1910, and despite the efforts of black leaders such as Booker T. Washington, W. E. B. Du Bois, and Marcus Garvey, the reality of discrimination against blacks did not change: in this respect neither the progressive administrations nor the New Deal devised any effective policy.

Nonetheless, through such measures as unemployment relief, the New Deal assisted impoverished blacks. Many of them therefore switched their allegiance from the Republican Party to the Democratic Party, and they came to constitute a powerful bloc in the Roosevelt coalition of 1936. Since then the blacks' support of the Democratic Party has remained basically unchanged.

During the Second World War, many blacks either were drafted into the army and went overseas or worked in munitions factories all over the country. Thus, in order to successfully mobilize blacks as human resources under the wartime emergency, America needed to promote "integration" both militarily and economically. Meanwhile, blacks were acquiring self-confidence; their experiences in the north and overseas taught them that discrimination was the exception rather than the norm, and they gradually began to unite behind a movement for desegregation. Under such conditions, in 1944 the Supreme Court declared the "white primary" unconstitutional (Smith v. Allwright), and in 1948 President Truman ordered the abolition of racial segregation in the military forces. In 1954 the Supreme Court handed down a decision which declared segregation in public schools unconstitutional (Brown v. Board of Education of Topeka). Overturning the 1896 "separate but equal" decision, the Court ordered the lower courts to advance, "with all deliberate speed," the integration of white and black students in public schools.

This epochal decision turned the tide toward racial integration, but for that very reason, public opinion became deeply divided. Beginning with the boycott of segregated buses in Montgomery, Alabama, in 1955, blacks determinedly pushed forward their desegregation movement under outstanding leaders like Rev. Martin Luther King, Jr. Further, beginning with the Freedom Riders in 1961, young white activists from the north joined forces with the desegregation movement in the south. The advance of industrialization and urbanization in the south itself was also weakening the foundation of racial segregation in the region.

As integration progressed, however, opposition among southern whites grew, and a violent anti-integration movement emerged in the south. In the summer of 1957 an incident at a public high school in Little Rock, Arkansas, necessitated the dispatch of federal troops for its settlement. After Kennedy's Democratic administration took power, the conflict between the south's regional practice of segregation and the national system, which made an integrated, multiracial nation its basic goal, became increasingly intense. In the south violent incidents accompanied by acts of murder occurred one after another. In Birmingham, Alabama, in May 1963 federal troops were sent against the whites who violently opposed the desegregation movement, but the anxiety and worry of the whites caused a "white backlash" which spread to every region. Kennedy's visit to Texas in November 1963 was a gesture of reconciliation toward the southerners, but it resulted in his tragic death in Dallas.

The racial problem was further complicated by the increasing migration of blacks to northern cities, transforming the peculiar problem of the south into a national problem. The northward migration of blacks, which had begun gradually after the First World War, accelerated in the 1950s and 1960s; by 1970 the number of blacks living in regions outside the south would reach one-half of the total black population. Such migration resulted in the creation of black sections in the large northern cities, and the black population of the large northern cites increased rapidly. Although the black urbanites had equal status legally, they were often severely handicapped in matters of employment, occupation, and residence. Under the administration of Lyndon Baines Johnson, the 1964 Civil Rights Act was passed. At the same time, however, blacks, who had obtained equality under law, grew impatient when social and economic advances did not accompany these legal rights, and within the black movement the advocacy of radical "Black Power" began to grow strong. The black nationalism movement sought not integration with the white race and culture, but the separation of the black race and culture from the larger society. Black nationalists considered the mainstream of the black movement, represented by men such as King, who advocated integration as their goal and non-violent action as their method, too moderate, and they began to take part in violent actions. Beginning with the riot in 1965 in Watts, the black district of Los Angeles, race riots occurred every summer in the large cities, evoking the fear and countering violence of the white low-income class. This violent atmosphere within the country, however, was not unrelated to America's grand-scale exercise of violence overseas, the Vietnam War.

In 1945, after the defeat of Japan, Vietnam, which had been a French colony under Japanese occupation had declared its independence (quoting from the American Declaration of Independence of 1776) and established the Democratic Republic of Vietnam under the leadership of Ho Chi Minh. France attempted to reestablish control over its colony and built a separate regime in the south, and war broke out between France and the Vietnamese people. At first the U.S. showed no particular interest, but after the stiffening of the Cold War confrontation, the Chinese Revolution, and the Korean War, it began to regard the Vietnam conflict as a link in the global Cold War system. It recognized the South Vietnam regime of Bao Dai, and promised military aid. It is said that by 1954 the U.S. had supplied 70 percent of the French war expenses. The "domino theory," which held that the communization of Vietnam would open the way to the communization of all of Southeast Asia, became the basis of American policy toward Vietnam. As soon as the defeat of the French army became inevitable, in 1954, the desirability of direct American military intervention was earnestly discussed by the Eisenhower administration, but ultimately it was postponed due to the opposition of England as well as of the U.S. army. The 1954 Geneva Agreement, which provisionally divided Vietnam at the 17th parallel, was concluded without American participation, but the U.S. continued to give economic aid to the South Vietnamese regime. Soon the dissatisfaction of the people in South Vietnam with their government exploded; the People's Liberation Front was created, and an indigenous guerilla war began in the south. The U.S. sent military advisory groups to aid the government forces.

The Kennedy administration, in addition to sending investigative groups and increasing the number of military advisers to 12,000, also interfered in the domestic affairs of South Vietnam, supporting a *coup d'état* and attempting to stabilize the political situation in the region. Lyndon Johnson inherited the staff and policies of the Kennedy administration. In the election campaign of 1964, the Republican candidate, Barry Goldwater, who regarded "me-tooism" as defeatism, criticized the Democratic New Deal policies domestically and supported the white backlash against black desegregation. From a position of firm anticommunism, Goldwater advocated positive intervention in the Vietnam War, including the use of tactical nuclear weapons, making the Johnson administration policy appear moderate by comparison. Johnson, using the Tonkin Gulf Incident of August 1965 as a pretext, ordered the bombing of North Vietnamese naval bases. Receiving broad military authority by Congressional resolution, he began to escalate the military intervention without a formal declaration of war. Having won the 1964 election by a wide margin, Johnson claimed that the public approved his policies and continued to escalate the bombing of the north. In the spring of 1965, American troops themselves were put into combat, and the expeditionary forces expanded rapidly. The civil war escalated into an international war, and the Vietnam War became an American war. However, the American forces, despite their highly modernized and mechanized equipment, encountered considerable difficulties in fighting a guerilla war in this distant and unfamiliar land. Figuratively, the situation can be said to have resembled the desperate battle of the British regular army when it encountered an army of farmers on the American continent two hundred years earlier. For the American forces, no victory meant defeat, and for the Vietnamese People's Liberation Front, no defeat meant victory. As the war escalated and was prolonged, the U.S. began to lose not only the support of the Vietnamese, but also that of the West European countries. The Vietnam War was leading to America's international isolation. Even within the U.S. it became increasingly unpopular with the people.

During the postwar anticommunist Cold War period, military as well as economic intervention for the purpose of preventing the spread of communism had the general support of the American people, including those in the labor unions and the universities, partly because it maintained prosperity through vast military expenditures. During the Johnson administration, however, as the number of American casualties increased and the conscription of American youth grew more widespread, public opinion changed. Beginning in about 1965, first on the college campuses, the voice of opposition to the Vietnam War grew louder, and debates and protests of professors and students through "teach-ins" began to take place all over America. The opposition of the "New Left" led by young historians and the like, the criticism of the war from a position of traditional power diplomacy by scholars such as Hans Morgenthau, rebuttal from such intellectuals within the government as W. W. Rostow, and the desertion from the Johnson camp of old Kennedy advisers such as Arthur M. Schlesinger, Jr., all exposed deep divisions among American intellectuals over the Vietnam War. In Congress also, as in the case of the War of 1812 against England, the conflict between the hawks who supported the war and the doves who opposed it intensified. The opposition of powerful legislators such as James William Fulbright, chairman of the Senate Foreign Relations Committee, became explicit. Within the government as well, even people such as Secretary of Defense McNamara, who had originally been the center of the Vietnam policy, recognized its failure, and some, opposing Johnson, resigned.

Under such conditions, confidence in President Johnson was lost both at home and abroad. All over America demonstrations against the Vietnam War raged, and thousands of young men refused to fight the war. Within the armed forces themselves, the number of deserters and drug addicts grew. Moreover, despite the increase in troops and war expenditures, the situation in Vietnam did not improve, and it became clear that day by day the U.S. was becoming stuck more deeply in a quagmire. The vast war expenditures were becoming a burden on the American economy, and some people in business circles began to criticize the war. In March 1968, Johnson announced a halt to the bombing for the sake of peace negotiations, and stated that he would not seek reelection in the fall.

The intensification and prolongation of the war, combined with the continuing racial strife, gave rise to division, deterioration, and violence within American society. On the one hand, such factors as frustration at the failure in Vietnam, economic distress due to inflation and heavy taxation, and anxiety over the emergence of black power intertwined, and the number of people who supported the radical right wing increased. The John Birch Society, established in the mid-1950s, was one radical right-wing organization; it rested on vigorous anticommunism and a simplistic Christian fundamentalism. This radical right-wing movement, which succeeded the McCarthyism of the 1950s, expanded its influence, centering in the southwest, and made the 1964 Republican presidential candidate, Goldwater, its spokesman on the main stage of politics. In the election of 1968, however, it found its representative in the governor of Alabama, George Wallace, who, having left the Democratic Party, organized the American Independent Party and became its presidential candidate. Wallace found his strongest support among the poorer white workers and farmers.

With the racial tension at home, the Vietnam War abroad, and the fear of the draft in their personal lives, young people lost confidence in the government, and in adults in general. They turned this distrust toward the education and administration authorities of the universities, which had become part of the managerial society, and student protests occurred on many campuses. This protest against the liberal intellectuals, who had been in charge of the system since the New Deal, was also funneled into the "counter-culture," which encompassed everything from long hair to sexual liberation. Politically, these young people tried to set a new course based on spontaneous and temporary organizations. One expression of this trend was the campaign activity of young people in 1968 in support of Senator Eugene McCarthy, the peace candidate of the Democratic Party. This New Left movement, while sharply critical of the establishment, was, except for the basic goals of withdrawal from Vietnam and the elimination of racial discrimination, not necessarily in agreement on concrete programs, and did not have unified plans.

In April 1968, Martin Luther King, Jr., was assassinated in Memphis, Tennessee, and enraged blacks rioted in various places beginning with the capital city of Washington. That same April student strife at Columbia University became violent; students occupied the office of the university president and were chased out by police. Similar incidents occurred all over the nation. In July, on a campaign tour, Senator Robert Kennedy, who was critical of U.S. involvement in Vietnam, was assassinated in Los Angeles, and the Democratic National Convention which opened in Chicago in August turned into a bloodbath when antiwar demonstrations were suppressed by the police and state troops.

The Democratic Party finally nominated Vice-President Hubert Humphrey, and the Republican convention nominated Richard Nixon. Nixon, since his defeat by Kennedy in the 1960 election, had strengthened his ties with the local Republican Party organizations. He ran under the slogan "law and order," trying to appeal to the masses who felt anxiety about crime and racial violence in the large cities. In the end Nixon was elected president by a small margin. The American Independent Party's Wallace received 9,500,000 votes, or 13.5 percent of the popular vote, an unexpected success for a third party.

Nixon appointed Henry Kissinger, professor of international politics at Harvard University, as special assistant in charge of national security, and developed the so-called Nixon-Kissinger foreign policy, which in a sense made classic balance-of-power theory its basis. Utilizing the conflict between China and the Soviet Union, it planned a détente between the U.S. and the Soviets and between the U.S. and China, and tried to maintain the international *status quo*. During the election campaign Nixon had said little about the Vietnam War, but in the Nixon Doctrine of 1969 he made clear his fundamental policy, which would combine a reduction of the American military force in Asia with an increase in the defense burden borne by the Asian countries themselves. This constituted a reorientation in America's foreign involvement, which had expanded continually after the Second World War, and attempted to limit intervention in proportion to America's national (including economic) strength. It also meant the Vietnamization of the Vietnam War, which had become Americanized, through the "withdrawal with honor" of the American military. However, before this withdrawal could be effected, it was necessary to achieve a normalization of relations between America and China in accordance with the logic of power politics. Nixon visited Peking in February 1972 and took a major step toward the improvement of Sino-American relations. In May, he visited the

Soviet Union and planned the "easing of tension" between the U.S. and the USSR. Nixon, champion of anticommunism and a hero of the Cold War, out of his thoroughgoing power-politics considerations, shifted American foreign policy out of the Cold War framework which had had as its principal axis the bipolar confrontation between America and the Soviet Union. Nixon changed this basis of postwar American foreign policy to a more complicated triangular structure including the U.S., the Soviet Union, and China.

In relations with American allies, the West European countries and Japan, Nixon not only took the alliance relationships for granted and therefore in a sense neglected them, but also began to perceive these nations as economic competitors. Indeed, the economic burden of the Vietnam War had markedly weakened the ability of America's economy to compete abroad, and Western Europe and Japan had recovered their economic strength. Japan in particular, through the rapid expansion of its productivity, came to stand in a competitive position toward the United States. At the beginning of the 1970s, the postwar relationship between Japan and America entered a new phase.

In the context of this détente with the Soviet Union and with China, the Nixon administration urged North Vietnam to negotiate a settlement of the still ongoing Vietnam War, using the threat of resuming bombings of the North. In the election of 1972 the Democratic Party nominated George S. McGovern, senator from South Dakota and a harsh critic of the Vietnam War. Not surprisingly, the Republican Party renominated Nixon. McGovern, who was supported by many amateur student campaigners, not only was an antiwar candidate, but was perceived by large numbers of Americans as a supporter of the "counterculture." Many in the established organizations of the Democratic Party and the labor unions were reluctant to support him. Nixon's spectacular diplomatic successes, the prospect of the end of the Vietnam War, and his appeal to white southerners put McGovern all the more on the defensive, and he suffered a crushing defeat.

After his landslide victory in the election, Nixon advanced his foreign policy with confidence. In Paris in January 1973, a truce was established. The American military began a complete withdrawal. Thus, insofar as the United States was concerned, the Vietnam War came to an end. This war had required forces of more than 500,000; fatalities exceeded those of the Korean War, and costs exceeded those of the First World War for the U.S. It was the longest-lasting war in American history, and the scar it had inflicted on American society was deep.

The postwar Cold War policy and the Vietnam War had expanded American military intervention overseas virtually without restriction; the U.S. had come to consider itself, and often acted like, a "world policeman." The quagmire of the Vietnam War, however, had demonstrated the limits of America's military, economic, and moral strength. This inevitably brought about devastation within the country, the result of what Senator Fulbright had called "the arrogance of power." The expansion and abuse of power abroad were paralleled by the concentration and abuse of power within, as the Supreme Court recognized in its ruling in favor of press publication of government documents in the Pentagon Papers case (see the excerpt appended to this chapter). National power centering on the military authority of the president in the name of national security had grown excessive and had begun to violate the rights of the people. The Watergate Incident was merely one aspect of the abuse and corruption of this abnormally expanded presidential power. Once the details of the Watergate Incident were brought to light by the efforts of the press, beginning with the *Washington Post*, people came to harbor a deep fear of the abuse of power. Criticism of President Nixon was heard from many quarters, until finally the opposition of the courts and Congress, including its Republican members, drove him to resign the presidency in August 1974. In the end, the tradition of constitutionalism—limited government, protection of human rights by the separation of powers, and the system of checks and balances—functioned effectively.

With Nixon's resignation, Vice-President Gerald Ford took office as the thirty-eighth president. Ford originally had not been elected vice-president, but appointed by presidential nomination. This meant that he became president without election. Ford retained Kissinger as Secretary of State, and continued the policies of the Nixon era. By advocating openness in contrast to Nixon's secrecy, he tried to restore the link which had been severed between the president and the people.[3]

In 1976 the United States of America celebrated its Bicentennial. During its two-hundred year history, the nation has faced many crises and turning points: the era of the Civil War, in which America experienced the collision of the south and the north over slavery and transformed itself into an industrial nation; the turn of the century, when the nation confronted the social crisis symbolized by the disappearance of the frontier and adjusted internally by progressivism and externally by becoming a world power; the 1930s and 1940s, during which America confronted the Great Depression and the threat of Nazi Germany and Japan and became, through the Second World War, a superpower. These can be said to have been periods of crisis and turning points in American history. In each of these eras, America, while passing through the crises, continued to expand and develop. However, are not the crises which America faces in the 1970s somewhat different from these? These crises must be conquered not by expansion, but by self-restraint; not by self-confidence, but by self-examination. Success in meeting the challenge will be measured not by quantitative expansion, but by qualitative change. This in itself may indicate that "America has come of age."

---

[3] I cite the tradition of constitutionalism (an expression somewhat more old-fashioned than the expression "democracy" used in the Japanese mass media, but for that very reason, a more appropriate one) as the ultimate cause of Nixon's resignation. Nonetheless, one must remember the importance of party politics as the more direct cause, and in particular that it was a voluntary resignation rather than a resignation due to impeachment. In the more than forty years since Franklin D. Roosevelt's assumption of office in 1933, the Republican Party had produced two presidents, Eisenhower and Nixon, but had held a majority in Congress for a mere four years. It had been a minority party for thirty-six years, a perpetual opposition party. The Republican Party hoped that Nixon, who advocated domestic "law and order" and a "withdrawal with honor" from Vietnam, would be the salvation of the entire party. If Nixon had been brought before an impeachment trial, it not only would have damaged Nixon himself, but would have been a fatal blow to the Republican Party. Because the American president not only plays the functional role of prime minister but also is expected to play the dignified role of a king as a symbol of national unity, it became a problem beyond that of the president as an individual. At this point, for the Republican Party leaders, retiring "tricky," "dirty" Nixon and substituting mediocre but "clean" Ford was a necessary calculation for the party, which must deal with the electorate. The relief with which the American people almost uniformly greeted Nixon's resignation and Ford's assumption of office demonstrated that this calculation was correct.

Documents

Harry S. Truman, Message to Congress, March 12, 1947

. . . At the present moment in world history nearly every nation must choose between alternative ways of life. The choice is too often not a free one.

One way of life is based upon the will of the majority, and is distinguished by free institutions, representative government, free elections, guarantees of individual liberty, freedom of speech and religion, and freedom from political oppression.

The second way of life is based upon the will of the minority forcibly imposed upon the majority. It relies upon terror and oppression, a controlled press and radio, fixed elections, and the suppression of personal freedoms.

I believe that it must be the policy of the United States to support free peoples who are resisting attempted subjugation by armed minorities or by outside pressures.

I believe that we must assist free peoples to work out their own destinies in their own way.

I believe that our help should be primarily through economic and financial aid which is essential to economic stability and orderly political processes.

The world is not static, and the status quo is not sacred. But we cannot allow changes in the status quo in violation of the charter of the United Nations by such methods as coercion, or by such subterfuges as political infiltration. In helping free and independent nations to maintain their freedom, the United States will be giving effect to the principles of the charter of the United Nations. . . .

George C. Marshall, Address at Harvard University, June 6, 1947

. . . The truth of the matter is that Europe's requirements for the next 3 or 4 years of foreign food and other essential products—principally from America—are so much greater than her present ability to pay that she must have substantial additional help, or face economic, social, and political deterioration of a very grave character.

The remedy lies in breaking the vicious circle and restoring the confidence of European people in the economic future of their own countries and of Europe as a whole. The manufacturer and the farmer throughout wide areas must be able and willing to exchange their products for currencies the continuing value of which is not open to question.

Aside from the demoralizing effect on the world at large and the possibilities of disturbances arising as a result of the desperation of the people concerned, the consequences to the economy of the United States should be apparent to all. It is logical that the United States should do whatever it is able to do to assist in the return of normal economic health in the world, without which there can be no political stability and no assured peace. Our policy is directed not against any county or doctrine but against hunger, poverty, desperation, and chaos. Its purpose should be the revival of a working economy in the world so as to permit the emergence of political and social conditions in which free institutions can exist. Such assistance, I am convinced, must not be on a piece-meal basis as various crises develop. Any assistance that this Government may render in the future should provide a cure rather than a mere palliative. Any government that is willing to assist in the task of recovery will find full coopera-tion, I am sure, on the part of the United States Government. Any government which maneuvers to block the recovery of other countries cannot expect help from us. Furthermore, governments, political parties, or groups which seek to perpetuate human misery in order to profit therefrom politically or otherwise will encounter the opposition of the United States.

It is already evident that, before the United States Government can proceed much further in its efforts to alleviate the situation and help start the European world on its way to recovery, there must be some agreement among the coun-tries of Europe as to the requirements of the situation and the part those coun-tires themselves will take in order to give proper effect to whatever action might be undertaken by this Government. It would be neither fitting nor efficacious for this Government to undertake to draw up unilaterally a program designed to place Europe on its feet economically. This is the business of the Europeans. The initiative, I think, must come from Europe. The role of this country should consist of friendly aid in the drafting of a European program and of later sup-port of such a program so far as it may be practical for us to do no. The program should be a joint one, agreed to by a number, if not all, European nations. . . .

Douglas MacArthur, Speech to Congress, April 19, 1951

. . . While I was not consulted prior to the President's decision to intervene in support of the Republic of Korea, that decision, from a military standpoint, proved a sound one, as we hurled back the invader and decimated his forces. Our victory was complete and our objectives within reach when Red China intervened with numerically superior ground forces. This created a new war and an entirely new situation—a situation not contemplated when our forces were committed against the North Korean invaders—a situation which called for new decisions in the diplomatic sphere to permit the realistic adjustment of military strategy. Such decisions have not been forthcoming.

While no man in his right mind would advocate sending our ground forces into continental China and such was never given a thought, the new situation did urgently demand a drastic revision of strategic planning if our political aim was to defeat this new enemy as we had defeated the old. . . .

I called for reinforcements, but was informed that reinforcements were not available. I made clear that if not permitted to destroy the enemy buildup bases north of the Yalu; if not permitted to utilize the friendly Chinese force of some 600,000 men on Formosa; if not permitted to blockade the China coast to prevent the Chinese Reds from getting succor from without; and if there were to be no hope of major reinforcements, the position of the command from the military standpoint forbade victory. We could hold in Korea by constant maneuver and at an approximate area where our supply line advantages were in balance with the supply line disadvantages of the enemy, but we could hope at best for only an indecisive campaign, with its terrible and constant attrition upon our forces if the enemy utilized his full military potential. I have constantly called for new political decisions essential to a solution. Efforts have been made to distort my position. It has been said that I was in effect a warmonger. Nothing could be further from the truth. I know war as few other men now living know it, and nothing to me is more revolting. I have long advocated its complete abolition as its very destructiveness on both friend and foe has rendered it useless as a means of settling international disputes. . . .

Supreme Court Decision, Public School Segregation Cases, May 17, 1954

Mr. Chief Justice Warren:

These cases come to us from the States of Kansas, South Carolina, Virginia, and Delaware. They are premised on different facts and different local conditions, but a common legal question justifies their consideration together in this consolidated opinion.

In each of the cases, minors of the Negro race, through their legal representatives, seek the aid of the courts in obtaining admission to the public schools of their community on a nonsegregated basis. In each instance, they had been denied admission to schools attended by white children under laws requiring or permitting segregation according to race. . . .

Today, education is perhaps the most important function of state and local governments. Compulsory school attendance laws and the great expenditures for education both demonstrate our recognition of the importance of education to our democratic society. It is required in the performance of our most basic public responsibilities, even service in the armed forces. It is the very foundation of good citizenship.

Today, it is a principal instrument in awakening the child to cultural values, in preparing him for later professional training, and in helping him to adjust normally to his environment.

In these days, it is doubtful that any child may reasonably be expected to succeed in life if he is denied the opportunity of an education. Such an opportunity, where the state has undertaken to provide it, is a right which must be made available to all on equal terms.

We come then to the question presented: Does segregation of children in public schools solely on the basis of race, even though the physical facilities and other "tangible" factors may be equal, deprive the children of the minority group of equal education opportunities? We believe that it does. . . .

Whatever may have been the extent of psychological knowledge at the time of Plessy v. Ferguson, this finding is amply supported by modern authority. Any language in Plessy v. Ferguson contrary to this finding is rejected.

We conclude that in the field of public education the doctrine of "separate but equal" has no place. Separate educational facilities are inherently unequal. Therefore, we hold that the plaintiffs and others similarly situated for whom the actions have been brought are, by reason of the segregation complained of, deprived of the equal protection of the laws guaranteed by the Fourteenth Amendment. This disposition makes unnecessary any discussion whether such segregation also violates the Due Process Clause of the Fourteenth Amendment.

Because these are class actions, because of the wide applicability of this decision, and because of the great variety of local conditions, the formulation of of decrees in these cases presents problems of considerable complexity. On reargument, the consideration of appropriate relief was necessarily subordinated to the primary question—the constitutionality of segregation in public education.

We have now announced that such segregation is a denial of the equal protection of the laws. In order that we may have the full assistance of the parties in formulating decrees, the cases will be restored to the docket, and the parties are requested to present further argument. . . .

Martin Luther King, Jr., "I Have a Dream," August 28, 1963

Five score years ago, a great American, in whose symbolic shadow we stand, signed the Emancipation Proclamation. This momentous decree came as a great beacon light of hope to millions of Negro slaves who had been seared in the flames of withering injustice. It came as a joyous daybreak to end the long night of captivity.

But one hundred years later, we must face the tragic fact that the Negro is still not free. One hundred years later, the life of the Negro is still sadly crippled by the manacles of segregation and the chains of discrimination. One hundred years later, the Negro lives on a lonely island of poverty in the midst of a vast ocean of material prosperity. One hundred years later, the Negro is still languishing in the corners of American society and finds himself an exile in his own land. So we have come here today to dramatize an appalling condition . . .

I say to you today, my friends, that in spite of the difficulties and frustrations of the moment, I still have a dream. It is a dream deeply rooted in the American dream.

I have a dream that one day this nation will rise up and live out the true meaning of its creed: "We hold these truths to be self-evident: that all men are created equal."

I have a dream that one day on the red hills of Georgia the sons of former slaves and the sons of former slaveowners will be able to sit down together at the table of brotherhood.

I have a dream that one day even the state of Mississippi, a desert state, sweltering with the heat of injustice and oppression, will be transformed into an oasis of freedom and justice.

I have a dream that my four little children will one day live in a nation where they will not be judged be the color of their skin but by the content of their character. . . .

Supreme Court Decision, The Pentagon Papers Case, June 30, 1971

Mr. Justice Black, with whom Mr. Justice Douglas joins, concurring:

I adhere to the view that the Government's case against The Washington Post should have been dismissed and that the injunction against The New York Times should have been vacated without oral argument when the cases were first presented to this Court. I believe that every moment's continuance of the injunctions against these newspapers amounts to a flagrant, indefensible and continuing violation of the First Amendment. Furthermore, after oral arguments, I agree completely that we must affirm the judgment of the Court of Appeals for the District of Columbia and reverse the judgment of the Court of Appeals for the Second Circuit for the reasons stated by my brothers Douglas and Brennan. In my view it is unfortunate that some of my brethren are apparently willing to hold that the publication of news may sometimes be enjoined. Such a holding would make a shambles of the First Amendment.

Our Government was launched in 1789 with the adoption of the Constitution. The Bill of Rights, including the First Amendment, followed in 1791. Now, for the first time in the 182 years since the founding of the Republic, the Federal courts are asked to hold that the First Amendment does not mean what it says, but rather means that the Government can halt the publication of current news of vital importance to the people of this country.

In seeking injunctions against these newspapers and in its presentation to the court, the executive branch seems to have forgotten the essential purpose and history of the First Amendment. When the Constitution was adopted, many people strongly opposed it because the document contained no bill of rights to safeguard certain basic freedoms. They especially feared that the new powers granted to a central government might be interpreted to permit the government to curtail freedom of religion, press, assembly and speech. In response to an overwhelming public clamor, James Madison offered a series of amendments to satisfy citizens that these great liberties would remain safe and beyond the power of government to abridge. Madison proposed what later became the First Amendment in three parts, two of which are set out below, and one of which proclaimed: "The people shall not be deprived or abridged of their right to speak, to write, or to publish their sentiments; and the freedom of the press, as one of the great bulwarks of liberty, shall be inviolable." The amendments were offered to curtail and restrict the general powers granted to the executive, legislative and judicial branches two years before in the original Constitution. The Bill of Rights changed the original Constitution into a new charter under which no branch of government could abridge the people's freedoms of press, speech, religion and assembly.

Yet the Solicitor General argues and some members of the Court appear to agree that the general powers of the Government adopted in the original Constitution should be interpreted to limit and restrict the specific and emphatic guarantees of the Bill of Rights adopted later. I can imagine no greater perversion of history. Madison and the other framers of the First Amendment, able men that they were, wrote in language they earnestly believed could never be misunderstood: "Congress shall make no law . . . abridging the freedom of the press." Both the history and language of the First Amendment support the view that the press must be left free to publish news, whatever the source, without censorship, injunctions or prior restraints.

In the First Amendment the Founding Fathers gave the free press the protection it must have to fulfill its essential role in our democracy. The press was to serve the governed, not the governors. The Government's power to censor the press was abolished so that the press would remain forever free to censure the Government. The press was protected so that it could bare the secrets of government and inform the people. Only a free and unrestrained press can effectively expose deception in government. And paramount among the responsibilities of a free press is the duty to prevent any part of the Government from deceiving the people and sending them off to distant lands to die of foreign fevers and foreign shot and shell. In my view, far from deserving condemnation for their courageous reporting, The New York Times, The Washington Post and other newspapers should be commended for serving the purpose that the Founding Fathers saw so clearly. In revealing the workings of government that led to the Vietnam war, the newspapers nobly did precisely that which the founders hoped and trusted they would do.

Appendix 1.   U.S. Presidents, Vice-Presidents, and Secretaries of State

No.	Year	Pres.	Party	Vice-Pres.	Party	Sec. of State
1	1789	George Washington	Fed.	John Adams	Fed.	Thomas Jefferson Edmund Randolph Timothy Pickering
2	1797	John Adams	Fed.	Thomas Jefferson	Rep.	John Marshall
3	1801	Thomas Jefferson	Rep.	Aaron Burr	Rep.	James Madison
	//		Rep.	George Clinton	Rep.	
4	1809	James Madison	Rep.	//		Robert Smith
	//			Elbridge Gerry	Rep.	James Monroe
5	1817	James Monroe	Rep.	Daniel D. Tompkins	Rep.	John Quincy Adams
6	1825	John Quincy Adams	Rep.	John C. Calhoun	Rep.	Henry Clay
7	1829	Andrew Jackson	Dem.	//		Martin Van Buren Edward Livingston
	//			Martin Van Buren	Dem.	Louis McLane John Forsyth
8	1837	Martin Van Buren	Dem.	Richard M. Johnson	Dem.	//
9	1841	William Henry Harrison	Whig	John Tyler	Whig	Daniel Webster
10	1841	John Tyler	Whig	. . .		// Hugh S. Legare Abel P. Upshur John C. Calhoun
11	1845	James L. Polk	Dem.	George M. Dallas	Dem.	James Buchanan
12	1849	Zachary Taylor	Whig	Millard Fillmore	Whig	John M. Clayton
13	1850	Millard Fillmore	Whig	. . .		Daniel Webster Edward Everett
14	1853	Franklin Pierce	Dem.	William R. King	Dem.	William L. Marcy
15	1857	James Buchanan	Dem.	John C. Breckinridge	Dem.	Lewis Cass Jeremiah S. Black
16	1861	Abraham Lincoln	Rep.	Hannibal Hamlin	Rep.	William H. Seward
	//			Andrew Johnson		
17	1865	Andrew Johnson	Rep.	. . .		//
18	1869	Ulysses S. Grant	Rep.	Schuyler Colfax	Rep.	Elihu B. Washburne
	//			Henry Wilson	Rep.	Hamilton Fish

19	1877	Rutherford B. Hayes	Rep.	William A. Wheeler	Rep.	William M. Evarts
20	1881	James A. Garfield	Rep.	Chester A. Arthur	Rep.	James G. Blaine
21	1881	Chester A. Arthur	Rep.	. . .		F. T. Frelinghuysen
22	1885	Grover Cleveland	Dem.	Thomas A. Hendricks	Dem.	Thomas F. Bayard
23	1889	Benjamin Harrison	Rep.	Levi P. Morton	Rep.	James Blaine / John W. Foster
24	1893	Grover Cleveland	Dem.	Adlai E. Stevenson	Dem.	Walter Q. Gresham / Richard Olney
25	1897	William McKinley	Rep.	Garrett A. Hobart	Rep.	John Sherman / William R. Day
	//			Theodore Roosevelt	Rep.	John Hay
26	1901	Theodore Roosevelt	Rep.	. . .		//
	//			Charles W. Fairbanks	Rep.	Elihu Root / Robert Bacon
27	1909	William H. Taft	Rep.	James S. Sherman	Rep.	Philander C. Knox
28	1913	Woodrow Wilson	Dem.	Thomas R. Marshall	Dem.	William J. Bryan / Robert Lansing / Bainebridge Colby
29	1921	Warren G. Harding	Rep.	Calvin Coolidge	Rep.	Charles E. Hughes
30	1923	Calvin Coolidge	Rep.	. . .		//
	//			Charles G. Dawes	Rep.	Frank B. Kellogg
31	1929	Herbert C. Hoover	Rep.	Charles Curtis	Rep.	Henry L. Stimson
32	1933	Franklin D. Roosevelt	Dem.	John N. Garner	Dem.	Cordell Hull
			Dem.	Henry A. Wallace		Edward R. Stettinius, Jr.
	//			Harry S. Truman	Dem.	James F. Byrnes
33	1945	Harry S. Truman	Dem.	. . .		George C. Marshall
	//			Alben W. Barkley	Dem.	Dean G. Acheson
34	1953	Dwight D. Eisenhower	Rep.	Richard M. Nixon	Rep.	John Foster Dulles
	//			//		Christian A. Herter
35	1961	John F. Kennedy	Dem.	Lyndon Baines Johnson	Dem.	Dean Rusk

36	1963	Lyndon B. Johnson	Dem.	. . .		Dean Rusk
		//		Hubert H. Humphrey	Dem.	//
37	1969	Richard M. Nixon	Rep.	Spiro T. Agnew	Rep.	William P. Rogers
	1973	Richard M. Nixon	Rep.	Spiro T. Agnew	Rep.	Henry A. Kissinger
38	1974	Gerald R. Ford	Rep.	Nelson A. Rockefeller	Rep.	//
39	1977	Jimmy Carter	Dem.	Walter F. Mondale	Dem.	Cyrus A. Vance

Appendix 2.   Candidates in Presidential elections, 1789–1976

Year	States	Candidates	Parties		
1789	11	George Washington	. . .	69	
		John Adams	. . .	34	
		John Jay	. . .	9	
		R. H. Harrison	. . .	6	
		John Rutledge	. . .	6	
		John Hancock	. . .	4	
		George Clinton	. . .	3	
		Samuel Huntington	. . .	2	
		John Milton	. . .	2	
		James Armstrong	. . .	1	
		Benjamin Lincoln	. . .	1	
		Edward Telfair	. . .	1	
		Others	. . .	12	
1792	15	George Washington	Federalist	132	
		John Adams	Federalist	77	
		George Clinton	Republican	50	
		Thomas Jefferson	. . .	4	
		Aaron Burr	. . .	1	
1796	16	John Adams	Federalist	71	
		Thomas Jefferson	Republican	68	
		Thomas Pinkney	Federalist	59	
		Aaron Burr	Anti-Federalist	30	
		Samuel Adams	Republican	15	
		Oliver Ellsworth	Federalist	11	
		George Clinton	Republican	7	
		John Jay	Independent Federalist	5	
		James Iredell	Federalist	3	
		George Washington	Federalist	2	
		John Henry	Independent	2	
		S. Johnston	Independent Federalist	2	
		C. C. Pinkney	Independent Federalist	1	
1800	16	Thomas Jefferson	Republican	73	
		Aaron Burr	Republican	73	
		John Adams	Federalist	65	
		C. C. Pinkney	Federalist	64	
		John Jay	Federalist	1	
1804	17	Thomas Jefferson	Republican	162	
		C. C. Pinkney	Federalist	14	
1808	17	James Madison	Republican	122	. . .
		C. C. Pinkney	Federalist	47	. . .
		George Clinton	Independent Republican	6	. . .
		Others	. . .	1	. . .
1812	18	James Madison	Republican	128	. . .
		De Witt Clinton	Fusion	89	. . .
		Others	. .	1	. . .
1816	19	James Monroe	Republican	183	. . .
		Rufus King	Federalist	34	. . .
		Others	. . .	4	. . .

1820	24	James Monroe	Republican	231	. . .
		John Q. Adams	Independent Republican	1	. . .
		Others	. . .	3	. . .
1824	24	John Q. Adams	⎰no party identification	⎰84	108,740
		Andrew Jackson		99	153,544
		Henry Clay		37	47,136
		W. H. Crawford		⎱41	46,618
1828	24	Andrew Jackson	Democratic	178	647,286
		John Q. Adams	National Republican	83	508,064
1832	24	Andrew Jackson	Democratic	219	687,502
		Henry Clay	National Republican	49	530,189
		William Wirt	Anti-Masonic	7	. . .
		John Floyd	Nullifiers	11	. . .
		Others	. . .	2	. . .
1836	26	Martin Van Buren	Democratic	170	765,483
		William H. Harrison	Whig	73⎱	
		Hugh L. White	Whig	26⎱	739,795
		Daniel Webster	Whig	14⎱	
		W. P. Mangum	Anti-Jackson	11⎱	
1840	26	William H. Harrison	Whig	234	1,274,624
		Martin Van Buren	Democratic	60	1,127,781
1844	26	James K. Polk	Democratic	170	1,338,464
		Henry Clay	Whig	105	1,300,097
		James G. Birney	Liberty	. . .	62,300
1848	30	Zachary Taylor	Whig	163	1,360,967
		Lewis Cass	Democratic	127	1,222,342
		Martin Van Buren	Free Soil	. . .	291,263
1852	31	Franklin Pierce	Democratic	254	1,601,117
		Winfield Scott	Whig	42	1,385,453
		John P. Hale	Free Soil	. . .	155,825
1856	31	James Buchanan	Democratic	144	1,866,955
		John C. Frémont	Republican	114	1,339,932
		Millard Fillmore	American Whig	8	871,731
1860	33	Abraham Lincoln	Republican	180	1,865,593
		J. C. Breckinridge	Democratic (S)	72	848,356
		Stephen A. Douglas	Democratic	12	1,382,713
		John Bell	Constitutional Union	39	592,906
1864	36	Abraham Lincoln	Republican	212	2,206,938
		George B. McClellan	Democratic	80	1,803,787
		Others	. . .	23	. . .
1868	37	Ulysses S. Grant	Republican	214	3,013,321
		Horatio Seymour	Democratic	80	2,706,829
		Others	. . .	23	. . .
1872	37	Ulysses S. Grant	Republican	286	3,596,745
		Horace Greeley	Democratic		2,843,446
		Charles O'Connor	Straight Democratic	. . .	29,489
		Thomas A. Hendricks	Independent Democratic	42	. . .
		B. Gratz Brown	Democratic	18	. . .
		Charles J. Jenkins	Democratic	2	. . .
		David Davis	Democratic	1	. . .

	Others	. . .	17	. . .
1876 38	Rutherford B. Hayes	Republican	185	4,066,572
	Samuel J. Tilden	Democratic	184	4,284,020
	Peter Cooper	Greenback	. . .	81,737
1880 38	James A. Garfield	Republican	214	4,453,295
	Winfield S. Hancock	Democratic	155	3,414,082
	James B. Weaver	Greenback-Labor	. . .	308,578
	Neal Dow	Prohibition	. . .	10,305
1884 38	Grover Cleveland	Democratic	219	4,879,507
	James G. Blaine	Republican	182	4,850,293
	Benjamin F. Butler	Greenback-Labor	. . .	175,370
	John P. St. John	Prohibition	. . .	150,369
1888 38	Benjamin Harrison	Republican	233	5,447,129
	Grover Cleveland	Democratic	168	5,537,856
	Clinton B. Fisk	Prohibition	. . .	249,506
	Alson J. Streeter	Union Labor	. . .	146,935
1892 44	Grover Cleveland	Democratic	277	5,555,426
	Benjamin Harrison	Republican	145	5,182,690
	James B. Weaver	People's	22	1,029,846
	John Bidwell	Prohibition	. . .	264,133
	Simon Wing	Socialist Labor	. . .	21,164
1896 45	William McKinley	Republican	271	7,102,246
	William J. Bryan	Democratic	176	6,492,559
	John M. Palmer	National Democratic	. . .	133,148
	Joshua Levering	Prohibition	. . .	132,007
	Charles H. Matchett	Socialist Labor	. . .	36,274
	Charles E. Bentley	Nationalist	. . .	13,969
1900 45	William McKinley	Republican	292	7,218,491
	William J. Bryan	Democratic	155	6,356,734
	John C. Woolley	Prohibition	. . .	208,914
	Eugene V. Debs	Socialist	. . .	208,914
	Eugene V. Debs	Socialist	. . .	87,814
	Wharton Barker	People's	. . .	50,373
	Jos. F. Malloney	Socialist Labor	. . .	39,739
1904 45	Theodore Roosevelt	Republican	336	7,628,461
	Alton B. Parker	Democratic	140	5,084,461
	Eugene V. Debs	Socialist	. . .	402,283
	Silas C. Swallow	Prohibition	. . .	258,536
	Thomas E. Watson	People's	. . .	117,183
	Charles H. Corregan	Socialist Labor	. . .	31,249
1908 46	William H. Taft	Republican	321	7,675,320
	William J. Bryan	Democratic	162	6,412,294
	Eugene V. Debs	Socialist	. . .	420,793
	Eugene W. Chafin	Prohibition	. . .	253,840
	Thomas L. Hisgen	Independence	. . .	82,872
	Thomas E. Watson	People's	. . .	29,100
	August Gillhaus	Socialist Labor	. . .	14,021
1912 48	Woodrow Wilson	Democratic	435	6,296,547
	Theodore Roosevelt	Progressive	88	4,118,571
	William H. Taft	Republican	8	3,486,720

	Eugene V. Debs	Socialist	. . .	900,672
	Eugene W. Chafin	Prohibition	. . .	206,275
	Arthur E. Reimer	Socialist Labor	. . .	28,550
1916 48	Woodrow Wilson	Democratic	277	9,127,695
	Charles E. Hughes	Republican	254	8,533,507
	A.L. Benson	Socialist	. . .	585,113
	J. Frank Hanly	Prohibition	. . .	220,506
	Arthur E. Reimer	Socialist Labor	. . .	13,406
1920 48	Warren G. Harding	Republican	404	16,143,407
	James M. Cox	Democratic	127	9,130,328
	Eugene V. Debs	Socialist	. . .	919,799
	P.P. Christensen	Farmer-Labor	. . .	265,411
	Aaron S. Watkins	Prohibition	. . .	189,408
	James E. Ferguson	American	. . .	48,000
	W. W. Cox	Socialist Labor	. . .	31,715
1924 48	Calvin Coolidge	Republican	382	15,718,211
	John W. Davis	Democratic	166	8,385,283
	Robert M. LaFollett	Progressive	13	4,831,289
	Herman P. Faris	Prohibition	. . .	57,520
	Frank T. Johns	Socialist Labor	. . .	36,428
	William Z. Foster	Workers	. . .	36,386
	Gilbert O. Nations	American	. . .	23,967
1928 48	Herbert C. Hoover	Republican	444	21,391,993
	Alfred E. Smith	Democratic	87	15,016,169
	Norman Thomas	Socialist	. . .	267,835
	Verne L. Reynolds	Socialist Labor	. . .	21,603
	William Z. Foster	Workers	. . .	21,181
	William F. Varney	Prohibition	. . .	20,106
1932 48	Franklin D. Roosevelt	Democratic	472	22,809,638
	Herbert C. Hoover	Republican	59	15,758,901
	Norman Thomas	Socialist	. . .	881,951
	William Z. Foster	Communist	. . .	102,785
	William D. Upshaw	Prohibition	. . .	81,869
	Verne L. Reynolds	Socialist Labor	. . .	33,276
	William H. Harvery	Liberty	. . .	53,425
1936 48	Franklin D. Roosevelt	Democratic	523	27,752,869
	Alfred M. Landon	Republican	8	16,674,665
	William Lemke	Union	. . .	882,479
	Norman Thomas	Socialist	. . .	187,720
	Earl Browder	Communist	. . .	80,159
	D. Leigh Colvin	Prohibition	. . .	37,847
	John W. Aiken	Socialist Labor	. . .	12,777
1940 48	Franklin D. Roosevelt	Democratic	449	27,307,819
	Wendell L. Willkie	Republican	82	22,321,018
	Norman Thomas	Socialist	. . .	99,557
	Roger Q. Babson	Prohibition	. . .	57,812
	Earl Browder	Communist	. . .	46,251
	John W. Aiken	Socialist Labor	. . .	14,892
1944 48	Franklin D. Roosevelt	Democratic	432	25,606,585
	Thomas E. Dewey	Republican	99	22,014,745

	Norman Thomas	Socialist	. . .	80,518
	Claude A. Watson	Prohibition	. . .	74,758
	Edward A. Teichert	Socialist Labor	. . .	45,336
1948 48	Harry S. Truman	Democratic	303	24,105,812
	Thomas E. Dewey	Republican	198	21,970,065
	Strom Thurmond	States' Rights	39	1,169,063
	Henry Wallace	Progressive	. . .	1,157,172
	Norman Thomas	Socialist	. . .	139,414
	Claude A. Watson	Prohibition	. . .	103,224
	Edward A. Teichert	Socialist Labor	. . .	29,244
	Farrell Dobbs	Socialist Workers	. . .	13,613
1952 48	Dwight D. Eisenhower	Republican	442	33,936,234
	Adlai E. Stevenson	Democratic	89	27,314,992
	Vincent Hallinan	Progressive	. . .	140,023
	Stuart Hamblen	Prohibition	. . .	72,949
	Eric Hass	Socialist Labor	. . .	30,267
	Darlington Hoopes	Socialist	. . .	20,203
	Douglas A. MacArthur	Constitution	. . .	17,205
	Farrell Dobbs	Socialist Workers	. . .	10,312
1956 48	Dwight D. Eisenhower	Republican	457	35,590,472
	Adlai E. Stevenson	Democratic	73	26,022,752
	T. Coleman Andrews	States' Rights	. . .	107,929
	Eric Hass	Socialist Labor	. . .	44,300
	Enoch A. Holtwick	Prohibition	. . .	41,937
1960 50	John F. Kennedy	Democratic	303	34,227,096
	Richard M. Nixon	Republican	219	34,108,546
	Harry F. Byrd		15	440,298
1964 50	Lyndon B. Johnson	Democratic	486	43,126,506
	Barry M. Goldwater	Republican	52	27,176,799
1968 51	Richard M. Nixon	Republican	301	31,783,783
	Hubert Humphrey	Democratic	191	31,271,839
	George C. Wallace	Am. Independent	46	9,899,557
1972 51	Richard M. Nixon	Republican	520	47,167,319
	George S. McGovern	Democratic	17	29,169,504
	John G. Schmitz	American	. . .	1,102,963
	John Hospers	Libertarian	1	2,691
1976 51	Jimmy Carter	Democratic	297	40,825,839
	Gerald R. Ford	Republican	240	39,147,770
	Eugene McCarthy	Independent	. . .	680,390
	Roger McBride	Libertarian	. . .	171,627

Historical Statistics of the United States: Colonial Times to 1957, U.S. Department of Commerce, Bureau of the Census, Washington D.C., 1960.
CBS News Almanac 1978, Hammond Almanac, Inc., 1978.

INDEX

INDEX TO DOCUMENTS